Sisters

Also by Susan Ripps:

A PASSION FOR MORE

Sisters

DEVOTED or DIVIDED

Susan Ripps

KENSINGTON BOOKS

The author has changed the names and all identifying
characteristics of every person whose story is told in this book.

KENSINGTON BOOKS are published by

Kensington Publishing Corp.
850 Third Avenue
New York, NY 10022

Kensington Books is a trademark of Kensington Publishing Corp.

Library of Congress Card Catalog Number: 94-076702
ISBN 0-8217-4679-0

First Printing: September, 1994

Printed in the United States of America

ACKNOWLEDGEMENTS

There are certain people to acknowledge: my husband, Richard, whose belief in my work propels me forward, Selma Shapiro, Herbert Shapiro, Mark Shapiro, Rose Ripps, and my dear friends for seeing me through. The professional voices in this book, those of Dr. Ronnie L. Burak, Dr. Donald Cohen, and Dr. Robin Meltzer, offer insight into the lives of these sisters. My excellent agent, Diana Finch, and my amazing editor, Sarah Gallick, deserve special thanks as do Lori Stuart and Jane Wesman for their tremendous support, and Gina Levy, my typist, for her tolerance.

A sincere thank you is extended to the many women who shared their innermost thoughts and feelings with me. To insure confidentiality, their names and identifying characteristics have been changed. Diverse and heartfelt, their stories are the lifeblood of this book.

My love and gratitude goes to my three children, two of whom are sisters and exist in a secret universe.

FOR MY CHILDREN
JENNIE, MICHAEL, AND ELIZABETH

Never praise a sister to a sister, in the hope
of your compliments reaching the proper ears.
—Rudyard Kipling

For there is no friend like a sister
In calm or stormy weather.
—Christina Rossetti

CONTENTS

AUTHOR'S PREFACE

Being without a sister, I have often eyed sisters and the world they share with awe and admiration. Watching my two daughters, the oldest and youngest in birth order, as they bond to the exclusion of my son, I recognize the strength and power of this particular relationship. While this is a familial tie which has existed throughout history, very little attention has been given to the ramifications of being a sister.

As I began this project, I asked myself if ever any sisters have inspired a legend as powerful as the tale of Cain and Abel. How many famous women are noted for their connection to their sisters? Modern sisters have choices and challenges that those who preceded us have not: the possibility of becoming a surrogate mother, mobility despite physical distance (no more excuses), longevity of parents. With the fast-paced lives we lead, if sisters are not near each other, will the relationship sustain itself? What place does birth order have in the role each sister plays?

Combining historical research with real-life, present-day stories, I have come to realize the strength and abundance of sister-to-sister connections. In sharing their stories anonymously, these sisters feel they are coming to terms with their relationships with their sisters. Working my way across the country, I interviewed women of various social stratas, ages, and walks of life about this attachment.

As Carl Jung views sisters, the siblings represent something very specific, both the perfect self and the "shadow." Sisters are immersed, regardless of age difference or birth order, in an experience of self-description. This connection is a life-long relationship. Although sisters may become estranged, the primary relationship does not dissolve as a marriage might, but is forever.

Living in a patriarchal society, sisters have not always received their due. In Greek mythology, Leda's daughters, Helen and Klytemnestra, were smitten with each other and their fate is a sad one, exemplifying Jung's "shadows." As young adults they shared a similar disappointment when each sister's husband left her. In turn, each took a lover—Helen turning to Paris and Klytemnestra to Aegisthus. The commonality in their situation was that each sister proved strong enough to reject being victimized by her spouse. How modern and admirable, a sister of today might note.

However, the sisters used dissimilar tactics. Klytemnestra turned away from her abusive husband while Helen maintained her notorious power over men. The sisters were united in their marital suffering, but Klytemnestra was finally defeated by her sister's beauty. Though they were sympathetic and understanding of each other's plight, Helen's great beauty was an ever-present factor. Is it so very difficult, then, for sisters to depart from the roles they are born into in order to fill a new and different need?

In my interviews with sisters, I have attempted to find as many different circumstances as possible. While birth order has had a tremendous influence, it is the impact of never having had a sister or sisters that is so remarkable to me. The nurturing that sisters offer, be it mothering or pure devotion and friendship, go beyond an outsider's wildest dreams.

I have found that sister/sister relationships fall into several categories. Interspersed with historical references is a professional voice as a method of providing insight into the inner workings of this blood tie.

Competitive sisters are a constant. We remember how Princess Diana was introduced to Prince Charles by her sister, who was not "princess material." The competition between the two sisters increased when Diana became a royal. Nancy Mitford, oldest of the six Mitford sisters, felt ignored at the age of three when her first sister, Pamela, was born. Her relationship with this particular sister suffered for years as the competition for their mother's attention raged on. Unity, the fourth Mitford sister, was part of Hitler's entourage, while Diana married Sir Oswald Mosely, head of the British Union of Fascists. Unity and Diana thus vied for recognition in the political world of their day.

The beautiful Soong sisters are said to have inspired the Chinese saying, "Once upon a time there were three sisters; one loved money, one loved power, one loved China." Daughters of perhaps the most westernized family in China and educated in America, each sister made an important marriage. Ai-ling married H. H. K'ung, a descendant of Confucius and the premiere banker for Nationalist China. Ch'ing-ling married Sun Yat-sen and was a supporter of the Communists against the Nationalists. And Mei-Ling became Madame Chiang Kai-shek.

Supportive sisters have existed throughout history. Abigail Adams, the wife of John Quincy Adams, got along well with her sisters. The only issue on which Abigail was unable to agree with her older sister concerned remarriage. Abigail viewed remarriage as lustful and unnecessary; she also admitted to her sisters that after twenty years of marriage, the romance was gone. Her sister advocated remarriage. Though they battled often, they still continued to support each other. What endured among these sisters was their spirit, intelligence, and sense of self.

The recent novel and film, *Like Water for Chocolate* by Laura Esquivel, explores the concept of a sister who takes her sister's lover. In a Mexican family where tradition dictates that the youngest daughter will never marry but must remain with her mother, Mama Elena, through her old age, Tita, the youngest, falls in love first, with Pedro. Mama Elena insists that her oldest daughter, Rosaura, marry Pedro instead. Tita, a culinary expert, becomes part of Pedro through her cooking. Rosaura, the unhappy wife, cannot win her husband's love. Only Gertrudis, the middle sister, who runs off with the renegade soldier and abandons her family, is set free. When Rosaura dies, it is Tita, ironically, who raises Pedro's daughter as her own. And in the film *Sex, Lies, and Videotape* we witness a woman engaged in an affair with her sister's husband. As if that is not enough, the sisters also share a lover. Woody Allen's movie, *Hannah and Her Sisters*, also addresses this; Allen's character marries one of his ex-wife's sisters while Michael Caine's character marries Allen's ex-wife, then has an affair with the third sister.

Sisters who act as surrogate mothers and bear their sister's child are becoming more common. A controversial issue, it is often thought that if a sister gives birth for her sister, there is less risk involved. This is one of the main themes in the popular NBC drama, "Sisters." When Frankie cannot bear a child, she is able to turn to her sister, Georgie, who already has children, to carry her baby. However, if Frankie gets divorced, it seems that Georgie might want custody of the baby. Such are the complexities of surrogate-mothering, even between sisters.

We have all come up against the exclusive sisters, those willing to join together and shut out the rest of the world. Perhaps the most notable were the Brontes: Charlotte, Emily, and Anne. Equally intellectual, ambitious, and affected by the tragic deaths of their two older sisters, they subsisted on the moors, molded by their physical environment and their motherless household. Writing their distinctive fiction under the male pseudonyms of three brothers, they spent their entire lives together. In this particular threesome, there was always an odd sister out, in a competitive and unending exclusivity. Emily refused to leave the moors, so Charlotte and Anne followed suit. The complexity of their lives centered around their childhood home, shutting out the rest of the world for the sake of their sistering and writing.

The unimaginable and foreign world of twins has long been a curiosity to outsiders. Whether fraternal or identical, twin sisters seem to share a secret connection. At the Museum of Modern Art in New York City recently, a portrait of adult twin sisters was featured in a Latin American Artists exhibit. Looking closely at the twins' faces, we see that one is happy and one embittered. Struggling to find a unique persona, the sisters, well over thirty, wear the same hairstyle and dress.

Identical twins such as Bridget Harrison and Dorothy Lowe, separated as infants and reunited thirty-four years later, often discover they share uncanny similarities. Both sisters had children with the same names, in reverse order. And they both wore seven rings on four fingers. Although raised apart, the twins had remarkably similar personality traits which indicated a strong genetic base.

Jealousy is common among sisters, as witnessed in the recent film, *Bodyguard*, where Whitney Houston's character has a sister so jealous that she actually hires a killer to remedy the situation. And one wonders what other motivation is possible when a character in Josephine Hart's novel, *Sin*, deliberately destroys her sister's marriage, bringing on the tragic deaths of both sisters' sons.

Devoted sisters brings the story of *Little Women* to mind. Louisa May Alcott and her sisters were the four daughters of an eccentric but brilliant man. It was Louisa, though, whose lifelong commitment to the family held it together. *Little Women* is not only a great work of literature, but it stands as a fictional account of the sisters' commitment and love for one another. Louisa's devotion to her sisters is apparent in her writing, and the devastating loss of her sister Elizabeth is a recurrent theme in her fiction.

There are explorations of joy, disappointment, and discovery in the name of true sisterhood. For those of us who do not have a sister, the book will provide insight into what it is that sisters share, or hope to share. For those of us who have lost a sister or a rapport with a sister, this book will offer hope and solace.

INTRODUCTION

by

Dr. Donald Cohen

Throughout history sisters have always banded together. They tend, however, to fare better as they get older and the competition lessens. The need for companionship becomes stronger and the desire to have a best friend overshadows any former competition and jealousy. This is not to say that these feelings dissolve; rather they diminish and the positive forces may dominate the relationship.

In the early years, there is always a problem with competition and envy. When the younger sister grows more socially adept, the older sister might resent it. Often the older sister or sisters pave the way in terms of parental approval. The youngest may be allowed more freedom at an earlier age and the older sisters might object to this. Then again, we have to remember that the older sister wishes she was the single daughter. Any sister who comes after her evokes the questions, Wasn't I enough? Couldn't I have been the only daughter?

I have also witnessed some fierce loyalties among sisters, who often bond in such a manner that they commiserate over life apart from themselves. They rally against the society beyond their sisterhood that can cause them harm. Despite their own issues of primacy and jealousy, they unite against these forces.

The attachment is especially strong between the oldest sister and the youngest, if there are more than two daughters in a family. It seems that with more distance and a significant age difference, there is less rivalry. In this situation, sisters can create a world of their own.

When a younger sister takes away her older sister's friends, there is a struggle between them. The oldest sister is often the most narcissistic and wants to control the situation. All these issues are part of the world of sisters. Eventually these girls become women, and continue to manipulate one another. The stakes are raised as they react to the frustrations of day-to-day life.

The relationship between sisters is very powerful, with many negatives and positives. Sisters become each other's confidantes, forming special and unique connections. When it works it really works, providing a sacred bond that few of us outside its realm can comprehend. Perhaps the greatest strength and greatest weakness of this connection is the fact that it does not evolve in terms of society. It is a timeless attachment, one that transcends generations. The manner in which sisters relate has very little to do with the times in which we live; it is an emotional bond and does not reflect our outer lives as much as our inner yearnings.

Those who grow up in a family without brothers lack the masculine influence. Although they are often unaware of it, they are missing the opportunity to learn how to relate to men. They do not gain confidence in dealing with males; instead they trade in the camaraderie of women, a sisterhood. The payoff is the soulmate that one sister becomes to the other. We constantly hear women say that they wish they had a sister to share their common experience. Women who do not have sisters are perpetually in search of this relationship. Sisters have an instinctive trust of each other, substantiating the idea that sisters provide a safety valve in the form of unconditional love for each other.

When sisters fail at their relationship it causes great damage, and they look for sisterhood elsewhere, in search of that special relationship. The loyalty they experience as adult sisters is tremendous and exclusive. I see it as an uncanny fidelity that seems to supersede all other relationships, eliciting the best and the worst from these women. Younger sisters are always looking for connections to older sisters, who are not always available which induces great pain. What we see is a negative triangle, where the eldest and youngest sister bond and exclude the middle sister, perhaps even irrevocably.

Sisters can be competitive with men as well, even with their husbands. It begins when they are adolescent and have a crush on the same boy. While they can share this fantasy, it becomes more demanding and less pleasant as they get older—they might fantasize about the man because of a deep-seated jealousy. In other words, the qualities that one sister has that the other hasn't are the very ingredients that capture the attention of this one man. Then they can fight it out. Recognizing one's own shortcomings by noting how it is measured by the opposite sex creates another triangle for sisters. It seems that any triangle which involves sisters can prove to be dangerous.

The complexities of the sacred bond of sisterhood are continually revealed. In a family of three or more sisters it becomes especially demanding. What prevails with sisters, however, is a unity that at some point in their lives, and in some cases for all of their lives, keeps the rest of the world out, enshrining their unparalleled alliance.

Dr. Cohen holds a master's degree in Social Work and a Ph.D in Clinical Psychology. He is a certified marriage and family therapist, and the host and creator of his own television/radio show, "Kids are Talking."

PART ONE

The Power of Sisters

INTRODUCTION

Ronnie L. Burak, Ph.D

Alfred Adler, a well-known psychological theorist at the turn of the century, believed birth order to be one of the most significant psychological influences in childhood. From it the individual develops many of the patterns of behavior that will continue as personality traits in adult life. Assuming that siblings of the same sex struggle with a closer identification than siblings of the opposite sex, birth order may have the greatest influence on same-sex siblings.

In this time of intensive research on women's issues, the relationship between sisters seems particularly relevant. Sister relationships may be especially close or distant, hostile or loving, but whatever their character most agree that the bonds of sisterhood are a powerful influence on women's lives.

Relationships between sisters may change dramatically from childhood to adulthood. Often the nature of the adult relationship is a reaction to the character of the childhood relationship. Sisters who are very close in childhood may remain close throughout their lives but others seem to grow apart. Certainly geographic distance, busy schedules, and family responsibilities stand in the way of maintaining close sibling connections, but there may be deeper issues involved.

Perhaps some sisters, because of their closeness in childhood, never had an opportunity to explore their individual uniqueness. Consequently, as adults the siblings need to separate in order to develop more fully as individuals. Sisters who were not so close as children may become closer as they mature. Feeling more comfortable with their adult roles, they begin looking for a closer connection to their roots.

Some sisters are competitive as children. Often the firstborn works very hard to please her parents, trying to recapture the place in their hearts that she feels she lost when the second child was born. She may be a "goody two shoes" or too achievement oriented. In response, the second sister may try to compete with her older sibling by developing skills in the same areas in which her sister has achieved recognition in order to top her; or she may try to excel in a different area where she won't be in competition with her older sibling. For example, if the older sister does well academically, the younger one may focus all her efforts on athletics. Some younger sisters, however, feel that it is too difficult to compete with an older sibling in any area and simply rebel, becoming the difficult child, the underachiever, or the clown.

When there are three or more sisters the middle one(s) may have an especially difficult time. The oldest has the identity of being firstborn. The youngest is the baby who is often still at home when the older siblings leave, becoming very special in her parents' eyes. The other sister(s) may be literally lost in the middle. The number of years between the births of these sisters also affects the situation. More time between births gives the parents a greater ability to focus on each child, thereby helping the girls to develop more individuality and self-esteem.

In adulthood the competition may continue in the areas of marriage, ability to have children, success of the children, career achievement, and financial security. Of course, many sisters are able to put their childhood competition to rest, having found comfort and security in adult identities. This may bring them closer than ever.

Physical illness and/or emotional difficulties of one of the sisters have powerful effects on the sibling relationship. A physically ill child demands a great deal of the parents' time and energy; the other sisters may feel neglected and, therefore, angry. Some sisters may respond with rebellious behavior—others may feel guilty about their angry feelings and try even harder to be helpful and please their parents.

Of course, the physically ill or handicapped daughter may also be jealous of her healthy siblings. She can respond by being particularly loveable and/or highly motivated to overcome her difficulties, in order to achieve in a very special way. Some physically ill or handicapped children may feel there is no way they can compete with their siblings and become depressed or respond with demanding or withdrawn behavior.

Sometimes in a family where there are only two children, and one child has a severe behavior or substance abuse problem, the other will try to make up for the difficult child. This child often becomes extremely perfectionistic and hard on herself. Anorexic and bulimic behavior are sometimes the result of this daughter's effort to be perfect. This dynamic can also occur with the death of the child, when the remaining siblings feel they must make up for the parents' loss.

In adulthood, sisters face the enormous task of coping with the illness and eventual death of their parents. In many families the females take on the responsibility for the care of aging parents. If one sister feels she carries the burden of caring for her parents alone, she may feel resentful toward her siblings. However, when the responsibility is shared it often brings sisters closer together. Shared caretaking leads to the realization that when parents die, siblings are the only tie with one's childhood history.

Because of the unique genetic and environmental bonds, friendships between sisters may be the most powerful and enchanting relationships we will ever have.

Personal Note

My sister buys me the best gifts. She knows my tastes like no one else. When we go shopping together, nine times out of ten we end up buying two of the same thing.

She often knows what I'm thinking better than my mom, my husband of twenty-five years, and my best friend. Even though we have lived far apart for most of our adult lives, when I spend time with my sister I feel like I can relax and be myself.

———————————

Dr. Ronnie L. Burak has a Ph.D in Clinical Psychology from the California School of Professional Psychology in Berkeley/ Alameda. She is presently teaching at the University of North Florida in Jacksonville and has a full-time private practice.

COMPETITIVE SISTERS:
The Need to be Number One

Competitive sisters take action. Suffering from an intense need to be number one in their parents' eyes, they are driven to top one another. Whether it is academic achievement, athletic prowess, beauty, popularity, or good deeds, these sisters never tire. Their efforts may have either a positive or a negative outcome, depending on their level of self-esteem and each sister's ability to truly care for her sibling.

—RONNIE L. BURAK, PH.D

Torn asunder in a bloody battle for the throne were Elizabeth I, daughter of Henry VIII and Anne Boleyn, and her half-sister, Mary I, daughter of Henry VIII and Catherine of Aragon. Each proved a threat to the other's security. When Elizabeth was born to Anne Boleyn, Henry actually considered naming her Mary in order to replace Catherine's daughter. Not only did this gesture not come to pass, but within a few years Henry had beheaded Elizabeth's mother, thus jeopardizing his daughter's future.

Elizabeth's birth altered Mary's life drastically. She was no longer called Princess Mary, but Lady Mary, while Elizabeth was called Princess Elizabeth. Mary saw that it was Princess

Elizabeth who blocked her chance at the throne. Despite an incessant battle for power, the two sisters were partially raised together. During Anne Boleyn's reign, Elizabeth was placed in the seat of honor at the dining hall, an event that Mary protested at every meal. When Anne Boleyn was beheaded, Elizabeth, at the age of two and a half, was declared a bastard. Mary then resumed the seat of honor at the dinner table, and Elizabeth did not appear at all.

Declared illegitimate, Elizabeth was nonetheless invited to her half-brother Edward's christening, where she is said to have held hands with their older half-sister, Mary. When King Henry lay dying, Prince Edward was only nine years old. Edward was then crowned king. Despite political unrest over religion, Mary insisted on remaining a Catholic. With religion at the heart of the matter, this seemed to aid Elizabeth's cause, as she was a Protestant. When Edward died, the sisters rode together to enter the capital. The sisters were divided over power and religion, but Elizabeth received the highest place of honor at Mary's coronation. Elizabeth vowed that she would embrace Catholicism, but Mary distrusted her half-sister's every word.

Any affection between the sisters deteriorated quickly. When Elizabeth appealed for clemency, she was sent to the Tower of London. By then Bloody Mary was burning Protestants, and was soon to die. Elizabeth became the Queen of England within hours of her half-sister's death.

A pair of famous acting sisters are the Redgraves, Vanessa and Lynn. Vanessa is said to have wanted to act since she was a child whereas Lynn, younger by several years, had no desire to pursue an acting career. In a family dominated by the father, the renowned actor, Michael Redgrave, it was Vanessa who held a special place. A description of a family game casts Vanessa as President, Corin, the brother, as Prime Minister, and Lynn as the royal pet. It is obvious that Lynn had to struggle for recognition.

Michael Redgrave watched happily as Vanessa became a successful actress. Lynn emerged later in the shadow of her sister, the star. It is notable, however, that when Vanessa turned down the lead in the film, *Georgy Girl*, it was Lynn who took it on. Believing herself to be second best, Lynn went on to create quite a career of her own in theater and film.

With an established name preceding Vanessa's daughters, we wait to see the extent to which Natasha and Joely Richardson are destined to compete.

Agatha

"I do wish she'd simply leave me alone and go away."

Agatha, forty-one, lives in Southern Florida and has two children. Her sister is younger by six years and childless. Agatha is a practicing attorney and her sister is an anthropologist.

"An age difference made my sister and myself very separate growing up. We were never close and I do not know why. I don't think it was my mother's fault in any way, although she definitely was a Donna Reed mother, which is a problem all its own. We shared a room for a while which was not a big deal, but basically we were not involved. My sister was a weepy, sickly baby and my mother had her hands full. Later on my sister became weird, which was no one's fault. I mean really very strange, which probably was indicated from the start but no one noticed."

What bothered Agatha was how her mother attempted to compensate for her sister.

"My mother was constantly telling me about my sister. I was in college when I first heard that she had learning problems. My mother felt very guilty. I remember how she made such a fuss over her. I definitely resented the attention lavished upon her when I came home to visit. Being away during this period without ever having established a rapport, there was nowhere to take the relationship. It has never developed but has always been a part of my life.

"To be honest, I do wish she'd simply leave me alone and go away. The point is that there was never any closeness and now there are times when it goes poorly—at family get-togethers, for instance. I understand now that she was never quite right, always odd and different. She never had any friends while I've always been very social and content. I suspect that she was jealous and resentful of me and my normal, boring, workaday life."

Agatha's sister has been married three times, and has no children. Agatha has been married to the same man for twenty years and has two children.

"She has not shown an ounce of interest in my children. She claims that I've never allowed her to be close to them. My interpretation of this is that her current husband insists that she be close because of family connections. He knows there is family money and he doesn't want her making any strategic errors. But the real point is not how my children and my sister get along but the fact that our husbands do not get along at all, to put it mildly. They dislike each other intensely and have even had physical battles. I also dislike her husband although I do not engage him. I see him as a bad person—an enormous emotional burden on my sister and a terrible influence.

"There was one juncture when I believed there was hope for my relationship with my sister, that we might finally bond and live happily after. That was when she married for the first time. I was very excited for her and he seemed like the right kind of guy. Then the marriage fell apart. And I see now that we have such diverse lives, with very different values. She was very religious for a time, devoutly so. That was during the first marriage. And it alienated me somewhat, despite my efforts. She is cult-oriented and her hook into religion was a manifestation of that.

"Perhaps these cults are a way of getting attention. Yet as an adult sister, I wonder if the basic intent behind all of it is a crusade to be odd, stranger than strange. She is undeniably drawn to emotionally needy people and then she pays the price. Three marriages speak for themselves.

"I do not know if we are opposites or the other side of the same coin. I have often thought about how divergent our lives are and how we have made such different choices. This is not the same as someone who was once close to her sister and it has fallen apart, or someone who in adulthood has been able to repair a relationship with her sister, and then reap those rewards. Mine is another scenario altogether. My sister and I have no real relationship nor have we ever had. One cannot miss what she has never experienced."

Agatha's story is unique because although she has a sister six years younger and they were raised under the same roof, she speaks of her as if they've had no interaction at all. She mentions her mother as having struggled with her sister's aberrant behavior, yet Agatha is detached from both her mother and her sister in certain ways. We never get close to the heart of the matter because of Agatha's detachment.

The only upset which Agatha relates to is the fact that her sister's present husband and Agatha's husband have had difficulties. There is a glimmer of insight in Agatha's narrative when she makes reference to her sister and herself as opposite sides of the same coin. She has not explored this concept further, however.

Cathryn

"There were conflicts from the start. I say it is the nature of the beast."

Cathryn, who lives in Houston, has worked in a family business for her entire adult life. At the age of thirty-three, she has never experienced any closeness with her middle sister and only on occasion with her youngest sister. Her mother remains close to all three daughters despite a family quarrel which has divided the family.

"My relationship with my middle sister was either strained or distant from the start. Today we do not speak although she lives nearby. The third, whom I do speak with, lives far away. The second sister is married and the third is not married. I have three children who have no connection to either of my sisters. When I think of what went wrong, I recall that as kids there was only the standard sibling rivalry. What has happened since is blown out of proportion. My middle sister is jealous of me and my lifestyle—yet she has the same lifestyle. Several years ago we stopped speaking. It has to do with the family business. She is not involved in it and I have been working there for my entire adult life. She has irrationally accused me of stealing from her. My parents have chosen to remain neutral, which makes me very angry. The bottom line is that there are deep, unresolved conflicts in our family, and the feud is simply a product of that."

Cathryn does not see this sister at all.

"I wonder how often our third sister sees this sister, since I never do. I see the third sister a few times a year. I do wish that she and I had more of a relationship. But growing up, I was often with the sister who is closest to my age, two years apart, and not with the one who is five years younger much at all. For years I tried to make my relationship with both sisters work. I even helped this sister, the youngest, with her wedding, but ultimately she rejected me.

"I have had screaming battles with my middle sister, but not about anything specific. Family events have been eliminated as a result of the break. It has caused a serious wedge in the family. The conflict existed, I would say, since my mother brought this sister home from the hospital and into the house. Obviously my mother did not deal with sibling rivalry as she should have, or I wouldn't feel this way. I am angry at my parents for not doing a better job. At two years old, I should have had more guidance in forming a relationship with my sister.

"This is not about favorites. As I recall, my mother took the blind eye of justice too far. She never recognized whose fault anything was. She tried to be evenhanded to a fault. What she could not allow for was the fact that one daughter might be wacko. As a parent today, I understand how we must listen to our children. She wasn't willing to do that.

"They would not acknowledge the fact that one child might be wrong. It wasn't the fault of either party in their final analysis. Meanwhile, my middle sister and I were in constant competition. It wasn't set up that way and still it happened. We went to different schools and were separated by choice. We were not consciously aware that we needed to be separated, but ironically it actually was the case. It happened because she chose to attend private school and I did not.

"The careers we have chosen are quite different. While the sister I do not speak with has a freelance job, I run a part of our family's corporation. I respect her education and achievements but I have no intimate knowledge of her career. In the past she has done interesting things. Her husband is a doll and a very bright guy. Our husbands like one another but have no real relationship because we do not see them. Yet it has become apparent over the years that they respect one another which is nice."

The relationship with her younger sister is cordial.

"I feel warmly toward my youngest sister. She has tried, to some extent, to fix the relationship with the middle sister and myself. But she is ill-equipped and too inexperienced. One problem is that my middle sister thinks the profits from the business are being mishandled. The youngest sister does not know enough about the business and is just as ignorant as the other sister in these matters. They both hold it against me without knowing how anything operates. I've tried to explain to both sisters how the structure works. To sum it up, the family battle is about money, family money.

"I have been very disappointed in my relationship with my sisters and the lack of family support. I am constantly looking for close relationships elsewhere. I really like women and have a lot of good women friends. But it does not compensate and I sense what is missing—I know it is not there. I have sort of given up on the entire thing. It never felt special to have sisters because my parents failed at making it work. It was flawed from the start. I am sorry that the opportunity was there and it never happened. I recognize the potential amongst sisters when it is successful. It is a specialness that can enrich one's life, that I understand."

Cathryn's theory is that the closeness in age between the middle sister and herself worked against them.

"Had there been more of an age difference, I wonder if my middle sister and I could have had something positive. With the sister who is five years younger, it seems to have worked better from the start. Being the same sex and close in age has to be difficult. There were always conflicts—I say it is the nature of the beast. We never had any shared secrets or confidences, my middle sister and I. I wish we had. Once, though, we went away together and she told me she considered me the brave one. She perceived herself as the shy one, who stayed near home. This is the only heartfelt exchange we have ever had. I feel it is too bad that there is nothing more. I regret what I couldn't have with either sister. I see it as a loss."

What is notable about Cathryn's story is that although she is convinced that her problems today exist because of family money, no one has stepped forward and been able to heal the wounds. Never close to either sister as a child, Cathryn's hopes for an improved relationship as adults have been discouraged because of the family feud. Since she describes her parents as unable to understand each sister individually as children, there is little hope that they can make peace today. While disappointed, she is matter-of-fact in her approach and conclusion.

Nina

"I have lamented that my kids do not know her . . ."

Nina and her sister grew up in the Boston area and live today in the Northwest. Eighteen months apart, Nina is older and has four children of her own. She does volunteer work in her community. Her sister, who lives near their childhood home, works in consumer products. She is married and has no children.

"Our childhood was bumpy. Our parents had a terrible marriage and finally broke it up when I was thirteen. They were both heavy drinkers. My sister and I ended up living for a while with my grandmother, then my mother, and then my father. The two of us shared all this and still we couldn't be close. During the ordeal, we were divided. I was my father's girl and she was my mother's. We were competitive about everything, but I was always better, especially in sports and academics. I excelled while she worked harder. She did not excel and she definitely resented me.

"We always shared a room. It was very difficult for our mother because she was left without money; that is the dark side of divorce, the part that no one spoke of when we were growing up—but she lived it. My sister and I were caught in the struggle but never felt like allies. We fought a lot—she was forever telling on me. Basically we were opposites. We never liked the same men or the same type of friends. We did not share a single friend, then I skipped a grade and did not have to be so close to her in school. I finished high school at sixteen. I could not wait to get out of that house and leave her.

"There was one time when I was in graduate school and my sister was in college when I wanted us to be close. It was a fiasco. She led a weird life; she was a lesbian, ending up as a bisexual. People were actually making fun of her because she was gay at a very straight college. Anyway, I let go of any expectation that we could be close."

As adults, Nina and her sister have not kept in touch.

"After a while I stopped speaking to my mother altogether because we had never gotten along. I'd been in a very bad accident and she refused to help me financially. So I decided it was time to let it go. As a result, my sister stopped speaking to me. She was so tied to our mother, and by then I was on my own. Whatever money my mother ever had was given to my sister, never to me. I got tired of it and left.

"I also saw their drinking together as a bond. I was totally out of the loop because I'd never been a drinker. During my first marriage, a short marriage, I'd tried to keep up with them. But they excluded me whenever I tried and then I let it drop. I've only seen my sister twice in seventeen years.

"She sends me a greeting card every year and I send her a copy of our family newsletter. I'm sorry that my kids don't know her and then I remind myself that she smokes like a chimney and has been in AA for years. My husband has met my sister twice— he wouldn't recognize her on a street corner."

Nina does not feel that she really has a sister.

"It's total hype that sisters are always close. I watch my own kids when they fight and I know very well that they might be very happy when they no longer have to live together. No one gave them a choice—they were thrown together from birth. That doesn't make it love, it makes it life. There are times when I wish it could have worked out with my sister. I think it would be nice to share what we love, like sports and books. But how can we? We're in different worlds. She doesn't want children while I have four. She's married to a man with several kids from a first marriage and the life they lead is not at all similar to mine.

"I blame my parents for this failed relationship. When they were divorcing, my mother purposely kept my sister away from my father and me. My sister had this need to please our mother even if it meant alienating our father. That's how it happened and has never healed. The tragedy here is that we were two sisters, less than two years apart, who came from a broken home. We were never able to work through our sibling rivalry. Somewhere along the line, we both lost. I look at my husband and kids and I know they're the only family I have. I say this knowing that my sister, my father, and my mother are alive and well somewhere. That makes me sad. Especially about my sister."

If Nina and her sister had not been alienated by the
circumstances of a messy divorce, one wonders if they would be

close today. Nina sounds as if she is in denial when she paints such a black picture of her mother and sister, as if convincing herself that there was no reason to try to salvage any part of the relationships. What is unhappy about Nina's narrative is that she and her sister were never able to find a common ground, so they have no history of joy together. There is only angst and disappointment from childhood onward. In order to protect herself and hold on to what she has established on her own, a marriage and four children, she has abandoned her original family and any chance of working out a connection to her sister.

Marcy

"She was given more by our parents and I had to work for what I got."

Forty-five years old, Marcy lives in Minneapolis where she is a freelance designer. Her sister, who is three years younger, lives in North Carolina. Although she is also trained as a graphic designer, Marcy describes her sister as "doing nothing but shopping."

"I cannot recall ever liking or not liking my sister. My early memories are of my mother pushing her on me so she could have some relief. When we were younger I did not appreciate my sister but as we grew older, we became friends. There was a period when we'd go on dates and then go home and whisper all night, sleeping in the same bed. We were secure in each other and got from one another what our parents could not provide. They weren't really there for us so my sister and I created our own homelife. I do not know if my sister feels that way but I know I do. I was more at ease with her than I was with my mother and it was more of a friendship. I'd go to my sister before my mother any day."

Marcy did not believe that her sister disrupted her friendships, despite their closeness.

"We fight today because I don't like some of her friends nor do I believe that they're good for her. But as younger women, there was no problem. There was room for us and for our friends. What I object to now is the friend of my sister's who is so controlling. My sister needs that and puts this friend ahead of me because she is so needy. Of course, the physical distance presents a problem. My sister sees her friend constantly while we are so far apart.

"When I moved to Minneapolis, my sister would invite our family to North Carolina but then this friend would be with her and she'd have no time for me. She'd put her first and it was very hurtful to know that she wasn't available to me on Christmas because she had so many plans with this friend. I knew she couldn't handle both of us so I backed out.

"Our biggest issue is our mother. We end up having big fights about her all the time. According to my sister, I've never been able to accept our mother as she is. Meanwhile, my sister cannot help support my mother because she can barely handle her own life. She is very wrapped up in her own problems—understandably. She has several kids and is getting divorced for the third time. She was married to a very sick man, emotionally ill. I don't know how she stayed with him all these years. She liked the lifestyle he provided, so maybe that's the answer. Then he found someone else and is leaving. She stayed because of the kids and the financial security. She's not a real strong person and allows people to run her life. She doesn't stand up for her own beliefs. My problem is that her personality is so similar to our mother's. I cannot relate to my mother at all. Of course my sister can, because she's so much like her."

Marcy's relationship with her sister is unconditional.

"I allow my sister to hurt me all the time because I make excuses for her. I expect there will be a day when I won't take it anymore. Then things might change. We've had huge battles and gone months without speaking. She's extremely self-righteous and not willing to hear what I have to say. When her divorce came through I went to visit her. We had this huge blowup and she told me how she sees our relationship. Her vision is so distorted that I began to understand why she can't be there for me. I have a child who has been in the hospital a few times and my sister never even visited, when she lived in Minneapolis. I thought she wasn't available at the time but she really had no idea of what was going on. She didn't even have the facts straight. She never bothered to ask me or to listen to what was happening in my life. I was shocked when we had this altercation and I realized how she thinks. It reaffirmed that she could never be there for me, at least not emotionally. I have to accept this."

Marcy allows her sister to be in control.

"I let her take charge because if I come on too strong she backs off. So I give in to her because I want our relationship to work. I help it along as best I can. I don't know what she wants, but I want it to be a positive thing. Then she upsets me so. The other day we were in the middle of a really serious conversation and she had to get off the phone and promised to call back. I waited and waited but she never did. I called her back several days later and she asked me not to hold it against her because that's just the way she is. Of course, then we have to discuss our mother and she tries to avoid me. She can't handle it.

"When I was nine years old, I became the mother and my mother became the child. My mother wanted me to take over and so I did. I might have been better at it than she was, or so she perceived it. Whatever the reason, my mother wanted it that way. But she remained a mother to my sister. Then she pushed my sister on me because she'd had it. I'd had enough also because of my mother insisting I be the mother. But becoming the mother made me strong. It made me able to say no, which my mother needed to do. My father was almost absent emotionally. He simply let things ride."

At this juncture, when she felt her mother no longer wanted to be in charge, Marcy began to break free.

"I soon became a teenager and began to date and have a life of my own. It was my salvation. By the time I was seventeen and my sister was fourteen, we were close. We do not look alike but have the same artistic spirit. We were never competitive, though. I was not jealous of her. However, if she had gotten more recognition from her friends, as I did, I might have felt differently. I might have resented it, but it didn't happen.

"Then I got married. I actually introduced her to her first husband, and the four of us were really close. I was very supportive of her when she divorced this guy, though. I was also quite busy having kids by then. She dated another man and moved out of town, staying with him until they married. I had the wedding in our home. Our father died soon after and her second marriage fell apart. By that time she'd met her third husband. I had two kids and was working. We were all close, her third husband, my husband, and the two of us. I'd have to go visit her which was tough, because she could never visit me. I think my sister has a problem being too far away from her home."

Today, living far from each other has worked in Marcy's favor.

"I know now that I cannot really count on my sister. Not living in the same town helps—I don't have to face it. It's nice to get back what you give but in her case, it can't happen. She's not capable of it. Despite this, I still believe that we'll end up together in our old age. We'll grow old and take care of each other. Then I cringe at the thought of how we treat each other after a few days in each other's house but still I hold onto this fantasy of spending our twilight years together.

"Now that I'm forty-five I understand that my sister was favored by our mother but that I'm the more stable and emotionally solid of the two of us. My sister can get very depressed and not function for days. She was given more by our parents and I had to work for what I got. I appreciate that now because it made me strong and that makes me happy. As kids even when my friends were more fun than my sister, I put her first. I had this sense of family and loyalty. No matter how I vowed never to put up with her behavior, I always relent because she's my sister.

"My sister can accuse and use me. We fight like crazy and she apologizes in the end. I know when I'm right so I wait it out. Basically we lead different lives and are very different people. But we *are* sisters. So if I think I've lost respect for her, I make an excuse. I know her limitations and how she needs me to be there for her. Can I ever get her to understand how much pain she causes me?"

The mother issue is ever-present in Marcy's relationship with her sister.

"My sister has to protect herself by accepting our mother for who she is. She shrugs it off because it's easier. I still try to help my mother get through life but my sister doesn't—she helps her materially, which I cannot do. I try to give her my insights, which I feel is my strong point. My mother doesn't live near either of us at present. Our approach would differ no matter where she is, though. My sister wants no emotional attachment to our mother.

She shrugs her off. I feel about my mother as I do about my sister. I owe her more than that.

"Over the years, I've realized I can count on my sister less and less. Whatever bone she tosses my way, I take. I keep getting shattered because I fall for her tricks. Then I remind myself of our old age. I know it will happen then—there will be no one else around."

Marcy has been bitterly disappointed by her sister but has not given up. For her, this relationship comes before all others. Both she and her sister have difficulties with their mother. For Marcy, who is a realist, the connection is pursued anyway and for her sister, it seems to be ignored. Although Marcy understands her sister's limitations, she hopes against hope that it can and will be otherwise.

Her perception that she took on the role of the mother by the time she was nine says a lot about the mother. Marcy is the strongest of the three women, and has been for many years. She is not exactly weary of her role, but frustrated that her sister, and her mother to a lesser extent, have not come through for her.

Leslie

"Our family was religious growing up. . . . Each sister broke away."

At the age of forty-one, Leslie has no children and has never been married. Working full time in hospital administration, she lives in a southern city. Leslie, the middle of two sisters, is six years younger than the oldest and five years older than the youngest.

Their background was middle class, and Leslie witnessed her father working several jobs in order to support his wife and the three children. Both of Leslie's sisters live nearby and each has one child.

"We come from a close-knit family. We all sang a lot and music was very important to our family, a real common denominator. It is still a bond but so much has happened since we were kids. My little sister was so much younger than we were, her experience growing up in our family had to be very different from ours. My own experience was that I had an older sister who left the house and I became the older sister. There was always sibling rivalry. I was closer to the older sister and then she was gone. I never felt close to my younger sister until I went to college. She was very smart. Of the three of us, I was the sister who did not live up to her potential. The other two were overachievers. Perhaps it was a middle-child syndrome. My younger sister has a holier-than-thou attitude and it's always bothered me. She told me that when she grew up she'd be a lawyer and I'd end up in the dog house but she would not get me out."

Leslie found being a middle child difficult.

"The first is the first and the baby is the baby. I think there are differences in how a same-sex, middle child is treated. I felt ignored. My grandmother made our clothes and we were all dressed alike. It was all very sweet when we were small. When my oldest sister left for college, the problems began. My parents did not want her to board. One weekend she disappeared and dropped out. We knew where she was but we had to leave her alone. My parents would cry on birthdays and Christmas. They took my sister to court for being a wayward minor. By this time it was so close to her twenty-first birthday it was hardly worth it. After fifteen years she returned to the family. During those years my younger sister and I saw her on occasion, but our parents did not.

"When this sister got married none of us were invited. She only returned to our family because our special uncle died. She got her priorities straight then, and by that time she was no longer married to the first guy. My younger sister missed years with this older sister but I already had a bond with her because I was closer in age."

Leslie does not identify with either of her sisters.

"I find it amazing that my sisters and I grew up in the same household and have such dissimilar views of the world. They had such a volatile relationship with our mother. Our family wasn't perfect but if our parents made mistakes, it wasn't out of not caring or not loving us. My sisters didn't see it this way— they would get furious because my mother was very domineering. I know how they felt. She was constantly telling us how to live our lives. My older sister rebelled against her overbearing nature by leaving. The youngest fought back by not speaking with my mother for months on end. When she had a child, she denied my parents any access to the kid. I thought it wasn't fair.

"I rebelled in my own way. I had an affair with a man of another culture, someone my parents, who are strongly ethnic, would definitely disapprove of. When they found out, they were horrified. They were ready to get the guns and machetes. Our family was religious and we had a strong Catholic upbringing. But all three of us broke away. I think we must have questioned the meaning and purpose of it. Separately we came to the conclusion that our parents' beliefs did not work for us."

Today Leslie feels she would do anything for her sisters.

"The lives we have chosen are not at all similar but we are older now and get along better. In fact, the family is close. I would do anything for my sisters but I also take some of the credit for the peace we have. I have always been the middle one, the mediator. Even when my youngest sister refused to let my mother see her child, I said I did not think it was right. She thought I was taking my parents' side. She began to distrust me and punish me as well. I also did not get to see her child as I had before I defended our parents.

"I was never friends with my sisters and I think that had to do with being separated by age. I could never sit with them and tell them my deepest, darkest secrets. To this day, it isn't what it's about. Yet I can do it with my best friend. What has made everything better with my sisters, although I do not confide in them, is that both our parents died recently. That brought us together. Now all we have is each other and that makes it more meaningful."

Leslie does not like her older sister's husband.

"I think my older sister's husband is probably good to her and the children but he was never nice to my mother. He dominates my sister and has kept her from the family. This is her second husband and she has made the decision to put him first. He resented the fact that our family was close. My other sister's husband is lovely. She dominates *him*. They have one child also and I'm close with this child but not with my older sister's. Her child came late in life and she is overly doting. We didn't have an adult conversation for a year. She was so absorbed with the kid—it was her one and only chance to be as perfect a mother as she could be.

"I see my sisters more now than in the past. We have all matured to a certain extent, and we finally know what family is all about. I had a strong sense of needing to be there for my parents. My sisters did not see it this way and today they are filled with guilt. I am not, as I feel I have always understood how much family counts. So now I see my sisters and we have a great time together, but they are not people I'd choose as friends."

At present Leslie has grown close to her younger sister.

"My younger sister and I are so involved with her child that it brings us closer. Basically I am happy to be with her and my other sister. It can be maddening, but we each remember certain incidents—each of us has a particular sensitivity. I question whether a brother could experience it in quite the same way.

"As I grow older, I appreciate my sisters more. As much as we hate to admit it, we see some of our mother in each of us. Unknowingly she kept us from being really close and alienated us by evoking certain feelings. She fought so much with each of us there was little time left for each other. And then the age difference kept us apart, because we each had different needs. We were raised with values and morals and there was no abuse in our family—that's what counts. My sisters are good mothers today and it had to come from somewhere. It all worked out in the end."

Leslie was in business with her father and considers herself to have been the favorite.

"When I worked with my father, there was an incident which caused my youngest sister to deny me the role of the baby's godmother. She claimed I was my mother's puppet, which meant I could not be her child's guardian. She wanted to hurt me very much. Two weeks later she called to apologize. At the heart of the matter, I think, was the fact that I got along with my parents. I never felt any competition with my sisters. I was the favorite child for one reason—I pleased my parents. The day before my father died he told me he knew I had always been there for him.

"My parents left all the money to me but I'm sharing it with my sisters because I have to live with them and don't want to cause any problems. If I ever needed anything, I would turn to my sisters. I count on them and they count on me. I love them because they're my sisters, and to fight now, with our parents gone, seems ridiculous."

It is interesting to note that Leslie, as the middle child of three sisters, perceives herself, in her final analysis, as the favored child. Her approach to her parents differed from that of her sisters, and ultimately she pleased them enough so they left her their money. Leslie, however, realizes that her sisters are her only immediate family, and is wise to share the estate with them. By making this gesture she is remedying whatever divisive gestures her parents used to keep the sisters apart.

Growing up with a strong mother in a religious family as Leslie did, she and her sisters each had to create their own identity. Her sisters married and had children while Leslie did not. Having suffered so much pain, her goal today is to hold the family together. To this end, the past is past and she is determined to go forward positively.

Janice

"My mother simply lumped us together and told us to take care of each other."

Living in a city in the northeast, Janice is forty-three and works in daycare. One sister is two years older and the other is five years younger. Recently her younger sister was relocated.

"When I talk about my sisters, I think mostly of the one closer to my age. She was the 'Queen' when we were growing up. She did everything in a ladylike way and was always favored by our mother. She was the obedient teenager and I was the rebel. We did a lot together so maybe we weren't as dissimilar as I think. I loved her then and I needed her. She was like a mother to me, she was there for me. I wanted and needed to be more like her, but I couldn't. As I grew up and learned what was expected of me as an adult, I did better. Once I got married, I stopped, finally, trying to be like this sister.

"The 'Queen' was married several years before I was. She led the way for me to marry the kind of husband I eventually chose. I really wanted to marry a farmer but I didn't dare. I was afraid it wouldn't be right for me so I followed in her footsteps and married a doctor. I threw myself into city life and never pursued living in the country. At the time I regretted repressing those urges but now I'm not unhappy. My life has worked out well."

Today Janice is disgusted with her sisters.

"In my maturity I realize that my sister has a more upscale lifestyle than I do. She throws it up to me, and seems to say that only the brightest and the best is good enough for her. I don't like this and it has bothered me over the years. She flaunts the fact that she has more than I do.

"Our oldest children are the same age. I have two daughters and she has two sons. I don't want to be in competition with her, especially not in terms of our kids' achievements. But she cares about that sort of thing. The way it is now, we are ostensibly close but what matters to my sister is of no concern to me. She is part of an upper crust crowd and her husband is a real social climber. At this stage I only see her once or twice a month. Even when she lived nearby, I only saw her at family dinners. She is not more important than my friends and I avoid the people we know in common. In her favor, I will say she has nice children."

Janice believes her father favors her and that her sister doesn't mind.

"My sister doesn't need our father. She doesn't need anyone anymore. She has even stopped caring about being our mother's favorite. She used to think our mother was terrific, but now she's beyond that, too. She doesn't want involvement. Her life is so full and she gets so much from her husband that she doesn't need us. That's the way she feels.

"My little sister is very babyish. She never grew out of her role as the youngest. She got lost in the shuffle and never recovered. She is no one's favorite and is detached from us. She stayed in the same hometown with our mother and is poorly educated, despite numerous opportunities. She surrounds herself with poorly educated people. She is happy with her limited existence because she seems to know no better. She is not close to me and I think I'm probably critical of her. It's as if she came from another family. She has married out of our culture and faith. It is hard to believe she grew up under the same roof. The same goes for my other sister, for that matter.

"What bothers me about my baby sister is that she has narrowed her horizons. She realizes how different my life is and yet she isn't resentful. She is completely closed off. She reminds me of our mother, a fifties mother. She is not the least bit enlightened. She had boyfriends who were cruel and horrible when she was younger. She never worked to better herself—her values are not mine or anyone else's in the family."

Janice's younger sister was the only one at home when her parents divorced.

"I know that when my father left, my little sister felt abandoned. That is why our mother is there for her today. Perhaps I should be close with her but it didn't turn out that way. I don't feel I'm missing out with either sister. This is the way my sisters are. Even my husband has strong opinions about them.

"I am grateful that my sister who is closer in age was there when we were kids. My mother simply lumped us together and told us to take care of each other. She knew I needed my sister. We even shared a room. Today, I'm not looking to be closer to either sister. I believe that when I'm alone with my older sister, it works. We are happy in a strange way. We have certain interests in common—we both work and are interested in the arts. If we weren't sisters, if we were just two adult women, it might be better. Then there would be a mutual appreciation. On the one hand, we can discuss the family and our parents. We have a shared history, we see eye to eye. On the other hand, we are still in the roles we assigned ourselves in childhood. That doesn't go away."

Janice does not desire closeness with either sister at this stage. One wonders if she is so disappointed by both women that it is a defense or if her needs have changed over the years. Although she and the older sister were close growing up, that stemmed from a tie that Janice feels is no longer there. The real barrier for Janice is that neither of her sisters has similar values. Her first sister is materialistic and her younger sister is undeveloped. Having made her own way, Janice has finally let go.

Fortunately for Janice, the marriage she chose in order to emulate her sister has worked out. She now distances herself from both sisters and does not aspire to any connection beyond familial duty.

Jody

"We were too attached and had to break free."

At the age of forty-five, Jody has been an office administrator in Chicago for over five years. Unmarried, she has a sister two years older who works for a corporation in New York City and is also single.

"We were very close growing up. We shared a room and when we were very young, I tagged along everywhere. My sister did not want me to, but I'd insist. I wanted to do whatever she did. If she stayed up late, then I did, too. It was sibling rivalry. I was the baby and, in some ways, I was favored. In other ways, I was not. My sister was initially the favorite in terms of appearance. She was adorable. I was favored later in terms of approval. I did more and was a more independent person in certain areas.

"I was more conventional but both my sister and I found our own ways to rebel. In the early years, I remained a tagalong and even attended nursery school at the age of two because my sister was there. Our parents treated us as if we were twins. That was fine up to a certain age and then we resented it. I wanted my own things and my own gifts. Neither of us wanted to dress alike anymore. I was the youngest, but I asserted myself more than my sister did. I wanted to make the break."

Jody and her sister kept each other company.

"We fought but we were pals. We played games and if no one else was around, we spent time together. When it came to friendships, we had separate friends. Sometimes we were competitive and I definitely wanted to be with her more than she wanted to be with me. By adolescence, my friends became more important than my sister. She and I are so different that we were attracted to very dissimilar people. I was more outgoing, my sister more introverted and shy. But we remained close enough to depend on each other if necessary."

Today Jody realizes how different her life is from her sister.

"My sister and I actually lived together in Chicago for several years, right after I graduated from business school. I learned that living with a sister is not the same as living with a friend. I do not believe that friends can be sisters. Sisters are sisters and friends are friends. It was all the history we brought to the table that made it so difficult. In order to survive living in the same house as adult women, we had to separate. First we established different lives for ourselves and remained in the apartment and then finally, to maintain our relationship, we separated physically.

"The perception I came away with is that sisters have to break away in the same way that kids have to separate from their parents. Siblings need the same distance. Growing up a certain way, how close you become to a sister depends on one's values and on a deep emotional love. But being friends or switching roles doesn't work. We are sisters, with unique personalities."

The physical distance has helped Jody and her sister.

"Since my sister has moved east, we speak frequently and see each other as often as possible. Sometimes I do wish we could be in closer contact. She did want me to come east with her, but my life is here and she's made a life for herself in New York City. Today she's more active and athletic than I am—she has a higher energy level. She's travelled the world alone. I would not and could not do that. Both of us have been involved in long-term relationships and neither of us is attached to anyone at present.

"I look back on the time that my sister and I lived together as a turning point in our relationship. We hadn't planned to do it originally—it was dictated by economics. She was the one who pressed for it. For the time it worked out, it was a positive experience. I think we ended up living together because our parents had died and we needed one another. There were economic and social circumstances, too, so we helped each other out. I was younger and very fearful of living in Chicago. She was less fearful in some ways.

"I think it can be wonderful to have a sister and it can also be problematic. The problems stem from the fact that each sister relates in her own way to the other. I had trouble with separation issues and my sister didn't. For me, growing up, I felt I was actually the older sister. My sister had another lifestyle and approach altogether. It took her years to come out of herself. When she moved away from Chicago and got to New York City she built a life for herself. She's not the same person she was when she left here, and I'm happy for her. She has developed as a person. I doubt if it would have happened if we had stayed together. I was not the best sister, I admit that. I was critical in the guise of being helpful. It might have been part of our family dynamic. It took me a long time to realize that people have to be themselves and you cannot tell them how to be. It doesn't work."

Jody sees the separate lives that she and her sister enjoy as a liberating experience.

"I was very worried about my sister until she finally moved away. We were too attached and had to break free. Today we can travel together and have fun, we can be close and get to know each other's friends. The sibling rivalry has lessened and in some ways, we are more comfortable with our real selves. I also know now that we are family and will always maintain that level of caring. The sensitivity and fighting have lessened but never entirely go away.

"With the distance, I've come to a better understanding of

who I am. I'm a more open person than my sister is. We would not intentionally hurt one another but she is more controlling. We deal with vulnerabilities quite differently and still have problems. I do not think it would work out to ever live together again. We are not a pair of sisters who will join forces in old age. I suppose it could happen but it isn't a goal for either of us. We are close enough in theory but in reality we do not get along when we are together for long periods of time.

"I do not imagine that sharing our old age would be a positive experience. If ever either of us was in need, the other would be there. But fighting with each other in our twilight years . . . I don't think so."

Jody and her sister had issues that were unresolved from childhood. Jealous and competitive when younger, they found themselves living together as young adult women. Having lost their parents, they clung to one another but Jody alludes to the fact that it was a destructive relationship.

The battle for autonomy was long and hard but finally the sisters established separate lives for themselves. Jody describes the bond with her sister as close today but is obviously relieved that they no longer are so intricately intertwined. The geographical distance has lessened the intensity so that Jody and her sister are able to appreciate one another.

Neda

"She simply followed my lead; I made it easier for her."

At the age of sixty, Neda and her sister, who are from India, practice different aspects of medicine in a city in the northeast. Neda, the oldest of six children, felt it was her duty to pave the way for her only sister who is four years younger. By choosing the medical profession, she believed she would have something to offer wherever she lived. Her sister has followed Neda so closely that today they work in the same area.

"We both studied in New Delhi, because our father wanted us to be doctors. My sister was the favorite but I was the first, so I pleased my father. My sister did whatever I did professionally. Today, we live nearby but do not see each other so often. Of course, we are both practicing medicine full time. Our children are grown and are quite close. In fact, our sons share an apartment in the city and work in the same profession.

"My sister and my husband do not get along very well, but it is her husband who has discouraged any real closeness between my sister and myself. I think that has caused the distance and I'm very disappointed. When I think of all that binds us, being foreign women who have achieved so much professionally, I'd like us to be closer in order to share our successes. My brother-in-law has actually pulled my sister away from me. I only see my sister every few months."

Neda recognizes that her sister is competitive.

"I do not respond to her overtures. My feeling is that I was first and there is no competing in my mind. She simply followed my lead—I made it easier for her. I am also more aggressive and we have such different personalities. I am more involved socially and in the community. I have other interests, while my sister spends most of her time being a physician.

"The fact that our kids are close matters to me. I identify with their struggle. They went to excellent colleges and yet they battle for their identities constantly, as my sister and I had to do. Despite a good education, being a foreigner in America is not easy. That is the common thread for both sets of kids, hers and mine. They need each other. My sister and I, for any differences we might have, also need to remember that we are Indian women, first and foremost. We are well-trained and hard-working, but we are female and foreign. That makes us sisters beyond anything else."

In their hometown, Neda and her sister are known as "the successful doctor sisters."

"I think we are known both as sisters and as physicians. My sister is more important to me than friends, especially with our identities so closely entwined, both professionally and as sisters. We entered the U.S. with our training and degrees from India. We shared the same experience there before coming here. That is another thread. It is a noble profession we have chosen and we both feel very grateful to our parents for pushing us. It has served us well. My sister and I understand this; no one else is in our shoes and no one else feels as we do."

For Neda, the relationship with her sister is tied up with their professional lives as well as their family life. She is pleased that their children are close. She is also pleased that her sister is successful in her field although it has been a competitive road. The other difficulty is her brother-in-law's control over the closeness the two sisters share. But the most compelling factor for Neda is how she and her sister have persisted to be where they are today. Ultimately, that bond is stronger than any negative aspects of the relationship.

Rebecca

"I am what I am and I am not ashamed of it . . . my sister worries about the peer pressure that my children will have to face."

At the age of twenty-seven, Rebecca is single and works for a pharmaceutical company. Living in a small town in Texas, she is one of two sisters. Her sister, who is two years older, is married and also works in pharmaceuticals. Both sisters are expecting their first babies.

"My sister and I get along fine on most issues. Growing up, we were definitely involved in each other's lives. We had our arguments but we defended each other against our parents. We were friends to each other when we were little girls. As grown women, it isn't the same. Today, she has remained in Colorado where we grew up and we don't see each other often."

Rebecca is pregnant with twins.

"I was artificially inseminated and my sister and my parents were not pleased about this. They do not approve of my choice and they feel I ought to be married to have a baby. Obviously I'd be married if I wanted to be. I do not plan ever to be married. I was worried about having a child before I got too old. I purposely chose a close friend to provide the sperm, someone whose history I know and who has not had many sexual partners. He is married and has a family and I am very comfortable with him.

"My sister is upset about my pregnancy and how I've gone about it. She has no concern for the babies I'm carrying, but focuses on the way I've gotten pregnant and the choice I've made. She thinks it's selfish of me and cannot accept it. I am still close to my sister but there is a wedge now. At a time when we should be sharing our pregnancies, she is reluctant to talk about mine."

Rebecca is a homosexual and lives with a partner.

"I am what I am and I'm not ashamed of it. I do not wish to be with men but that doesn't mean I don't want children. Gay people often deny themselves families because it isn't the thing to do. My partner actually lost her child to her husband in a custody case. She and I plan to raise our twin babies together. She is totally involved with the birth and was there for the artificial insemination. She cannot medically have children which is why I wanted to do this. My sister worries about the peer pressure that my children will have to face. My response is that I will not be denied something I feel so strongly about—mothering a baby. My parents would like to disown my homosexual lifestyle and the fact that I became pregnant as I did.

"My mother is a twin, which is ironic. I didn't think it would happen to me. Despite the fact that I'm having twins, my sister and my mother cannot deal with it. I have explained that women have maternal feelings whether they're gay or straight. I wanted to have a baby so badly that I would cry at diaper commercials on television. This went on for three years until I finally found the right person. Financially and emotionally I wanted to be set, and that's where I am today. I was determined to have a baby before I met my partner but the timing became perfect once we'd met. To have twins makes it even better; we'll have our whole family immediately."

When Rebecca told her sister she was pregnant, her sister was shocked.

"My sister and my mother are so close, it's as if the umbilical cord has never been cut. I purposely told my sister about the pregnancy first. Then I decided to tell my mother first about the twin part. She went crazy. She called my sister and had a fit.

"When I think back, I remember my parents were very supportive of my athletic abilities when I was in high school and college. My sister was left out of that particular loop. By the time I was in college they knew about my sexual preferences. I have had serious problems with my father but he was the one who would listen. My mother and sister would not discuss the life I've chosen. They simply could not face it.

"I would like to be close to my sister and mother, but on my terms, not theirs. The way they behave is controlling and stereotypical. No matter what I say, my sister believes I ought to be married. They are embarrassed by me, because they are sheltered and traditional people. They have never been out of Colorado."

Rebecca was molested by her father as a child.

"For years my mother knew. She blamed me and no one would believe my story. That was the way it happened, and still happens. We were a well-respected family and my parents had successful careers, both in the field of law. But this was what was kept hidden—it was a terrible secret and I was the victim. My sister doesn't know, she hasn't any idea; it was too awful to tell her. And I don't think it's the reason I don't choose to be with men—it's simply what happened to me, a part of my life.

"Recently I've lost any hope that my family will accept me. I've become more concerned about my own family, the one I'm creating. I've never really felt that my original family is *my* family. What they've done has taught me what I do and do not want to put into my new family. I realize what's missing in them, and why I never really belonged."

Rebecca's twins and her sister's baby are due within a few months of each other.

"My sister has never come to visit me in Texas, nor have my parents. I doubt they will when the babies are born because my mother has made it clear that she will be helping my sister with her newborn at that time. And for the holidays, she's already committed to being in Colorado with my sister. I keep thinking it might be different, that my sister will accept me on some level. The problem is that there is so much tension with my mother, who finds my situation impossible. It's so difficult with her. I want her to treat me like a daughter and be able to talk to her. I want a mother-daughter relationship that works.

"I don't believe the trouble with my mother began when she found out about my sexual preferences. But it escalated when I chose an alternative lifestyle. My mother feels she must disown me now because I choose to live with a woman. But deep down, she knows what happened."

What Rebecca is concentrating on today is the life she and her partner have established for themselves.

"I can't compete with my sister. So I've made my own life, and my future is centered around my children. I hope for normal, healthy babies. Somewhere down the line, my sister could be there for me. My whole family could, maybe, but I can't count on it. I need to be accepted now, not when the babies are born. My sister has to be there now. When we talk on the phone she won't ask about my pregnancy, but I ask about hers. I wonder if we're really talking at all."

In a complex situation fraught with pain and disillusionment, Rebecca has emerged as a woman who understands her own needs. The price she pays is that her relationships with her sister and mother, both of great value to her, have been seriously altered by her choice to live with a woman. It seems that when she became pregnant, the entire state of affairs escalated. Rebecca feels she is not treated fairly and does not belong with her family.

After many disappointments, Rebecca cannot completely give up the possibility of a reconciliation between her sister and herself. Despite everything, she craves the closeness and her sister's and mother's acceptance. The original competition, which centered around Rebecca's athletic ability, is now focused on the impending birth of both sisters' children. Because Rebecca has chosen an unconventional way of having children and raising them, her sister has ammunition against her. Her sister has finally usurped her place. Even after Rebecca's father's abuse, and her sister's and mother's inflexible attitude, she still wants a fair shot at being accepted and invited into the warmth of the family.

SUPPORTIVE SISTERS:
There For Each Other

Supportive sisters share a healthy relationship. Sibling rivalries and striving for attention from the parents have ended. The fears and anxieties of childhood are over. The sisters react maturely and realize that a sister is a special person in one's life. Supportive sisters enjoy their genetic and environmental bonds and are able to count on each other.

RONNIE L. BURAK, PH.D

Bonded to one another, Loretta Lynn and her sister Crystal Gayle share a past they were able to leave behind. Lynn, known as the "coal miner's daughter," is perhaps the most famous female country singer. Her sister, Gayle, is sixteen years younger and known for her own type of music, including "Cry me a River" and "Don't It Make my Brown Eyes Blue."

What is dissimilar about the two sisters is that Loretta Lynn was a mother at thirteen and a grandmother at the age of twenty-nine. Crystal Gayle did not have her children until her career was established with the help of her sister, who was already a star. That their singing skills are not alike works in their favor. Another factor is the age difference. Because the sisters were not exposed to the same environment growing up, Crystal was influenced by pop as well as country singers. There for each other, Loretta has paved the way for her younger sister's talent to shine.

When we speak of sisters, it is difficult not to comment upon Olga, Masha, and Irina, the famed sisters of Anton Chekhov's play, *The Three Sisters*. Olga, at the age of twenty-eight when the play opens, is the eldest. Successful in her career, she has no personal life. Masha, the middle sister, is in an unhappy marriage at twenty-four, frustrated by the constraints of her existence. Irina, at twenty, is young, hopeful, and engaged. Each sister, inextricably connected to the others by locale and personal disappointments, searches for what she cannot have. In the end, all three sisters, disparate as they seem, realize they are bound by blood.

Again we are informed of an unusual sisterly support system in Marilyn Robinson's novel, *Housekeeping*. When the mother drowns herself, leaving her young daughters in the care of their two maiden great-aunts, the great-aunts, as a team of sisters, decide that the candidate best suited to care for these young sisters is their niece, the surviving sister of the mother. Raised by an eccentric aunt, one child grows up to enter the mainstream, eerily reminiscent of her mother, while the other resembles the aunt, dysfunctional and good at heart. Ultimately the three-tiered sisterly support team splinters and we are left to absorb the tragic impact of the story.

What of the sisterhood of Beth Henley's play, *Crimes of the Heart*? When one sister is accused of murdering her husband, her two estranged sisters reunite in their hometown to show their support. And again, in the film, *Gas, Food, Lodging*, we watch two adolescent sisters as they support each other's dream of escape from an impoverished existence. Choosing different methods, in the end these young sisters are separated by circumstances. What makes the tale so poignant is their connection as sisters.

* * *

Debbie Allen and Phylicia Rashad are determined sisters—as well as two of the most sought-after women in show business. Seeing each other as best friends and yet enjoying separate careers, each is thrilled with the other's success. Because Debbie lives in Los Angeles and Phylicia in New York City, it isn't a day-to-day relationship. However, when just out of college, they were roommates. A year apart and both graduates of Howard University, Debbie as *cum laude* and Phylicia as *magna cum laude*, the sisters were raised to succeed. Prepared for the difficult road to stardom by their mother, Vivian Ayers, a poet, they were encouraged to be educated and accept challenge. Debbie starred in the television series "Fame," several Broadway shows, and "One Life to Live" while Phylicia is best known as Bill Cosby's wife on the sitcom "The Cosby Show."

Despite the fact that Debbie's success came more rapidly than Phylicia's, the issue has never come between them. Today both enjoy their stardom and are recognized for their unique talents in acting, singing, and dancing. Each is married to an athlete—Phylicia to Ahmad Rashad, a former star of the Minnesota Vikings, and Debbie to Norman Nixon, an NBA all-star who retired from the LA Clippers. Motherhood is one more joy that the sisters happily share.

Emily

"My mother was told when my sister was born that she might never have the capacity to learn anything."

At the age of thirty-six, Emily is the oldest of three children. Her sister, who is the youngest in the family by five years, is deaf and aphasiac. She lives in northern California and has two small children, while Emily lives in Atlanta and has three children.

"During my childhood, it seemed normal to have a handicapped sister because I had no basis for comparison. Looking back, I know now that I grew up in unusual circumstances, with a handicapped sister and an overachieving middle child, my brother. As I grew older, I began to understand how different my life was, yet it was acceptable to me. I did not quite notice how life revolved around my sister. I thought it was the way things were—that was it.

"Although I did not actually take care of my sister, my brother and I were expected to teach her things. My mother spent a tremendous amount of time with her when my brother and I were at school. At the same time, my parents were able to create a life for themselves; they traveled and had friends. There was a lot at stake, but they still fought to have their life separate from us. So while I was conscious that my sister needed more attention, I was also aware of my mother's life away from her. So much in my mother's life revolved around my sister's needs—her juggling act was terrific. It was never obvious that she did what she did."

Emily has always missed having a "regular" sister.

"By the time I was a teenager, I had seen enough wonderful sister relationships to know I was missing something. My sister and I could not be close because she could not communicate with me for years. When she began to do so, I was already in college. I was never able to catch up. And even though she could communicate, it was not the same as the relationships between sisters that I admired.

"I still believe that whatever was possible was better than nothing. I'm grateful to have a sister, although she was never available to me in the way I had hoped she might be. I know what a heartbreak that is, but I also know that I benefit from the rapport I have with her children. I'm very attached to my sister's children. I find her exasperating to this day, but I'm extremely proud of what she has accomplished. She is married to a deaf man who works full time and together they have two hearing children. I find it quite remarkable.

"My own children have difficulty communicating with my sister and that bothers me, although I understand. But they also love her children very much. They are simply crazy about those kids. We live far away, my sister and I. That's another factor, because she is on the west coast. I see her three times a year at the most. My mother sees her much more, but her relationship with my sister has always been at the heart of everything."

Emily views her mother's manner of dealing with a deaf child as amazing.

"I admire how my mother coped with my sister's situation from the start. She was told when my sister was born that she might never have the capacity to learn anything. It was my mother's energy and love that made my sister who she is today, a college graduate. In the past eighteen years of my life, since I became a young adult, I have realized how hard my mother worked with my sister. My mother and I became a team, concerned and fearful for my sister. I think she values my input, and it has strengthened our relationship.

"I was very aware during my own pregnancy and the birth of my children how fragile and blessed we are to have normal, healthy children. I felt I tempted fate with the third pregnancy because of what had transpired with my mother's third. So I see life in terms of gifts, not givens, because of my sister. It has also given my mother another dimension. She is not just another up-scale, materialistic, suburban woman. She could never be that, because she had to face this challenge and it made her more human.

"To have a sister like mine has taught me tolerance. I could never be superficial or glib. I had a sister at home who needed special care, who could never have the freedom or experiences I had. My mother wanted me to fit in desperately because my sister did not. Thank God I learned what mattered. My sister made me sensitive to other people. There was no need to fit in so perfectly—it was overrated. I realized this after years of introspection.

"I'm disappointed because of what my sister and I have missed. I watch my two daughters and I know what I never had. But in retrospect, my sister helped me escape the shallow world that surrounded me. Early on I recall my sister making it impossible to do things as a family. She had a behavioral problem, to the point where there wasn't a family meal that wasn't disrupted. The five of us could never go to a restaurant together. She could not be included because she couldn't function. I felt terrible about this. I felt terrible about the things that did not happen—family trips, cultural outings. If we took a day trip she couldn't go."

Emily never felt ostracized by her friends because of her sister.

"I escaped my friends' awareness of my sister's situation because of the age difference—their paths and my sister's never crossed. Soon enough she was in school all day and that helped ease things. What I came to know as an adult was that it is more difficult for me to feel really close to women because of my sister, although I like having women friends. I never had a built-in role model of an appropriate sisterly relationship. I felt removed and remote, not drawn in. I spent a lot of time alone as a kid. I've learned to rely on myself as a result of my sister. I became a loner by choice, and grew accustomed to it.

"I cannot give up the dream that I have an okay sister. There is no way to have a discussion with her to this day. Because of her impairment, she sees things in black and white—there are no shades of grey. She is very literal, not philosophical, which is limiting. But when she first had children, she called to ask questions and looked to me as a role model. It's very interesting that for us, as adult sisters, the common bond is our children."

During high school and college, Emily and her brother were excellent students.

"My brother and I are very smart—we have always excelled. It was painful to watch my sister and know how boxed in she was. She has always existed in her own world; she craves acceptance in the handicapped universe, and couldn't care less what the speaking, functioning world expects of her. Her bitterness focuses on where she fits into the world of the deaf, her place in her own sphere. What I do has little impact upon her. And I cannot forget our separateness—it goes beyond any connection we create with one another."

Emily's story is one of hope and loss. She has always understood that her sister and she could not be equals. Recognizing that her sister's condition evoked strength in what Emily would consider an otherwise ordinary suburban family, she continues to be acutely disappointed that she has a sister she can never be close to.

The admiration she has for her mother indicates there is no resentment or unhappiness on Emily's part. She is not envious of the attention her sister received, nor does she resent her neediness. Rather she feels extraordinarily attached to her mother as a result, and appreciative of her method of handling her sister. Emily has accepted the good that has come about: her mother's determination to help her sister become a functioning person, her sister's marriage and children, and the relationship she has established with her sister's children.

What cannot exist between Emily and her sister is a true meeting of the minds, and for this Emily is extremely sad and disappointed. She has worked through many of the issues, but the facts remain: her sister is deaf and aphasiac, and her interests do not lie in the speaking world.

Sarah

"I have a sick child and a dead sister, so two circuits are shut down for me."

Having lived her entire life in southern Florida, Sarah is the oldest of three sisters. The youngest left home by the time she was eighteen and never returned. Her middle sister was Sarah's best friend during childhood and for much of their adult lives. Ten years ago, Sarah's middle sister died. Today, at the age of sixty-one, Sarah misses her sister as if it happened yesterday.

"My middle sister and I shared a room as kids—I can still see the twin maple set. We were only two years apart and while we did not share the same interests, we were devoted to one another. She was much quieter and more academic. I was the social and popular one. My middle sister had one boyfriend and he became her husband by the time she was eighteen. I was married by the time I was twenty. That was how it was in those days."

Sarah had many boyfriends before she settled down.

"I was so full of fun and my sister was so serious and reserved. There was no competition because we were so different. She was very homely and I was not. But my sister had lovely skin and deep-set eyes. The truth was that she had a terrible nose. Once she decided to have it fixed, she went from being an ugly duckling to a swan. She became a smashing young woman, but she didn't do it until she was a mother with a young child. I remember when I went with her to see the plastic surgeon she asked him what she'd look like. He looked over at me and said you'll look like your sister. She asked why she should pay so much money to look like her sister and he explained that he could not make a Cadillac out of a Ford. Once she had the surgery, however, she became more outgoing. Had she been married to a more adventurous man, she might have really let loose."

In the early days of their marriages, Sarah and her sister lived half a block from each other.

"We chose to live nearby on purpose. We had always lived in the same city and we saw one another constantly. My sister had three children and I had two. After our mother became ill and died, we became even closer. The baby sister was never a part of the fabric of our lives—it was just the two of us, my middle sister and myself. We shared everything: family, children, households, holidays. Our children are close to this day. We continue to spend the holidays together.

"When my sister was forty, she developed breast cancer. For eleven years she fought five bouts of it. It did not metastasize until the end. Each cancer that my sister battled was different and localized. I was with her throughout each ordeal. She'd say to me she knew that she was going to die, but we all knew we'd die someday. She said what set her apart was that she knew what she would die *from*. She taught me how to die properly and with dignity. At the end my sister was at home in a coma and was totally prepared for her own death."

Sarah's sister's husband married one of her sister's best friends.

"I do not believe that my sister had the advantage of having been married to someone special. She married her husband because of her lack of confidence. As I said, she was not pretty until her nose was fixed. Our kid sister was gorgeous and I was considered really pretty. Our poor middle sister really suffered. That's how I'm able to come to terms with her marriage. I'm not surprised he married my sister's close friend."

Sarah feels that her entire life has been altered by her sister's death.

"My sister and I did everything together. We played tennis, went to the theater, raised our kids, and because we had each other, I did not need a best friend. There is no replacement for this kind of loss. Nothing is the same, a part of your heart is missing. I have a sick child and a dead sister, so two circuits are shut down for me. Sure I go on, but I'm always aware that something is missing. It's not pain, but a dull ache.

"When something special happens in my life, I wish my sister was here. My connection to her kids helps me and I go to the cemetery. These are my ties. It's almost as if we become accustomed to loss and sickness when we grow older. My sister was an integral, functioning part of my life. Emotionally I am closed off because she's not here."

There are certain issues which Sarah believes only her sister could have supported.

"If ever I'd gotten into terrible trouble, my sister would be the only one there for me. I could go to her and tell her anything. Things I'd tell no one else. Her home was my kids' home and she was their second mother, and vice versa. The loss of my sister is like losing an arm. I miss her so, there are days I say to my husband, *If only she was alive.* My life is changed irreversibly. And while we have to expect loss, my sister died at a relatively young age and I feel absolutely cheated. When you're younger, you don't expect it to happen."

Sarah feels she can never recover from her sister's death.

"Once my sister brought home a painting of two old sisters and said it was us in our old age. We used to laugh about it. My husband assumed I would outlive him and she and I would be together one day. But it never came to pass. It was a fall-back position that never had an opportunity to happen. Our thinking was so similar—we balanced each other out. That was why it might have been a good way to spend our later years.

"If you don't have a sister to begin with, you might not experience the meshing of two souls. There probably aren't four people one meets in an entire lifetime where there is truly that meshing. Each of us is lucky if we have it once, and we know in our gut what it is, what sets that attachment apart. I had it with my sister."

Sarah's commitment and love for her middle sister goes without question. For her the loss is so all-encompassing that it has affected every aspect of her life. She has lost her support system. What one wonders about her story, however, is where her younger sister fits in. As Sarah tells us, she dropped out of the family quite early on. Once her middle sister died, why didn't the younger sister step forward?

The way it is described, it is almost as if Sarah had only one sister. Now that she is gone, Sarah carries on, but feels her life is diminished. Her sister's death is an everpresent sadness to her.

Dana

**"My next youngest sister, who I feel closest with, calls
herself an overeater and an alcoholic."**

*Dana, who grew up in southern California, is the second eldest of
four sisters. While her entire family remains near her hometown,
Dana lives and works in New Canaan, Connecticut. All four
sisters are married and work part-time. All the sisters are
married but only the two youngest have children.*

"My two younger sisters have a different father because my
father died before I was two. My stepfather definitely became a
father to me but there is quite an age range in the family. I am
two years younger than my older sister and then there is a five-
year gap between me and the next sister and then five more
years between her and the youngest. The oldest sister and I
would seem the most similar superficially; we both have husbands who are professionals and have a similar socioeconomic
existence. However, I feel closer to the third sister, the one who is
five years younger. The oldest sister and I are no longer very
close because she has a very strange, manipulative husband who
dominates her completely.

"What is interesting about my oldest sister is that our husbands have the same kind of background, while she and I come
from a completely different orientation. Our stepfather is an
Episcopalian minister and our husbands are Jewish, northeast-
erners. But my brother-in-law has tried to tear our family apart.
As a result, my sister has really closed herself off from me. She is
so blinded by her husband, she has cut me out in order to justify
being with him. He is a control freak. I know my older sister and
I are there for each other, but we aren't close. Once when he was

out of the picture, we were closer. But then she made the decision to remain with him. So only when they were separated did she try to come back into the family. It was a brief effort."

Dana's closest attachment, to the third oldest sister, remains intact.

"My next youngest sister, who I feel closest with, calls herself an overeater and an alcoholic. She had a bulimia problem which she has overcome. I see her as needing acceptance and support. I am not close to her physically, but I'm emotionally available. And she knows it. I often wonder if the geographical separation I've created by living in the northeast was intentional. I realize I'm the only one to make that break and I think it's fine. It works for me.

"I speak with this sister three times a month. I write to the youngest because we never use the telephone—it just doesn't seem necessary in this particular relationship. I only visit my sisters every other year but I'm aware that they see each other very often because they live nearby. I send my old clothes to them and they do not see them as castoffs but are grateful. That's the nature of our relationship. I don't feel excluded, and I know that having children has provided a common bond. They make an effort to get together because of the kids."

Dana views having sisters as the ultimate sharing process.

"Although I am not close by, I know what being one of four sisters has done for me. It has taught me about sharing and responsibility. I was so lucky to learn this way, to have to pitch in around the house and babysit for the younger ones. It was expected of me and it enriched me as a woman in terms of human relationships. I see how it helps me as an adult. I don't believe that a brother is the same kind of attachment. We have one brother and he is not in the loop nor is it part of his value system to be there. While we might say he was outnumbered, I also think it's his makeup, that of brothers versus sisters.

"There are such poignant moments growing up as sisters. My sisters and I are individual and unique so it's difficult to realize that we all grew up in the same house. I cannot imagine how some sisters end up being similar because it's not the case in my family, not at all. I don't know any sisters who are much alike. I do find it easy to have female friends because I relate well to women. Observing my sisters with their own distinct styles has made it easier to have various and assorted women friends."

At certain times, Dana has felt more attached to one sister than to another.

"I have felt closer to the older one in times past. When I was in college she and I were very close. Then the third oldest and I began to bond and it has been the strongest. I think the oldest felt that she carried a burden by being first and having to carve a path for the others. She's definitely the one with a dark side. I have always been the most independent. I wanted my own life from the age of five, and it came naturally. I didn't want to divorce myself from the family but I stood on my own two feet. The others lean more on each other and are more interconnected. I do not feel excluded. I was always a thread but I never needed to be physically placed in the same room. I was never threatened by being absent."

Dana recalls the fact that her mother changed radically in the past and is aware of the toll it took on all four sisters. Religion is a strong force in all four sisters' lives, as well as the mother's.

"My mother became a religious fanatic. It affected all of us greatly, but me the least because I'm here in Connecticut and it isn't a day-to-day thing. She refused to come to my wedding ten years ago because of her newly found religious beliefs. And my stepfather was officiating, which made it doubly hurtful. She was the coolest, most popular mother when we were growing up, and my sisters and I were always the ones to have kids over. Everyone came to our house, filled with four sisters and the neat mother. Then all of a sudden she's someone else, another person.

"I suspect that my sisters are bonded to each other more closely than ever because of this change in our mother. We no longer consult her because she doesn't fulfill our needs. She is too religious and self-absorbed to pay any attention or give advice. I think religion has put a real tailspin on my family. My oldest sister converted to Judaism. My choice is to remain as I was raised, an Episcopalian. My third sister is now Catholic and the fourth is a Jehovah's Witness, like my mother. Ironically, she still has difficulty with my mother, despite the same religious affiliation.

"The way I see it, each of us has made our own choices, independent and individual from each other. The more independent we are, the more connected we become, almost as a way of getting closer. I'm aware of the support system and strength I have because I'm one of four sisters."

The fact that Dana is the only sister to move across the country and establish a completely separate lifestyle does not impinge on her role as a sister. Rather she feels anchored and grounded in her decision and the life she has chosen. There seems to be no competition or jealousy among the sisters; each woman appears quite committed to the life she has created. What Dana feels as a result of having been one of four sisters is a source of comfort.

She notes that religious beliefs have affected the family and that each woman, sisters and mother alike, have made serious personal choices. Yet no one is intolerant of the others. She does not sound regretful about her mother's sudden decision, either. Her approach is to live and let live, and while she describes each sister in very individualistic terms, this philosophy seems to permeate the entire family.

Kim

"I feel very strong because I am a part of these women. I am one of the sisters."

At the age of thirty-four, Kim still views herself as the baby in the family, the youngest of four sisters. Living in Chicago, she laments how infrequently she is able to be with her three older sisters. Growing up without a father, Kim believes that she and her three sisters were connected in an unusual and powerful bond.

"I lost my parents early in life and I remained the baby because of my older sisters. I'm the baby no matter how old I become. We have a unique relationship because there is less competition and jealousy in a family where there are no surviving parents.

"Although at times I have a favorite sister, we all get along. My oldest sister and I have more of a mother-daughter relationship. She is the most maternal and a mother figure to me. My second oldest sister is the brightest and was always the achiever. The third settled for everything in life and I see her as a middle child almost—and then I was the baby, spoiled rotten."

Kim describes the attitude her three sisters had toward her as unconditional love.

"My sisters don't see me as a responsible adult and yet I'm unconditionally loved. I'm the most financially secure because my husband is a lawyer. I don't see my sisters very often and when I do, there is a sense that my lifestyle is different from theirs. Two of my sisters live in Georgia and one in New York. I make the most effort to travel to see them because I can afford it. I have a good relationship with everyone's husband and kids.

"We're devoted to each other because it's all we've got. There are no parents and so we cling together. I won't say that there is no pettiness, but it isn't serious and passes quickly. An example of this has to do with gift giving. When we go in on a family gift for another sister, it never goes smoothly and I'm consulted last because I'm the baby. Another issue is our children. During family get-togethers, we all try to put our children in the best light. When we're on someone else's turf, it's difficult."

There is an age discrepancy between Kim and her sisters.

"I'm eight years younger than the next youngest sister, then there are four years and then three. I shared a bedroom with my oldest sister, who was like a mother to me. I loved that, but then she married and I cried and cried. I knew I'd become less important to her and I did. To this day I envy the relationship my oldest sister has with her daughter. Her daughter's importance to her is almost a mind game for me.

"The two middle sisters are a pair. I had always bonded with the oldest as a child and because of our age difference and the fact that she lived at home through college, we spent the most time together. Today, I am the least close with the sister who is closest to my age. She and I have children of a common age, but the closeness is not there. It isn't about competition, either. I can't figure out what it's about. My closest relationship at present is with the sister who is second oldest."

Kim and her sisters look very much alike.

"Our mannerisms and ways are strikingly the same. When strangers see us all together there's no doubt that we're sisters. I feel very strong because I am a part of this group, I am one of the sisters. I wonder if they perceive it as I do, or if it is because I'm the youngest and happy to be a part of it all that I feel so much strength.

"When our mother died my sisters and I laid out her beautiful jewelry. Then we distributed it. I'll never forget how I sat there— my oldest sister was in charge. She kept saying who should have what. To this day I resent her telling me and the others what we should have. She seemed to think that my husband could afford anything I might want that my mother had, so why was I entitled to hers? But I wanted these things *because* they were my mother's. That was what mattered to me. My sisters saw it another way and in the end the one whose husband provided the least got the most. I knew that as the youngest I'd be the last to be consulted, even about that jewelry. They won't admit it, but they still see me as the spoiled baby."

Kim sees the physical distance as a factor in her relationship with her sisters.

"I feel lonely because my sisters and I live so far apart. I know that my primary family is my husband and children but I long for my sisters. All of us are married with kids and we do have our own lives. But I fantasize about how much closer we'd be if we lived in the same town. I yearn for a family. I watch mothers with their daughters and see sisters together and I'm jealous. It's so special to be together. It's lonely without them and I choose friends who are older and younger to have an assortment, as if it can somehow take the place of my sisters. If my mother were still alive, I might not feel so lonely.

"Realistically speaking, the last time we were all together, several years ago, it was a disaster. We had a bull session and it was devastating. Each of us cried and felt hurt by the time it was over. We haven't had a reunion since, but we need to make the effort and forget the pain. It's not like any other relationship I know, being a sister to sisters."

The portrayal at the beginning of Kim's interview changes as she opens up. Her first description of her sisters is close to perfection.

Then we learn that she is the most financially secure and that there is resentment among the sisters regarding her lifestyle. This is obvious in the jewelry episode, where Kim's feelings are not considered relevant. She is doubly punished, first for being the youngest and then for having a comfortable life.

The attachment to her oldest sister, a mother figure, is significant because her parents are deceased. The loneliness that Kim describes is poignant; she wants her sisters to be closer both physically and emotionally. She understands the uniqueness of the relationship, but she hasn't yet figured out a way to make it a reality.

Marissa

"She was spoonfed while I worked hard to get everything that I achieved."

Living in Sante Fe, Marissa is forty-two years old and has one sister two years younger. Marissa works for a public relations firm and her sister is a nurse, living in southern California.

"We were very close growing up, my sister and I. We were dressed alike and did everything together. Once when we were very small we were in a recital and my parents specified that we were to perform together. It bothered me that we were dressed alike and treated like twins from the start. As a very young child, it was an unhappy experience.

"Later my parents varied the colors, but the theme remained the same. Now we were in the same outfits, but I wore pink to her blue. We had adjoining rooms with the same decor, in different tones. I was pink again and she was pale blue. I did not want to be my sister's twin, but I had no choice. We were forced to be very close and we were very close. We attended the same school but had different friends. My best friend's younger sister was my younger sister's best friend. Everything was cookie-cutter perfect."

Marissa and her sister remained very close once Marissa married.

"I married young and she remained single for a long time. I would fix her up constantly. She was engaged to a friend of my husband's but it didn't work out. Later she married a man who insisted that she distance herself from me and from our entire family. She is not estranged but the closeness is no longer there. We never speak. I feel very bad about this because I want that sisterly relationship. I miss her. We saw each other all the time until she married this guy. We were always together as adults, as we had been as children.

"My sister was very involved with my children until she married. She was so good to them and spent time with them. Presently, I have no closeness with her kids because of her husband. I have never confronted her because she is not the same person she was and I don't understand it. She has acquired her husband's characteristics, obnoxiousness being the worst of it. She seems like the typical woman who married late in order to have children. The clock was ticking for her, that I understood. What I don't understand are her other choices, such as eliminating our relationship."

Marissa realizes how much her sister disliked being single.
Ironically it was Marissa who never expected to marry young.

"As a child my sister always talked about marrying and having a family. She never had any career ambitions. She became increasingly uptight as the years went by and she remained unmarried. Her marriage is worthwhile in terms of the children it has produced—she's happy because of her children. On the other hand, I have never stopped working for a day of my married life. My children have been incorporated into that structure. I never expected to marry as young as I did and I kept moving onward with my career.

"We are not competitive because we are so different. Now it's not an issue because we don't see one another. My children are older so they can't really be compared, in any case. We always developed separate tasks, even as children. I was the smarter child, the bookworm. She was not a great student. I saw her as the favorite child, favored by both parents. She was spoon-fed while I worked hard for everything. I always had to help her with her homework. If I had a date in high school, and God knows how hard I worked to get it, I had to drum up one for her so we could double. I was expected to provide for her on every level.

"Because my sister stayed close to my parents in her adult life, they became wrapped up in each other's lives. I watched it from afar since by then I was living in Sante Fe. I was too removed to resent it. Of course, in our family, we were not allowed to resent one another. What I feel today, instead of resentment, is a sadness and a disappointment that my relationship with my sister is non-existent. We were close as young women, as children, as adults. The emotional distance is what bothers me, not the physical distance. To have had a sister and lose her later on is more painful than never to have had one at all."

Marissa has many female friends in an attempt to fill the gap.

"I'm always looking for my sister, a sister, to connect with. Because she's missing, it's a preoccupation with me. I seek that closeness all the time with my women friends. I know I can no longer confide in my sister so I have created several close friendships which help fill the void. Often I think of my sister's husband and how he has influenced her with an artificial jealousy. It was never what my sister and I were about. We were always happy for one another. We were not the kind of sisters who shared the same boyfriend or friends, so there was room to cheer each other on. This estrangement is shocking and seems irreversible."

What is unusual about Marissa's story is how truly committed and supportive she and her sister were as children and young adults despite their parents' tactics. Sisters who are forced to be close don't always feel good about one another. Yet their closeness prevailed until her sister's marriage, when Marissa feels her sister became almost brainwashed. It is unfortunate that she sees no remedy in the future and that she and her sister are permanently estranged.

Claire

"The loss with my mother is somehow replaced in the attachment to my sister."

Living in New England, Claire, in her mid-forties, is a nutritionist. Her younger sister, who lives in Georgia, is a nurse. Ten years apart in age, Claire only wishes she were able to spend more time with her sister.

"I love my sister very much. Initially, it was difficult because I was jealous. I was ten years old when she was born and my jealousy quickly turned to love and protection. I never felt like her mother but I was very aware that I was the big sister. She still looks up to me today. The only issue for us is our age difference which creates a real distance. For instance, she was eight years old when I left for college.

"I wasn't there for her teenage years, so we know very little about each other's lives. I had to get to know my sister as an adult—it was too late to know her as a child. Several years ago we began to call each other a few times a week, when our kids were in school. These conversations were very valuable for her because she hadn't felt she was a part of our family for years. I now know that it was the relationship we have with our mother which has been so difficult. Our mother is so hard to handle that my sister was in search of some kind of affirmation. She needed to know how special she was to our parents late in their lives and to me, as her sister."

Claire feels that age, distance, and time has kept her apart from her sister.

"I only see my sister once a year. Her lifestyle is much simpler than mine. She is also involved in things that I cannot relate to, such as hands-on healing. I don't meditate like she does. My sister is also very much a homebody and doesn't venture out much. While I'm no social butterfly, I do get about.

"Physically we are very similar, and that pleases me. My sister lives near my mother—they're close geographically but not emotionally. My mother is unable to show her feelings—my sister and I had to work hard to overcome her sarcasm and the way she treated us. We have both tried not to be like her. My mother pushed both my sister and me, and there were always conditions.

"As a result, my sister and I often discuss our unconditional love for our kids and for each other. We've learned how not to be like our mother, not in every way, but in many ways. We raise our children as we think best and our method of mothering differs from our mother's. I do wish that I lived closer to my sister so we could do things and spend time together. I'm aware that my sister should come first but she's so far away. In other words, I can't evaluate time spent with my sister because she's physically unavailable."

The satisfaction of her relationship with her sister replaces the closeness Claire did not have with her mother.

"I've never shopped with my mother or gone to lunch with her. Not that I have to pal around with someone every day, but we've never done anything. When we get together my sister and I do things, and so it's not a total loss. The lack of relationship with my mother is somehow replaced in the attachment to my sister. What bothers me, however, is my sister's preoccupation with her meditation and beliefs. It actually gets in the way of our closeness. I find it distancing, her need to find her inner self. It's so personal—how could I be a part of it?

"This is an area where my sister and I are not in sync. I try not to let it get in the way, but it is a serious issue. I watch our daughters play together and I know there's a special connection. I remind myself that whatever she believes in, sister-to-sister is more important. I'm waiting, though, for her to get past this preoccupation so she can come closer to me."

What is unusual about Claire is that she points out the obstacles to an ideal relationship with her sister even while she convinces us of how good it is. The common enemy for Claire and her sister is the mother; and because Claire is older, she's the one on the front line. They are linked in their need to make up for a lost ten years and considerable physical distance.

The real factor for Claire is her sister's interests, meditation and healing. Claire sees herself as the pragmatist, and her sister's preoccupations seem unrealistic and escapist, thus not tolerable. She waits patiently, reminding herself of what she and her sister do have together.

Constance

"There was no favoritism which is why I think we could be friends."

Constance is thirty-two and works part-time in publishing. She has three children and lives in Hartford, Connecticut. The second of four sisters, two of her sisters live in Boston and one in Rhode Island. Constance is the only married sister in the family.

"We are from a close-knit family. My oldest sister and I are best friends and always were. The other two are not a pair, however. It's a very competitive situation with the last two. The oldest sister and I do not compete because the chemistry is such that we are completely complementary. She is laid-back and casual, very easy-going. I'm not but between us, it works. She is getting married soon and I'm so happy for her. For eight years I've been the only one married. Although outwardly none of my sisters has said anything, I think they've felt slightly estranged from me. Every time I have a baby, it becomes more obvious how different my life is. No one has shown any envy but I sense it. The youngest sister is very much like me and also works in publishing. She might have resented the fact that I found a man at such a young age, but this is speculation."

Constance realized that she was making a break from her family when she married.

"It was tough on my sisters when I no longer visited with the family without my husband. They could never really be alone with me again in quite the same way. I have continued to think of myself as one of four sisters, however. Especially now that I have three little boys. I find it distinguishing to have three sons or four daughters, several of the same sex. It is very insular to have each other. With sisters it is especially so.

"As kids we led a very isolated life. Our parents wanted the four of us to get along. We traveled a great deal and it was not tolerated if we didn't treat each other well. Our mother couldn't stand any fighting. We were so terrified of her wrath that we whispered when we fought. The eldest and I never fought, never. The third and I fought over dumb, possessive stuff; the youngest and the third were the big fighters—they fought constantly. The third was the jealous one—she was jealous of me and the first sister. It was wild."

Constance's parents were very fair and had no favorites.

"My mother and father treated us all exactly the same. There was no favoritism, which is why I think we could be friends. Fairness is something I try to set as an example for my sons. If one of us got something, then all of us got it. That included attention, not just material things.

"I don't identify with any sister in particular in terms of temperament. I am more like my mother than the others. I think the life I lead is closer to my mother's than to my sisters'. I do things with my husband and take care of kids, and that's how my mother has lived her life. I'm the most conventional of the daughters. My oldest sister is like our father, cool and detached, very Scandinavian. She is completely unruffled and I like that. She is great to be with and is almost like a mother to me—I feel very anchored when I'm with her."

Everyone in Constance's family expected her to marry her husband.

"My sisters watched my relationship with my husband closely. Each sister is connected to our children in a very sweet way. The youngest is their godparent because I wanted to bring her into the family. Although I'm closer to the oldest, I didn't need to bring her in so I deliberately chose the youngest. The third sister never cared about being a godparent because she is so devoted to her career. If she was upset initially she isn't now.

"I definitely put my sisters ahead of my friends. We are devoted and loyal. I speak with my oldest sister every day. The other sisters and I speak every two weeks or so. My oldest sister and I are very close and I feel close to number three right now. The youngest and I can fluctuate, depending on who is doing what. I do wish they all lived closer. They're my support system.

"Our mother is the center of the wheel. All the news is heard through her. I speak with her daily. She is very much involved with my children and I like it."

Constance and her sisters attended the same private girls' school and the same college.

"We all attended the same Ivy League college. There was no competition academically because we all did well. What we did do was borrow clothes from our mother. Finally she put a lock on the door because we were all the same size and we all look alike. My oldest sister and I used to be called twins. It's obvious we all come from the same family. When we go out in public, there is an immediate reaction. It's obvious to everyone that we are sisters."

Constance's husband appreciates how protective her sisters are of her.

"My husband was under tremendous scrutiny at first. They resisted him and were afraid he'd hurt me. He had to win them over. It was a tough task but finally he succeeded. If he had been faint of heart, he would have given up. Our parents' attitude has caused this suspicion in part. We have always had to depend on each other and fight for each other. Our parents were so clannish. It's been a positive force, and I believe that good sisters are able to be friends to each other. My sisters have not done so well with men, however. I think it has taken a long time for the younger two to learn to interact with them. They've had little exposure to men and only recently have they begun to catch up.

"Although I am close to all of them, I know my oldest sister is my confidante. I view all three of them, though, as my foundation. From there I can jump into life. I would not have wanted to grow up any other way. My ties to them are so strong, as strong as anything I've known or ever will."

Constance is pleased and proud to be one of four sisters. She realizes that growing up in an all-female family has given her identity and strength. Although she is more connected to her oldest sister, she is also close to the others. She believes there is little jealousy among the four of them and only positive feelings. However, she also mentions how difficult it was for her husband to be accepted by the family and how separated she felt once she was married. We question if she purposely created the space, and then found the balance between her sisters and her spouse, or if it was happenstance.

Nancy

"Our mother did not encourage any closeness between us. She simply hoped that we'd get along."

Nancy is the youngest of three sisters. Having grown up in a middle class home in a midwestern town, Nancy works out of necessity. At the age of forty, she has one daughter. Today she and her sisters live near each other, not far from their hometown.

"There is a big age difference between myself and my first sister. She is fifteen years older, and my second sister is four years older than I am. As a kid I have little memory of my oldest sister and then she was gone. The middle sister and I grew up together and were close.

"When I was thirteen my older sister moved back after her divorce. At that point we got reacquainted. There was sibling rivalry between myself and the middle sister. We'd argue over clothes and everything else because we were peers. We had terrible fights until she went to college and I saw how much I missed her. Once we were separated, we understood what we'd had. The oldest sister relationship was based on friendship and there was no jealousy. It is only now, as an older woman, that I really appreciate my sisters and the fact that I have them. I have one child and I realize that she is missing out."

Nancy's mother has been very ill which has united the sisters.

"We communicate often these days because of my mother. We share the responsibility and speak a few times a week and see each other weekly. Our mother has been difficult and the only sister who can reach her is the middle one. I believe she was always favored. She was good in school and never got into trouble. I was the more rambunctious of the two of us and definitely more rebellious. I expressed my opinions and thoughts, while she was quiet. Maybe she was favored because she was the first child after a very long time—I think my parents were thrilled to have another child. I might have resented the fact that she was favored when we were teenagers. I don't think any of this affected the oldest sister one bit. It was as if she was from another family, almost. But in my teens, I felt that my middle sister got more—and then it stopped seeming so important.

"Our mother did not encourage closeness among us. She simply hoped we'd get along. We were each at a different level in school, with four years between us, so we had our own friends. To me, growing up, my best friend was more sisterly than my sisters. She and I told each other everything. She really came before my sisters and she does to this day. We have been friends since we were five years old. That's how I would imagine sisters to be, the way she and I are. If I needed anyone, this friend would be there for me. My real sisters and I are not confidantes. But I'm pleased that they live nearby."

Nancy's older sister never remarried.

"My older sister has been single for many years and has one child. She has a boyfriend and has made a conscious choice not to marry again. I see her as a sweet woman, yet very set in her ways and from another generation. She has gone about her life in a way I never would. She says she likes the independence. My middle sister has been married to her childhood sweetheart for over twenty years and I happen to like him. He's brotherly. She's been there for me and I feel I can count on him, too. They have two children and I'm very close to their kids. When my child and my nieces were small, they were often together. The control lessens with these relationships as the kids grow up, but the importance remains. I want my sisters' kids to have a relationship with my kids.

"My sisters and I have devised a system to share caring for our mother. Because I work, she is their responsibility during the day; on the weekends, I'm responsible. We have learned to cooperate and since none of us had any problems with our mother when we were growing up, we have managed during her illness. We each have a different saturation point. When one of us is fed up, another takes over. It can be extremely difficult to take care of an elderly parent, but having the support of my sisters is the saving grace. We have had to make major decisions about her health care. Sometimes we do argue over this—my oldest sister is not big on decision making. So the middle sister and I, who are more outgoing and decisive, do it."

Nancy knows that she and her sisters have three distinct personalities.

"My oldest sister is not a doer or a traveller—she's content to simply do nothing. My middle sister and I love to go places, yet we have other diverse interests. I never saw my oldest sister as maternal toward us but she's been a good friend. It's just that there's nothing maternal in her personality. I don't think she resents me or my middle sister. Then I remember that she was alone all those years and wonder how she really feels about us. Our mother is seventy-five and our sister is fifty-five and I often tell my middle sister that we'll soon be taking care of our older sister.

"Sometimes I imagine I'll be left alone with my middle sister. The two of us will grow old together and it makes sense, as if we're going back to our roots. If my mother's sisters were alive, they'd be living with our mother, helping her out. She was one of three sisters also. She is the last in her family, and as I watch her fading, I know it is the end of an era.

"The older I get, the more I appreciate family. When we get together, my sisters and I, at Christmas and on other holidays, I see how few we are. We have a need, an obligation to hold it together. My older sister never entertains so my sister and I take turns planning family gatherings. I don't want to lose what we have. It would be devastating."

Nancy has not had a deep involvement with her sisters—the relationships seem to exist on a superficial level. In a family where the oldest sister is set apart by age, it is interesting to note how the two sisters close in age, Nancy and the middle sister, form another entity altogether. The commonality at present is the mother's illness, but even within this context, Nancy identifies with her middle sister and not with her oldest.

The oldest sister, on the other hand, does not seem to mind. Whatever her reasons, she has chosen a separate life for herself and seems unperturbed. The years spent alone, as an only child, have molded her. Her sense of independence and disparate ways belie her need to continue in that role.

It matters very much to Nancy that she and her sisters remain connected as they grow older. This reaction, that maturity brings an appreciation of family, is not so much about her sisters as individuals as it is about what they represent, which is family unity.

Michelle

"When I look back on our childhood, I see that my sister had this proclivity from birth. . . . She was never with us when we played with dolls . . ."

One of four sisters and two brothers, Michelle lives in Baltimore where she works in advertising. At the age of thirty-six, she is the second oldest daughter and the only one who has never been married. Her first sister is a sociologist, her youngest a homemaker with five children. Her third sister works for the phone company. The homemaker is the only sister who has remained married.

"We grew up in a suburb of Baltimore and come from a close-knit, religious family. Half of my siblings have remained religious and the other half have not. I feel that my strong Christian upbringing has had a positive impact on me so I've stuck with it.

We had a happy childhood and I felt connected to my three sisters, to different degrees. My oldest sister did not get along with the third sister, though. This is my one caveat—our oldest sister was on such a different wave length. At present I am closest to my sister who has all the kids. I don't see my third sister too often and my oldest sister has chosen a different life for herself."

Michelle's oldest sister is a recovered alcoholic and a lesbian.

"My sister who is a sociologist has had problems and is now finally happy. She was married for a period of time, which was a disaster, and that's why she drank. Her sexual preferences are such that being married destroyed her. When she left the marriage she gave up drinking. Today she is a much happier person. When I look back on our childhood, I see that my sister had this proclivity from birth. As toddlers she was never with us when we played with dolls or did female things. Once she came out of the closet, our entire childhood made sense to me. I hate to sound stereotypic, but if we played with makeup as young kids and with dolls or dressed up, she never did. That was how it first manifested.

"She never dated in high school although she had a close male friend. Then she got involved with a man who was married. She had an interesting and powerful relationship with him. Ultimately they married and it lasted for six years. Then she left her husband for a woman. That was when it began to fall into place for me, and I began to feel she was better off. I'd watched her suffer in her marriage—and it just wasn't right, it wasn't fair.

"We come from a tolerant, open-minded family. All my siblings know about my sister and all of us accept it, as do our parents. My parents' attitude is different—they kind of look the other way. My relationship with this sister has not been changed because of her current lifestyle; she was never the one I'd pour my heart out to. The youngest sister, the homemaker, is the one I confide in."

Michelle's parents have come to terms with her sister's choice.

"My parents always include my sister's lover on holidays. They are very good to her but they do not acknowledge the lifestyle. I think my sister waited until we were all aware of her preference before she made it clear. She never made an announcement but this has been going on for years. When she left her husband under these circumstances, he was devastated. Since then, except for holidays and birthdays, she has purposely kept her life separate from ours. She has had several lovers in the past ten years. I have preferred some over others. I like the present one very much."

Michelle was the prettiest sister in her family.

"It was not a competitive family but I know I was the pretty one. Each of us was encouraged to pursue our own goals. Our family did not emphasize looks and superficial things. Ironically, the family was not divided over my sister's lesbianism, but they were divided when she got married. My parents were really upset that she was marrying a man who had been married and whom she might have lived with before they married. They refused to attend her wedding. Now things have changed and they have come a long way. What my parents had to understand was that my sister's happiness was at stake. While she seemed to want to marry her husband at the time, now she has made another choice. They are, at last, behind her.

"My parents don't see this sister much, either. Everyone sees the conventional sister who has the kids. My interests were never the same as my oldest sister's. Lately she and her lover have been discussing having a baby, which interests me. But they can't decide who should get pregnant and neither wants to. I thought that she'd have kids with her husband, way back. I was very close to him and I believe she loved him but preferred women. That's why the marriage failed."

Michelle has no problem with her sister's lifestyle.

"I watched those tortured years my sister put in. I know how she must have felt—it never worked as it has for the rest of us. Alcoholism was her escape and fortunately that's behind her. I miss seeing her sometimes, though, because when she led a heterosexual life she obviously fit in with the family more and I saw her often. But the level of emotional intimacy I have with my sister today is improved although we are together less. It seems more honest."

Family members have gotten beyond societal pressures and are happy for Michelle's sister.

"I'm crazy about my sister's girlfriend and I'm so happy for my sister. I can't be caught up in what people will think. Both women have high-powered positions and make good money. They lead a life that celebrates accomplishment and is very positive. How can I be anything but happy about it? My sister has found what she wants."

Michelle, coming from a traditional, religious family, did not anticipate that her oldest sister would be gay. In retrospect, she feels that the signs were there. Because she has empathy and cares about her sister, there is no judgment, only relief that her sister has paved her own way. Michelle witnessed her sister's misery when she attempted to lead a conventional life. The drinking problem and unhappy marriage are past, and her sister has decided to be bold and go forward.

A positive story all around—not only Michelle but her other sisters, brothers, and her parents, in their own fashion, have come to accept this sister's choice. It is surprising that Michelle's parents put up a fight over her sister's marriage and then, facing a usually more controversial issue, became more tolerant. But for Michelle, it is significant that no one harbors ill will; they are truly happy that her sister has found herself.

SISTERS WHO STEAL:
Husbands, Boyfriends, Lovers

It is the ultimate sibling rivalry to steal a sister's husband. The act creates a serious wound that may never be healed. To the family members the situation can feel incestuous. Basic trust in the family structure is gone and when this happens it leaves the victims feeling as though they can never trust anyone again.

—RONNIE L. BURAK, PH.D

When Jacqueline Kennedy was first introduced to Aristotle Onassis, both she and President Kennedy were aware of her sister Lee Radziwill's carefully thought-out plan to eventually annul her marriage to Stas Radziwill in order to marry Onassis. It was believed that Onassis wanted very much to be the President's brother-in-law. During her first meeting with Onassis, in the early sixties, Jacqueline Kennedy, at her husband's insistence, was accompanied by Mr. and Mrs. Franklin Roosevelt, Jr., and the Radziwill's, aboard the *Christina*. If there were any undercurrents during the trip, it was between Onassis and Lee.

It might have been there that the competition began. Onassis gave Jackie a diamond and ruby necklace and presented tokens to the other women aboard. This included Lee, who realized then that Onassis was not going to marry her and that he had become a great admirer of her sister's.

Although Onassis had been involved with Lee before he met Jackie, once the tide turned and Onassis and Jackie announced their engagement, Lee publicly supported her sister's decision. If she experienced any jealousy, it was kept quiet. By 1970 Jackie's marriage to Onassis was less than perfect, paralleling her sister's separation from Radziwill. Jackie did not obtain a divorce but was widowed for a second time. Despite the fact that Jackie won Onassis, the sisters maintained their relationship and their attachment seemed unaltered.

In the Book of Genesis we read that Jacob, the son of Isaac, laid eyes upon Rachel and wanted to marry her immediately. Laban, her father, insisted that Jacob work for him for seven years to earn his right. But on the wedding day Laban fooled Jacob and delivered Leah, his oldest daughter. Laban explained that it was his obligation to see this daughter married first but if Jacob was willing to work for seven more years, he could marry Rachel also.

Thus, in the days of polygamy, Leah, the oldest, "weak eyed" daughter, became Jacob's first wife and Rachel, her younger, lovelier sister, became his second. Jacob's passion was for Rachel no matter how many sons Leah bore him. For many years Rachel could not conceive and became jealous of her sister despite Jacob's affection for her. Finally she gave birth to a son, Joseph.

Later, when Jacob decided to take his wives and many sons back to his father, Isaac, the sisters became inextricably connected. By leaving their native land, they had no one but each other and the one husband that the two sisters were destined to share.

Elizabeth

"My husband moved into the city proper and so did my sister. That was when I became very suspicious."

At forty-two, Elizabeth is the mother of three children and lives outside Atlanta, Georgia. Thirty years ago her father remarried and her stepmother's children and Elizabeth and her siblings were raised as one family. Consequently, Elizabeth has nine sisters and four brothers.

"The sister I want to talk about is not my biological sister. We grew up together. She is seven years younger and I was like a mother to her. Our parents married when she was only four. I remember how she would watch me in the mirror when I used to get ready for dates. I took care of her and in some ways it was a maternal relationship. I had a conscious sense that I was her older sister. She worshiped the ground I walked on.

"I think that for a long time this sister wanted whatever I had, which I did not realize at the time. I felt very close to three of my sisters and she was definitely one of them."

When Elizabeth got married and moved to the midwest, her sister followed.

"My sister finished college and came to live with us. Wherever we moved, she moved, too. Obviously, there was an attraction which I didn't pay attention to—my sister was definitely after my husband. He adored our entire family but called me the 'cream of the crop.' I was confident and did not notice what was going on. My sister didn't make a move without consulting my husband. She even consulted him about the men she dated. The only time I was jealous was when he seemed to spend a little more time with her than necessary.

"This sister lived with us several times during my twenty years of marriage. There was a real camaraderie among the three of us. She was still single and I was busy raising three kids. My husband was in-between jobs and so was she. They spent a lot of time together. At that point I admitted to myself that it was bothering me. I mentioned it to my husband first, not to my sister. He always took the defensive. He asked me how I could suspect him of such a thing. I have since learned that a defensive person is a guilty person. There was something going on, even when he denied it. I think my sister wanted a fatherly, brotherly figure and he fit the bill.

"I always thought my sister and my husband would butt heads, and I took the role of pacifier. Finally, my husband made me feel very guilty for questioning him about my sister. But the writing was on the wall. This sister got married in the mid-eighties, and my husband behaved very strangely. In retrospect, maybe it bothered me, but that's twenty-twenty hindsight. I look back and I can put two and two together.

"Then we moved to Atlanta. My sister was married then and I was consumed with getting everyone settled in a new place. We were very busy renovating our home. That was when I found out that my husband was having an affair with his secretary. I did not tell anyone this was going on. I put my energy into trying to save my marriage. My husband left for awhile, and that was when things spun out of control."

During this period Elizabeth spoke with her sister only on occasion.

"My sister and I were no longer close. There was such emotional upheaval that I found it impossible to chat with anyone. I was trying to save my marriage, but the truth is, I did not trust my sister. Our closeness had come as a result of her need, not mine. I fulfilled her needs but she did not fulfill mine. I got very little out of the relationship and never trusted her once she was an adult. She was a bad seed and my instincts told me not to confide in her. She went after my husband because she wanted my life.

"I knew that if I told one of my sisters my problems, she'd hang up the phone and call another sister. I didn't want my problems known throughout the family. My true confidante was my sister-in-law, my husband's brother's wife. She seems more like a sister to me than anyone.

"For several years my husband and I tried to save our marriage, then we got a divorce. My sister moved to Atlanta at the time, contending that she wanted to help me. She lived in my guest house. My husband moved into the city proper and so did my sister—that was when I became very suspicious. I asked my sister point-blank. She denied everything just as my husband had, but it was a lie. For a long time I made myself crazy. I confronted my sister about my husband and she blatantly lied."

After her sister had lived in Atlanta for one year, Elizabeth ran into her with her ex-husband.

"Once I'd run into them together, she decided to meet with me. She called and asked if I would. I agreed. We met in a restaurant and she told me that I looked sad. She had asked me several times since I'd been divorced if I had a boyfriend or if I was involved with someone. I believe my sister asked this because she still felt threatened. She has never been without a man. If she lived with someone, she would never leave him until the next one was in the wings. That was her style.

"At that point I asked her if she and my ex-husband were involved and she admitted they were. I asked her if they were in love and she said yes. Then she complained that my husband was difficult, as if I'd agree. I told her our relationship was over and I never wanted to see her again. We have not spoken since."

Elizabeth believes that she and this particular sister are similar types.

"This sister and I are very much alike physically. But she is not an honest person. I'm not talking about how strong-willed she is, but about her integrity. When we were younger and our entire family was together, we were always mistaken for biological sisters. I was there for her and always helped her out. As youngsters we were close when we lived in the same house. And when my kids were young, she was the one I counted on to babysit."

Recently Elizabeth's sister and her ex-husband have married.

"The repercussions of their getting married have been enormous. The family is totally divided. I'm still close to his family but my family refuses to accept their relationship. They feel that of all the people in the world, they could have found two other partners if their first marriages didn't work out.

"I've made a deliberate decision for the sake of my kids. He's their father, and they need a relationship with him. However, they do not need one with my sister. My ex-husband is still very upset about my attitude but that's how I feel. My daughter is very protective of me, and sorry for the pain I've endured. My kids are grown and off on their own, and I've had to face this problem alone.

"As far as I'm concerned, she's no longer my sister. I want nothing to do with her. She orchestrated the entire affair. She went after what was mine with complete determination. I was naive not to see it. In retrospect, there were clues. For instance, when I was helping her move to Atlanta, I was in her apartment. At this stage I was getting divorced and didn't know anything for sure, I just suspected it. I kept trying to convince myself that it wasn't true. She lied to me that day and said she planned to unpack that evening but when I left, she made plans to meet my husband. I know because my daughter was there visiting her father and saw them.

"Now I know that my sister was calling my husband ten times a day. And I remember that when I walked into a room they'd exchange looks and then there would be an awkward silence. It was so obvious but I didn't want to believe it—it was too painful.

"It's so difficult to believe, to this day. It has had a terrible effect on our family. My husband was like a brother to my siblings for twenty years. Now all that has been destroyed. Having sisters should be very special. I've always had sisters, even before my father remarried. I loved all my half-siblings. The great irony was that our parents worked so hard for so many years to keep outsiders away. As one of my sisters pointed out, it was a person from the *inside* who ended up tearing us apart. We can never be one big family again.

"Today, my sister and my ex-husband live two towns away. I keep hoping that as our kids are completely grown and independent, they'll move away. I have lost both a husband and a sister, and two very special friends. I realize now that my sister wanted the comforts of wealth—she is quite materialistic. My ex-husband can certainly provide that, so she took what was mine. He would say that the marriage was going sour anyway, but it isn't so. He told me at one point that she tried to convince him to return to me. If so, it was out of pity."

Elizabeth feels nothing for her sister anymore.

"I have lost all feeling for this sister. If she died, I wouldn't care. I never want to have anything to do with her. When my husband called as a courtesy to tell me he was marrying my sister, I told him I hoped he'd be happy, but that if it didn't work to walk away. I still care for him because he's the father of my children. It's not easy to hate someone you once loved. I once loved my sister and I once loved my husband. Had he married someone other than my sister, I could have accepted it. My sister is an obstacle to an amicable relationship with my husband. I resent her completely. I hate what she has done to our entire family. Maybe I don't actually hate her, but when someone asks if I hate anyone, she's the first person who comes to mind. Sometimes I wonder if my sister liked being the other woman in some perverse way. She's full of denial over what she's done. Otherwise, how could she live with it?"

Perhaps Elizabeth did not want to see the telltale signs that her sister and her husband were having an affair. To this day she blames her sister more than her husband. In retrospect, although Elizabeth cared for her sister, she was not thoroughly at ease with her. The fact that her sister, from her college years onward, made a beeline for Elizabeth's husband is enough to discourage any relationship.

Elizabeth pitted hope against hope, suffering great anguish over her sister's and ex-husband's decision to marry. Realizing today that her sister coveted what she had, Elizabeth finds the most unacceptable aspect of her sister's behavior to be that she lied repeatedly.

Her ex-husband is held to another standard altogether. Elizabeth does not resent him in the same way that she does her sister. For her the real heartbreak and devastation has centered around an almost incestuous relationship initiated by her sister.

Sheila

"I really adored both my husband and my sister. I feel that since that day, I have lost them both."

Having lived her entire life in a suburb of Chicago, Sheila and her younger sister grew up in a home filled with privilege and strong moral standards. Her parents saw themselves as old world WASPs, firmly entrenched in the community. Sheila's sister is five years younger than she. Both sisters married happily and the two couples were close for years. Fifteen years ago, Sheila's sister married Sheila's ex-husband.

"My sister and I were close our entire lives. Although I was older, we were both considered good-looking and received lots of attention from men. My husband was handsome but so was hers. We enjoyed a high standard of living as married women, as we had in childhood. Although I was older, I didn't look it. My sister and I often spent time together, socially and with family. We were known as a pair around town, even after we were married.

"I was married first and my kids were several years older than my sister's. We always vacationed as a family, staying at my parents' compound on the lake. At some point, my husband and sister began an affair. I didn't know about it. I was in my late thirties and my sister in her early thirties. I suppose there were telltale clues if I'd been suspicious, but I wasn't."

Sheila came home unexpectedly from a trip one day and found her husband in bed with her sister.

"When I found them in bed together it was so ugly. It was one of the ugliest moments of my life. It divided the family irreversibly. I really adored both my husband and my sister. I feel that since that day, I've lost them both. The family will never be the same. My husband cannot be forgiven by our children. They'll never be able to accept it."

When Sheila and her husband split up, he decided to marry her sister, who was also getting divorced.

"This affair was great gossip. We lived in a small town and everyone knew us, as sisters, actually. The country club set was scandalized and everywhere we went, be it skiing or scuba diving, people seemed to know. What has always bothered me was that I thought my husband was happy with me and that my sister was happy with her husband. He was a successful man and really loved her. It seemed to me that she had everything she could wish for. But I guess what she really wished for was my husband. We were so young and pretty when it happened. This was years ago. We were known as the sisters who really had it together."

Once the marriage ended, Sheila went into a decline. She purposely sought men who were inappropriate.

"For years I'd find men in bars and sleep with them. I was that hurt and vengeful—it went on endlessly. Most of the men were younger. I was so upset that my ex-husband and sister were married. I didn't know how else to get back at them. I grew very bitter and old before my time—a direct result of what happened.

"I've tried to remove myself completely from their lives but it isn't easy with children in common and family occasions. My ex-husband and sister no longer live in the same suburb, which is a blessing. But it took me years to recover. I really felt I'd lost everything when it happened.

"I've heard other stories like mine and my heart goes out to the sister who's left behind. I had to pick up the pieces and begin a new life. It wasn't bad enough that my husband left, but he left to be with my confidante, my sister, my closest connection beside him. I felt totally betrayed. I know I'll never forget it."

Today Sheila feels she has gained some perspective on what happened.

"I cannot imagine anything worse. There's no one left to trust in a story like mine. But I still don't know what motivated my sister. She's been gone from my life for a long time and so has my ex-husband. After a series of revenge affairs, I'm trying to find my way. I'm older now and I have the perspective that time provides. I'm healed in some capacity, thankfully. But it never really goes away. I wake up each day and it flits through my mind. Then I wonder what they think of when they wake up each morning. How can they live with it?"

Completely devastated by the betrayal of her sister and her husband, it has taken Sheila a very long time to begin to heal. The impact was so harsh and unexpected that she sought revenge blindly. In choosing inappropriate men, Sheila was trying to make a statement, however ill-advised. Her family was also shattered by the affair and marriage of her sister and ex-husband. Despite the tremendous pain they have caused her, Sheila still mourns the loss of her sister's companionship. There is irony in her contemplation of how her husband and sister wrestle with their decision.

Roberta

"It didn't occur to me right away that she wanted him.
Not my children or my life, just my husband."

*Roberta, at the age of seventy, lives in Taos, New Mexico. She is
the youngest of three sisters. Part Navajo, Roberta has identified
strongly with her culture and has been influenced by the
hierarchy of the family.*

"I was the youngest of three and had to be very respectful of
my older sisters. I was very shy. I felt I had no talent while my
sisters were quite gifted. One was artistic and the other a writer. I
had no apparent skills and was simply smart, while they were
exceptional.

"When I was little I was closest to my oldest sister. She mothered me and she'd buy me toys if she had a penny or two. Growing up, my middle sister and I became closer. She was much
more socially oriented and I began to identify with her. I wanted
to be more like her. The oldest became reclusive, which didn't
appeal to me."

*The middle and the oldest sisters in Roberta's family did not get
along.*

"The oldest felt she was supplanted and her personality was
typically that of a firstborn. She'd been touted in the family as
being very intellectual, and never developed socially as a result.
The middle sister was so outgoing. She always had a smile or a
laugh. I think my oldest sister was admired by the family but the
middle sister was adored, understandably so. I was the 'Johnny
come lately' in the family of three girls; I was the last hope for a

boy. By the time I was born, my mother worked and I was left with a wicked woman to watch me. My two older sisters were in school. This woman only spoke in our native tongue, and she was terrible to me. When I was in kindergarten, I was so traumatized by her that my sister had to be asked to come in. I couldn't speak English. I remember feeling isolated, being separated from my sisters. I'd lost my confidence.

"It took me a while to emerge. My sisters attended all-girls schools but I rebelled. I wanted to be with boys. I joined a community club and worked hard to be independent, and then came into my own. At that point, my oldest sister was really distancing herself. She no longer needed to protect me so she didn't have much to do with me. The plot thickened when I met the man who would become my husband. I was only fifteen. He was my oldest sister's age and she had known him first. I think she liked him before I really knew him, but she never said anything. Neither of my sisters had met any potential husbands when I met this man. I was very serious about him and the family was concerned. Especially my oldest sister, who was vehemently against it."

Soon after, Roberta's middle sister met her husband. The two sisters had a double wedding.

"Our father could not afford two weddings. I was so anxious to get married, I didn't even care. My oldest sister began to push men away. I don't think she wanted a relationship. My parents insisted she be included in anything my husband and I did. They made me feel, although I was the youngest, responsible and protective of her. She tried to put me down. She realized that the middle sister had her own life and she despised her husband. It was mine that she liked. I didn't realize it at the time, but she was barely civil when my husband was around.

"My oldest sister, who accompanied us everywhere, treated me badly but was wonderful to my husband. She resented me, and I just didn't get it. I thought she was simply respectful of him. She knew that he would not tolerate being treated the way she treated the middle sister's husband. He respected her and expected the same. It didn't occur to me right away that she wanted him. Not my children or my life, just my husband. My oldest sister never babysat for my kids. She only came around when my husband wasn't working, on weekends.

"Control was a big issue for my oldest sister. She would give wonderful gifts but never knew how to accept them. And she had been with me constantly during my courtship with my husband. My father had insisted. She would not even leave the room so that my husband and I could kiss good night. She did not want to see me happy, especially with him. He was her peer, someone she had known first. She kept reminding me of this."

In retrospect, Roberta feels that her oldest sister abused her mentally.

"She could say whatever she wanted when my husband wasn't around, but she knew I had the prize, I had my husband. During all of this, our mother urged us to be close. She wanted us to settle our problems. But they were complex and my oldest sister was difficult. My middle sister lived far away by then and had kids the same age as mine. Our lives were similar and there were no problems, no anguish.

"I think my oldest sister's jealousy over the double wedding never subsided. She didn't show it at the time and I didn't pick up on it until later. She was called an old maid at the reception. She certainly didn't envy the middle sister's marriage, but it was obvious she envied mine. In our generation, everything was repressed. If this happened today, maybe it would have been out in the open—the story of a sister who really wishes she had her sister's husband and acts on it. But nothing was said or done. Today, we are older women and my sister is still so angry that I've had the life I've had.

"Through all these years, my husband served as a buffer. He found her impossible, but never showed it. It's ironic that she thought he was so special because he knew she was difficult and treated me badly. She browbeat me—she was just plain mean."

After many years, Roberta and her sister live near each other.

"Recently I moved back to New Mexico. The frustrations with this oldest sister continue. I worry about her; we are all older now and she lives alone. Her hostility is almost worse today. It's as if I've lived the life she wanted and she's really out to punish me. While we've never stopped talking, the tension is there."

Roberta's feelings of obligation toward her oldest sister have persisted, despite her awareness that her sister envied her marriage and acted almost as if Roberta had somehow stolen the older sister's opportunity. Entrenched in family obligations, Roberta has remained a faithful sister. Her story is representative of her generation, where feelings were swept under the rug.

Subconsciously Roberta lived the life her sister coveted, yet has remained an obedient sister. Perhaps her knowledge of how her husband perceived her sister was reassuring. She did not feel threatened by her sister's inner yearnings and fantasies.

Kara

"I knew something was up but I had no idea she was sleeping with my boyfriend . . ."

Kara lives in a suburb of a midwestern city and is the oldest of three sisters. One sister lives several miles away and the other has moved to the northeast. Kara works as a dental hygienist, while her sisters have held various jobs in the last year. Kara has two children as does each of her sisters.

"My sisters and I were very close growing up. I have remained involved with one, the youngest. The other sister and I are no longer in touch as a result of something which happened when we were both first divorced. We had always been very competitive. I was the goody two-shoes and she was not. I did what was expected of me and kept being punished for it. All she ever said to me was that she was sorry she couldn't be that perfect."

Kara and her sister began to spend time together after their divorces.

"The sister who had been so competitive began to invite me places. We began to be close, hanging out as two single women with kids. That was the bond and finally it seemed that she was letting go of all her high school jealousies. We began to date two guys who were friends. One of them and I became pretty serious. I slept with him and he was my boyfriend for a long period of time. My sister knew all that, she was with me when it started.

"I really liked him. We were dating each other exclusively to the best of my knowledge. What happened then was one of those sneaky things. One night my sister and I did not go out to the clubs together. I was somewhere else and she'd gone with a friend. She unexpectedly met my boyfriend at a club, or so I've been told, and they left together. I knew nothing at first. They began to sleep together. My sister either seduced my steady boyfriend or they had felt something for each other and left me out in the cold."

*Kara's sister began to behave strangely. She was no longer
friendly or inclusive.*

"Then my sister began to act funny again. She was nasty and made fun of me just like in high school. She called me 'Miss Perfect' and got very cold. I couldn't understand it. I kept asking her what was going on. I still hadn't picked up on it. Suddenly she confessed and then I confronted him. If I had not pushed her, I'd never have known. I really cornered her. I knew something was up but I had no idea she'd been sleeping with my boyfriend for months. That was it for her, and for him, of course.

"I think she felt guilty or she wouldn't have told me. I also think it was revenge that drove her to it. No matter that we seemed to be getting along, she was still jealous of me and will always be. After years of her treating me badly, I finally realized that she resented me. Maybe she realized she had gone too far, that sleeping with my boyfriend was a mistake. The bottom line is that she did it. She did it to get back at me."

*After this, a wedge was created between Kara and her middle
sister.*

"We had been doing well but she couldn't resist temptation. I thought our goal had been a more truthful, closer relationship. But she was only camouflaging her true feelings. To this day I don't trust her. I love her because she's my sister, but I can't depend on her and will never trust her again as long as I live. She was not really happy for me because she is so unhappy with herself. She saw me happy with my boyfriend and had to take it away. I never questioned his motives, I simply cut him off. But for me the real devastation had to do with my sister. She was the one who hurt me so much. I told her I forgave her because she was my sister but I will never forget.

"This sister and I have never been the same type and actually we didn't go for the same kind of men. I told my boyfriend that the party was over but I told my sister, at the time, that what she did disgusted me. It was incestuous that we were both sleeping with the same man at the same time. I don't know how she stood it, because she knew it was happening, but I didn't. I continued to sleep with him unwittingly while she did it on purpose."

Kara's youngest sister also had difficulties with the middle sister.

"Our middle sister has always behaved badly. Even before she did such a terrible thing, I had to psych myself up to be around her. I just don't have the patience to get along with her. My middle sister never made an effort with us, never tried to make it work. After this episode, we returned to our former pattern. I behaved toward her as I had before our divorces. I distanced myself and yet remained close to my baby sister. I would tell her anything—she is a true sister. I have one close friend who is like a sister to me and I have a younger sister. But my middle sister and I are finished.

"I'm very close to my mother—both she and my little sister knew what the other sister had done, but they were hesitant to take sides. They saw that we had worked it out superficially and that was what they wanted, so they stayed clear of it. In our family no one minds anyone else's business—we respect each other's privacy. My mother is relieved because on the surface everything seems fine. My middle sister does not live close by and that makes it easier. When she comes for a visit, I rarely see her. I don't feel I'm missing anything. I see my other sister all the time and we speak on the phone constantly. When the middle sister is around and joins us, she changes the atmosphere. There's tension and a feeling of discomfort. She's sharp and jealous, which she was long before she did what she did to me."

Recently Kara has had another issue with her middle sister.

"My sister has a child who is very much like her. I've distanced myself from the kid, too, so the separation between my sister and myself now extends to our children. What she did by sleeping with my boyfriend has really changed everything, and it doesn't go away."

Although Kara says she still loves her sister by definition but cannot forgive her, we wonder how much love is really there. Once she learned that her middle sister, who had been jealous of Kara all along, slept with her boyfriend, it seems that any hope for closeness between the two sisters was lost. So deep is her anger that Kara now finds issue with her sister's child, too. The repercussions are undeniable; Kara is connected to her mother and youngest sister, and has simply severed any real tie with her middle sister.

As for her sister's motivation, Kara sees it as revenge against her for being the good daughter, and a winner. Since neither sister ended up with this particular man, Kara's theory could be correct. It does not seem that her sister and her boyfriend fell passionately in love and could not resist temptation. Her sister's behavior was about something else—a competitive and destructive gesture.

Valerie

"He always cheated on me, so why wouldn't he go after my sister?"

Valerie is the oldest of four sisters, and has never been close to her youngest sister. Viewing her as the baby, she felt she was over-protected by her parents and there was no possibility of developing a relationship with her. Living in southern California, Valerie recently married. Several years ago, her youngest sister married Valerie's former fiancé.

"When I was in medical school I met a man and was really taken with him. I liked him enough to invite him to my parents' home one weekend. He met my entire family. My youngest sister was leaving a live-in relationship at the time. I think her initial opinion of this guy was that he was obnoxious. Anyway, he and I continued to go out and were about to be engaged. The next thing I knew, he had broken it off. I was devastated. I did not confide in my sisters but my parents knew what was going on. What shocked me so was they also knew that my baby sister had taken up with this man. They took a strange attitude, almost defending her behavior."

Valerie knows that her youngest sister is very attractive.

"My youngest sister is eight years younger, while this man I was involved with is my age. My sister proceeded to leave her boyfriend and begin to see this man. There was nothing I could do. I had been with him for two years and the attraction was very strong. I couldn't get over it. He was a cheat to begin with, I have to admit. He always cheated on me, so why wouldn't he go after my sister? By the time I learned that they were really dating, their relationship was very hot and heavy. My sister's attitude was that I didn't need to know. She was actually afraid to tell me—we already didn't get along so well. She was the favorite in the family, so I don't know why she was worried, but she was."

Valerie saw the fact that she wasn't told as a conspiracy.

"I was deeply embarrassed to learn that he was being intimate with one of my sisters. She never apologized and, in fact, behaved as if I'd barely dated the guy. She made light of our relationship in order to justify theirs. My parents acted the same, as if bygones should be bygones. They also were under the impression that with me it had been unrequited love. The great joke was that this guy still called me and behaved the same way as before. My sister hasn't a clue, to this day, as to how important it is for him to keep his options open.

"My sister and I became further estranged. We spoke only at family gatherings and I tried to avoid those. Then in the past years, two things happened: We all gathered together because a family member became very ill, and then I pulled my life together. I have practiced medicine professionally throughout, and I finally lost the weight that I had gained during the ordeal. I met a man and we got married. I'm finally happy but it took me years. I will never forgive my sister completely for trying to put something over on me. Our family is trying to heal from such a difficult situation. I went through a tremendous amount of pain as a result of what my sister did. I ended up in therapy which was probably a good thing."

Today, Valerie believes that her sister saved her from a cruel fate.

"I understand now that this man is not a good person. I believe he deliberately went after my sister. He is a very successful doctor—that's how he attracts women. I think of him as a liar and a cheat and he doesn't treat women well. He enjoyed being part of a family with four sisters; then he saw that she was a younger, prettier package with the same anchor, the same family, and went after that. I watched how he treated my sister. I think his attraction to her was that she didn't fall all over him. But the bottom line is that we were from a wealthy, good family of the same culture and religion. He was ready to marry and my sister was younger with a sensational body so he went for it.

"Both of them are so superficial and materialistic. They actually suit each other perfectly. But it has totally split our family. My relationship with this sister, beyond being polite if the circumstance demands it, is nonexistent. I have such animosity and hatred toward her. If she's the winner, she got quite a prize. She never stopped to wonder how I felt. She was too caught up by him."

Valerie has come a long way from the initial shock.

"When it first happened, I could barely get myself to work. I fell into a deep depression. Then I analyzed the entire experience and saw them for who they are. This particular sister and I have never been close—it wasn't how we were raised. I see her as completely empty and unfeeling to do what she did. In the end, since there is a happy ending for me, it's fine that she married him and it's fortunate for me that I did not. She's really perfect for him and they're in material pig heaven. I'm well out of it. I haven't lost a terrific man nor have I lost a great sister. The situation ultimately reflected what was missing in both of them. Their marriage suits them and I've learned who my sister and her husband really are."

Valerie knows intellectually that she escaped an incompatible marriage with a disappointing man. The proof of this is found in his choice of a wife. It seems as if the lack of closeness between the two sisters is what allowed the younger sister to justify her behavior. For Valerie, it has been a tedious, unhappy experience.

Jessica

"My sister acted as if I'd torn her heart out. . . . She did not come to my wedding . . ."

The youngest of three sisters, Jessica is thirty-two and lives in New Orleans. Growing up, Jessica was close to her middle sister but not her oldest one. Today she is married to her oldest sister's former live-in boyfriend.

"I went to school back east and lived with someone from college by the time I was twenty-three. When I was twenty-seven I left him and went home to be near my sisters and my friends. At that time, my oldest sister was living with a man. I can honestly say that the relationship was going nowhere, and if I hadn't come along, I doubt he would have married my sister. It wasn't like that.

"I met him at a friend's party. All of our family was invited. I thought he was good-looking and I was surprised that he'd hooked up with my sister because she is not the prettiest one of us. I was attracted to him. I knew he liked me but I stayed clear. Finally we met for coffee, and that was the beginning."

Jessica did not tell anyone in her family what had transpired.

"He wanted to talk about my sister. He said that he wasn't happy living with her. I knew that no one would believe me, that my sister would be devastated. If he'd left for another woman, fine, I suppose. But for her sister? I knew I was in trouble but I wanted this man. I really liked him. He was just the kind of person I was looking for. We dated seriously, sneaking out whenever we knew that my sister was traveling on business. She is three years older than I am and he is five years older. I think he wanted a younger version of her. I began to see that my sister and I were somewhat similar. But growing up, I never knew it. I spent all my time with our middle sister, who seemed more nurturing and more interested in me. Suddenly I was thinking about my older sister nonstop. The relationship that was developing with her boyfriend made me face who my sister was and who I was. I knew I had to make a decision."

Jessica's sister's live-in moved out at this point.

"Once he moved out, I knew it had to be made public. So, I began with my mother. She was surprised and then kind of supportive. She felt that the relationship my sister had had with him was not successful. She believed me when I said I wanted to marry him but she knew it would disrupt our family. I think my parents wanted me to be happy but in the end they'd hoped I'd find someone else. They knew deep down what would happen.

"Next I told my oldest sister. She went nuts. She said that with all the women in the world for him to choose from and with all the men for me to go after, it wasn't necessary. I tried to explain how I felt about him. We were madly in love, and I knew he'd never felt this way about her. If he had, it had been a long time ago, when I was away at school. She realized that because I'm a very determined person, I would pursue this to the end."

After several months time, Jessica announced her engagement.

"My sister acted as if I'd torn her heart out. He had never proposed to her. As I stated earlier, it wasn't in the cards. But she was devastated. She did not come to the wedding and she stopped talking to me completely. I played it down, but I knew that my sister was really suffering. I also knew that my life mattered, too. I'd had very unhappy relationships with men. I was looking for stability and someone to adore me. He did."

Today Jessica and her husband have three children. Her oldest sister is also married.

"My sister married soon after our wedding and has a family. She met someone on vacation and was swept off her feet. Despite the fact that this happened to her, which proves that the live-in situation with my husband was doomed, she has severed all ties with me. She will not speak to me and if I go to my parents' with my husband and kids, she refuses to go, including Christmas and Easter. If she accepts an invitation, she makes sure I won't be included. It's been going on for years. My other sister probably thinks I was wrong. Neither she nor our parents sees it as I do.

"The sad part for me is that our kids don't know each other. Mine think they only have one aunt. I watch my daughters as they bond and I wonder if one day something like this might happen to them. And would I understand? I suppose I feel some guilt, but not much. My attitude is that if my husband had wanted to marry my sister, he would have. Instead, he chose me."

Until the end of Jessica's story when she expresses remorse, there is a notable absence of guilt. In order to go forward she has detached herself. She denies it was her sister who was the spurned woman. With this take on it, it is understandable that Jessica felt able to go forward.

Jessica was capable of marrying this man and confronting her sister because she justified her actions. Working through a half-truth and reestablishing the facts to suit her needs might be the only way Jessica can live with herself. Her sister has married and found a new life. She harbors great resentment toward Jessica, which is something Jessica minimizes in order to lead her own life.

Sonya

"No matter where I went, no matter who I met, I always thought about my sister."

At the age of ninety-eight, Sonya, a grandmother and great-grandmother, is widowed and lives in a city in the northeast. Although her marriage was dignified and produced six children, Sonya is convinced that her husband married her as part of an arrangement once her sister stole Sonya's boyfriend.

"My husband and I knew each other in Europe. We all came from the same village. My sister, who was several years younger, was smitten with my boyfriend. I really wanted to marry him but my sister and he fell in love. This was not America but Europe and it was many years ago. My sister took my boyfriend, and for every year I was married I thought about it. My sister and my boyfriend ran away to South America. Then I ended up marrying this man my father chose. I lost both my sister *and* my boyfriend."

Sonya and her sister were very close as children.

"My sister and I were true sisters until we were teenagers. We did everything together. It was only when my boyfriend walked through the door of our father's house that everything changed.

We both wanted him. We were so young, only in our teens. In those days, everyone married early. I assumed that I would marry him and I thought he felt the same. Instead he chose my sister and my father insisted I marry someone else. There was little I could do. There was no way I could have convinced my father otherwise.

"It destroyed our family. There was no love between the man I married and myself. My father knew how hurt I was by what my sister had done. He matched me up and sent us to America. He made a deal with my husband, no question. Because there were only two sisters, it made it a more difficult situation. It was so painful."

Sonya and her husband began a family.

"Once we got to America, I began to feel better. My sister was far away and I hoped I could forget her. What happened instead was that my husband, always a good provider and a perfect gentleman, had affairs. I never had proof, but I knew it. In the same way that my father had insisted I marry this man, I felt I had to stay with him. I accepted that what existed between us was not love but tremendous respect.

"We had six children and they became my entire life. I was involved with them and that was how I filled the void. My husband and I treated each other civilly and were never unkind to one another. It was a marriage without emotion—it was about dignity and respect. My children became the most important thing to me. My husband often went out alone—he loved the opera and going to restaurants. I stayed at home and focused on family life."

Sonya never forgot what her sister did.

"No matter where I went, no matter who I met, I always thought about my sister. And once my children grew up, I felt there was no longer a reason to live. I never believed that my daughters-in-law or sons-in-law could ever become like my own. And so my children moved away; they had their own lives.

"I know that my marriage succeeded because I was willing to look the other way. And what was most difficult about it was that it all hinged upon my sister. She and I did not remain in touch. I could not forgive her for marrying the love of my life. She had to know how I felt and she did it anyway. Even though neither of us still lived in Europe, the hurt was not diminished. It had nothing to do with my day-to-day life and still it was difficult for me. I never really recovered."

Sonya took what she could from her marriage.

"What makes me so sad is the loss of contact with my sister. It has been so many years now, but I'm still very aware of it. The children fulfilled me and my husband and I did things together as a family. But my sister was on both our minds, no matter what each of us was doing. My husband understood how he and I ended up together."

Forced to marry a man after her sister took her boyfriend, Sonya believed she had no choice but to do the best she could under the circumstances. Pouring herself into motherhood, she found her own separate happiness in a loveless match. One wonders if her relationship with her sister was severed by the marriage or possibly by the different parts of the world the sisters found themselves in.

Sonya's tale is one of compromise, and her sentiments are understandable. In a marriage that could be described as cordial at best, the ghost of her absent sister and her former lover seem constant.

SURROGATE MOTHERS:
Sisters for Sisters

The whole concept of surrogate parenting is so new that we are just beginning to study the consequences of this medical manipulation of sperm and egg. As the years go by and the children of surrogate parents meet the developmental challenges of life we will be able to see the effects of our scientific engineering on the physical and emotional well-being of these children. So far, we know that the emotional factors in surrogate parenting are complicated. Some surrogate mothers have difficulty giving away the baby, even though they fully intended to do so from the beginning. Other women don't seem to have a problem carrying a baby and handing it over to others to raise.

Certainly when a woman carries a child for her sister the issues become even more complex. The surrogate mother will become the aunt of the child she gives up. How will this relationship work for both surrogate mother and child? How does it affect the relationship between the two sisters? The possibilities seem endless.

RONNIE L. BURAK, PH.D

Kandice Righetti, wife of Dave Righetti, relief pitcher for the Giants, had one of the most unusual stories involving sisters and surrogate motherhood. When Kayla, Kandice's sister, offered to carry her sister's fertilized egg, she did not anticipate that she would give birth to triplets. At the time Righetti had signed with the Giants and Kayla's surrogate pregnancy was kept quiet. When Kayla underwent an emergency cesarean section, Kandace missed the birth of her children. Born prematurely and weighing in at less than three pounds each, the babies are in good health today. Her sister's gift of love gave Kandace the family of her dreams.

According to Dr. Hugh Melnick, Director of Advanced Fertility Services in New York City, the number of sisters who serve as surrogate mothers for their sisters is on the rise. "When it works out positively, it is a happy situation all around." Dr. Satti Keswanni of Livingston Fertility in Livingston, New Jersey, believes that sisters are genetically compatible and a better choice because they are less likely to have a change of mind after the birth of the baby.

In January of 1990, another surrogate mother-sister scenario took place. Pamela Better, a woman in British Columbia, was artificially inseminated by her sister's husband. The mother of a young daughter, Pamela did not expect to be so overjoyed when she delivered a baby boy to her older sister, Virginia. Having experienced four unsuccessful pregnancies, Virginia thought she would never have children until her sister offered to bear her a child. Not the least bit threatened by the question that she might fall in love with her sister's child and want to raise him, Pamela told the newspapers that she had given her sister the "baby of her dreams" and that she was delighted to gain a nephew.

There have been an estimated five thousand surrogate births in our country since the late seventies. And while the control and screening of the possible surrogates is strict, there is always a danger. At the Surrogate Parenting Center in Beverly Hills, parents and surrogates undergo medical and psychological testing.

Among sisters who surrogate for sisters, the risks appear lower and the complications less significant.

Despite the obvious motivation of a sister who surrogate-mothers her sister's child, be it as egg donor or carrier, there remains the possibility of repercussion. Noel Keane, an attorney who devotes his entire practice to contracting for surrogacy and is personally responsible for over five hundred births, views sisters who surrogate mother as a very specific situation.

"It depends on the sisters and their relationship whether it is easier for them. In some cases, a sister can be too close and too possessive of the child. Then it is not a good set-up. Generally, it is a non-fee arrangement between sisters, and financially it may be the only option for certain women. However, not everyone has a sister. When a sister surrogates her sister's child, it is usually an act of devotion."

A recent and successful surrogate mothering of a sister's child involved three sisters. James Alan Mack, Jr., of Bandon, Oregon, was born as the result of the fertility and selflessness of his two aunts. Jim's sister, Kathy Huemann, had offered to carry a baby, but the egg had to be supplied by someone who was not a blood relative. Ann Scacco, the mother of two, had previously offered to help her sister Linda, but chose not to carry the child. Thus the egg for the baby was supplied by Ann, the maternal aunt, and the carrier was Kathy, the paternal aunt.

The impressive result, that of the birth of James Mack, Jr., is testimony to the triumph of modern science and the ultimate gift of sisterhood.

Deirdre

"I see what happened between my sister and myself as a miracle."

In her mid-forties and living in New England, Deirdre is the mother of one child. Her sister, who lives in South Carolina, already had two children when she became the surrogate mother for Deirdre's daughter. Both sisters are full-time mothers.

"My sister and I were not close growing up. As adults we are quite close, but it wasn't until we were grown up that we felt this way. Because we are so close, I was able to ask my sister to donate an egg and carry my child. Before either of us had kids, we spent so much time together. To this day, we spend our summers together with all our children."

Deirdre knew from an early age that she could not have children.

"I had a hysterectomy when I was twenty years old. For the most part, though, I had pretty much accepted it and was resigned by my thirties. My husband wasn't wild about adopting a child but I wanted to. He has a child from a previous marriage and his ex-wife has used this kid as a weapon. His feeling was that he had difficulty caring for his own kid so how could he handle someone else's?

"Finally I asked my sister if she'd ever heard of surrogate mothers. She looked at me kind of funny and once she understood my intention, she asked me why I hadn't asked her right off the bat. She was that supportive. We decided to discuss it with our spouses. The four of us had a number of meetings and discussed every single possibility. We were all very clear about what each expected of the other if the unexpected happened. For example, we agreed to amnio because my sister was in her mid-thirties. If the fetus was spina bifida or a Down's baby, it was my decision whether she should abort or not. I needed to know how my sister felt morally in certain situations because we both worked with mentally retarded kids. We went over everything until we were in agreement."

Knowing that it was her sister made it much easier for Deirdre.

"We have the same blood pumping through our veins. It didn't bother me that she would be an egg donor as well as a carrier. When she became pregnant and throughout the pregnancy, I visited her. I flew in when she had her amnio and spent the last six weeks before she delivered with her. She decided to deliver near me because we were both crazy about the doctor we'd found and I wanted the baby with me immediately after birth.

"I didn't pay my sister a fee but I paid any bills that were not covered by insurance. And I bought her maternity clothes. There were no legalities because we're sisters, and there was no need to draw up any papers. Had my sister said no, I would have paid someone else what I could afford. But this was in the mid-eighties and the going rate was ten thousand dollars. My husband and I didn't have that kind of money. In retrospect, knowing what I know about surrogacy, I'm so happy it was my sister who carried the baby and that it wasn't complicated."

Deirdre and her sister are as close today as they were before the baby was born.

"We're not closer because we were so close from the start. But there are certain times of the year when I feel very sentimental, such as Mother's Day or when I see a card about sisters. She gave me the ultimate gift. And while I don't get to see her any more than before, the knowledge that she did this for me is always there. We go away together every summer. She treats my daughter as her niece. She had her own baby fourteen months after she carried my daughter.

"I am absolutely in love with my daughter. She is the best kid in the world. When I think back to my childhood, I see traces of my younger sister in her. My mother says that she looks just like me but I see only a little of me and more of my sister. She looks more like my sister than her own daughter or son does."

Deirdre's husband is very pleased with their daughter as well.

"My husband is so happy that we wish we had more. If I were younger by ten years, I'd do it again—and I think my sister feels the same way. If she were ten years younger, she'd do it again. We never even discussed it when my daughter was three or four. At the time I was so consumed with my only child and my sister had two to look after.

"I see what happened between my sister and myself as a miracle. What upsets me about surrogacy is the negative press it receives. I've yet to see a happy ending on television but I know from first-hand experience that there are lots of happy endings out there. Look at me. My sister made it possible."

Deirdre's story has a happy ending indeed. What is notable is that she and her sister were so comfortable with one another that there were no papers drawn up and no exchange of money. Sitting down and discussing every aspect of the procedure was important, but beyond that it seems that the trust these sisters share is all encompassing. There wasn't any hesitation on either sister's part. Today each sister knows her place as mother and aunt, there are absolutely no second thoughts. Theirs is truly a story of love and devotion.

Margaret

**"I had total empathy with my sister throughout
the pregnancy . . . her attitude was that her body
was mine . . ."**

*At the age of forty-five, Margaret is a designer and her sister is
an environmentalist. Margaret lives in northern California and
her sister in the midwest. Margaret and her sister were not close
growing up, but as adults they became close enough for
Margaret's sister to surrogate-mother her child.*

"What happened was the culmination of a growing relationship with my sister. She was the youngest and my brother and I
didn't pay much attention to her. We grew up tolerating one another and yet we were competitive. There was such sibling rivalry. When we left home we realized that the family we had
taken for granted was very special. That was when we began to
bond.

"I have always loved kids and I was the babysitter. My sister
loved sports and boys. She married early, however, which was
surprising and had kids right away to please her husband. Then
she was deeply disappointed because her husband wasn't there
for her. He was very traditional and liked children when they
grew older. But I was there, the doting aunt. I did not marry for
years afterward. I gave her kids my energy and while I didn't
choose to be married at the time and have my own kids, I loved
hers."

*At this point, their mother died and she and her sister became
closer.*

"When our mother died both my sister and I realized the value of having a sister. I got married soon after and I was ready for children. The nest was ready—and the income. But what if I didn't get pregnant, I asked myself. Then I learned that the Dalkon Shield causes infertility problems and just as I had dreaded, my tubes were blocked. I couldn't have children without years and years of surgery. Finally they were opened up but I still did not conceive. My sister shared my pain and heartache for six years. She didn't want any more children but she could get pregnant at the drop of a hat. Had she become pregnant, she'd have had an abortion. That was how opposite our situations were.

"My marriage began to suffer. After six years of trying everything under the sun, we were financially drained. But my husband refused to adopt. I would have compromised on surrogacy—I kept thinking my sister might do it, but it wasn't the kind of thing you asked of someone. So my husband and I worked with my attorney and a psychologist to find a surrogate. This was the mid-eighties and we went to the Surrogate Parenting Center in Beverly Hills, which is a most impressive place. We were presented with a psychologically and medically screened surrogate.

"What happened to me was that I needed an egg donor and I also needed someone to carry my child. I told my sister what I was going to do. A few days later she called and offered to carry the child for me. Her offer, at her instigation, had to be an unconditional gift or it wouldn't work. It had always been my hope, in the back of my mind, but I never had asked."

Margaret flew her sister's family to her home after they had created the structure.

"Logistically it was difficult. We all got together, including my father and stepmother, to ask the family. Our stepmother was against it—she's very conservative. But finally our entire family was supportive.

"My sister refused to be paid. I insisted she take the standard fee, but she kept refusing and finally I explained that I viewed her role as work. We met with an attorney and discussed the legal aspects. It never worried me for a moment that my sister might want to keep this baby. Her fear was that my husband and I would be in a plane crash while she was pregnant and she'd get stuck with my child. Another factor was that she lived in a small community where everyone knew she was pregnant. She had to think of how it would affect her children. It was definitely difficult to explain in her small town. I was ecstatic when she finally decided to do it, despite the obstacles. And our father's support, which mattered to us, was there.

"Then I found out I was pregnant, and a few weeks later I miscarried. I was told that my tubes were inoperable. It was a blessing in disguise because then my sister and I knew beyond a doubt that I couldn't have a baby. The first time she was inseminated by a doctor and it didn't take. The second time we were told how to do it. We put the sperm in a cervical cap and the two of us went into the bathroom. We were laughing as she shoved the cap inside her. And then she got pregnant.

"My sister was so wonderful while she was pregnant. She lived in her hometown but we saw each other as much as possible. I was there for the delivery and it was a girl—she had had two boys. From the beginning she made it clear that she was handing over her body—it was my child. My sister's children and my father and my husband were all there for the delivery. I had total empathy with my sister throughout the pregnancy. She let me touch her body and photograph her nude. Her attitude was that her body was mine for that period. She was truly thrilled to be able to do this for me—it brought us much closer. I look at our child and she is the greatest gift one sister can give the other. She treats our daughter as her niece."

Today Margaret and her sister see each other and their families several times a year.

"What has transpired between my sister and myself is beyond my wildest dreams. Not only did she do something for my marriage, but she showed me the better side of human nature. There is a special biological connection to a sister and she did what no one else could do in the same way."

As a result of her experience, Margaret began an organization for surrogate mothers.

"Not everyone can have their sisters do this. A surrogate mother, related or not, brings great joy, so I began a referral service for women who are seeking alternative birth methods. It is called OPTS, Organization of Parents Through Surrogacy. Having a sister who will do it is the best of both worlds but it isn't always possible. There is a big difference between a sister and a stranger, of course. You can't just walk away from your sister if something goes wrong. My recurring fear was that my sister would die in childbirth. But in the end it worked out beautifully and with a sister, it is such an amazing tie. I would not ask, but I have often wished she'd do it again."

Having her sister surrogate-mother her child completed the cycle for both sisters. After a detached childhood, it seemed appropriate due to their closeness as adults. Their mutual desire for family approval, that of their father and even their stepmother, reveals their strong family ties.

The manner in which Margaret's sister handed over her body for the nine months that she carried the child displays a generosity of spirit. Margaret was able to feel totally involved in the process, and with no lingering doubt that her sister was selfless and committed to her task. Another healthy aspect of her story is the roles that both women assumed after the birth of the baby—that of motherhood for Margaret and that of an aunt for her sister. There is no residual regret on either woman's part, but a positive sense that what they agreed upon has been enormously successful.

Angela

"My sister will go to the ends of the earth to find an egg that is compatible if I refuse."

Angela, at the age of thirty-two, is the mother of four small children. Her sister, who is two years older, has recently married and discovered that she cannot have children. The two sisters are very close, and both live in Delaware. Knowing that her sister is devoted to her children and to her, Angela has recently begun to explore the possibility of being a surrogate mother for her sister's child.

"I would do anything for my sister. She was single for a long time. When she had the opportunity to get married, she was so happy. Both she and her husband are in their mid-thirties and are professionals. I'm a full-time mother and I had my babies so easily. My sister came to me because they really didn't want to adopt a child. She is desperate to have a baby; in fact, before she married this guy, she actually considered having one out of wedlock. Then she met her husband and they immediately began to try."

Given the choice, Angela's sister would want her to have the baby.

"I'm the one who's hesitating at the moment. The only reason I've held back is that my sister needs an egg donor, not a carrier. I would gladly be the carrier for a fertilized egg but I think it's too weird that her husband and I would end up producing a baby together. I couldn't bear it. Even if she carried my egg, I'd know. Our genes are so similar and we look so much alike. But I'd be its biological mother and that's not what I bargained for when we first began this business."

The egg donor aspect of surrogacy bothers Angela.

"Way before my sister and I discussed this, I'd read about surrogate mothers who donated their eggs. I always thought that
was odd and uncomfortable. It's such a shame that my sister and
I can't work it out the other way, so I'd carry her egg. If she could
provide the egg, I'd gladly do it. But this aspect of surrogacy
makes the baby mine. I don't want a biological tie. We've explored this at great length and she's hoping against hope that I'll
change my mind. The real problem is that when I agreed, we
thought she only needed me as a vessel.

"My sister will go to the ends of the earth to find an egg that is
compatible if I refuse. She knows how complicated it is for me,
but she's obsessed with this and won't rest until it happens. I
keep saying I don't want my child to be raised by her. I feel great
sympathy for her, but I have to think of the future. I'd go crazy if
my kid was being raised by her. And I can't be sure of how I'd
feel, knowing the child is half mine, and my sister can't accept it.

"I feel terrible about this and recently I've felt very guilty as
well. I know I'm capable of helping her physically but not emotionally. I have a wonderful family and she has been on the side-
lines looking in for every baby I've delivered. It's a real joke.
She's finally happily married and I had promised to do anything
I could to help her. But I've explained that donating an egg
would create very serious problems."

Despite Angela's hesitation, her sister continues to seek her help.

"She's been asking me repeatedly. As her only sister, I want to
make her happy. We're struggling with it. Before this episode,
my sister and I were so close. I know that as a sister, until this
occurred, I'd have done anything for her. We've been there for
each other our entire lives.

"I also know that donating the egg would create problems in
my marriage. My husband would find it strange, and probably

unacceptable. I often wondered, when I thought I'd be the carrier, how it would affect my marriage and my children, but this is more difficult. Then I project and say to myself that if she was raising a child that was half mine, I'd certainly let her know if I didn't think she was doing a good job."

Another factor for Angela is the knowledge that her sister has been unhappy much of her adult life.

"I've been happily married for years. My sister has been very involved with my kids because she was so alone. I thought she'd be the spinster aunt; I never even expected her to get married. Every Christmas and Thanksgiving she would be at my house. For a short time, she was married and blissfully happy, but then she found out she's infertile. Now I feel it all rests on me because she won't turn to someone outside the family.

"I think this problem is harming her marriage at this point. The doctor told her that it's her problem, not her husband's which makes it worse. She's absolutely obsessed and it's driving a wedge between us. We have to make a decision very soon."

Angela's relationship with her sister seems to rest on her choice to be or not to be the donor for her sister's child. Although she alludes to the fact that her sister wants what Angela has, Angela does not want to provide it under the circumstances. Unexpectedly and ironically, it is against her wishes to do what her sister is asking. As she states, she would gladly have been the 'oven' in a surrogate arrangement. Believing she would do anything for her sister, Angela is in a bind.

In an unfortunate situation, she finds herself up against her personal beliefs for the sake of her sister's happiness. She feels doubly obligated, knowing she has led the life her sister yearns to have and because she had initially promised to carry the baby. Since Angela finds the concept of being an egg donor intolerable, it seems a no-win situation for both sisters.

Lucinda

"The closeness came about in full circle—first she
delivered her own baby and I was there. Then she
delivered mine and I was there."

*At the age of thirty, Lucinda is the oldest of four sisters and four
brothers. Working in a hospital, Lucinda did not want to have a
child until five years ago. Unsuccessful after many attempts, she
decided to accept her second sister's offer to be artificially
inseminated by Lucinda's husband. Today she is the proud
mother of a year-old baby girl. Lucinda lives in Palm Springs,
California.*

"I'm very attached to two of my sisters. The other is the black
sheep of the family, a drug addict. I'm very close to her daughter
but I cannot stay close to this sister. It is the life she has chosen
for herself that makes it so difficult. We grew up in a lower middle class, hard-working family. I think she got stuck in adolescence after our father died. It's very sad. All of my sisters live
nearby and we grew up in such a happy family. I'm so involved
with my troubled sister's child that I would adopt her in a minute if my sister would allow it."

*Lucinda did not anticipate having any difficulty conceiving a
baby.*

"Both of us, my husband and myself, are from large families,
eight kids in each. I learned there were problems when I went to
a doctor and was told I had to have my tubes opened up. We
went through this procedure several times and I still could not
get pregnant. We decided to try for a test tube baby which failed.
My tubes closed up again. By this time the sister who is two

years younger already had a baby. She was so upset about the devastation that my husband and I experienced. It really hurt her. That was why she offered, because I never dreamed of asking her. She told me that she and her husband had decided a year earlier that she would do this for me."

Lucinda made the decision, although her eggs were intact, that her sister should be artificially inseminated.

"There is a tremendous amount of hormones required in order to implant your eggs in someone else's body. I didn't want my sister to take so many hormones because I knew she wanted more kids of her own. So we decided, since we all look alike and have similar traits and personalities, that we would use her eggs. When she first offered, I had no idea how this process worked. Nor did she. We found a counselor and ended up in the Center for Surrogacy in Beverly Hills. No money was exchanged because my sister refused, but we promised them a vacation whenever they wanted to go. And I bought her maternity clothes.

"I would have done anything to help my sister through this. Her insurance covered most of the expenses and that was fortunate. We were told that we could actually use a turkey baster to get her pregnant but we used a syringe. We did it at home and it was much better and friendlier than going to a clinic. It wasn't until the second cycle that she became pregnant. My sister couldn't sleep with her own husband during this period and she used an ovulation kit to track herself. It was an amazing process. We felt extremely close throughout, from the day we decided to the day the baby was born."

During the pregnancy, Lucinda's sister lived several blocks away.

"I saw my sister constantly but then they had to move because of her husband's business. She was an hour away and I was sad but I thought it might be good for us, too. We still saw each other on our days off. I was very involved with her child as I had always been. I think one reason she offered to do this is because when she had problems with her first pregnancy, I was there for her. I was also there for the birth and that also increased her support. Our parents were behind our decision to do the surrogacy one hundred percent.

"It was a shock to the entire family that I couldn't have kids. I was the perfect aunt and the perfect babysitter and our family is very tight. It seemed unbelievable that I couldn't do what was so natural to all of us. My youngest sister did not quite get what was going on, and then she realized what a joyful experience my second sister and I were sharing. I don't think that this sister was jealous, however, but she's not like the sister who offered. The sister who carried my baby always understood that it was not her child. My other sister is very maternal and very emotional. In the same situation, I doubt if she'd be able to separate herself from the baby. The sister who carried my baby understood it was for me and she did it only because I'm her sister."

Everything went smoothly during the pregnancy and delivery.

"My sister is a very private person. Even her way of telling me that the pregnancy had happened was subtle. She left a bottle of champagne and a positive pregnancy test outside my front porch. We told family and close friends that we were pregnant. Both her husband and mine were at the delivery and, of course, I was there. It was a C-section, which had been scheduled, as with her first pregnancy.

"Today my baby is almost a year old and I am thrilled and in love. My sister is a perfect aunt, which was what I expected. I feel sorry that she didn't feel well during the start of the pregnancy. She came to my house quite pale and tired—that was when I helped her with her child. I hated seeing her that way."

Lucinda and her sister are closer now than ever before.

"I am so grateful to my sister for what she did. The closeness came about in full circle, first she delivered her own baby and I was there. Then she delivered mine and I was there. I know that we could not have afforded to hire a surrogate but my sister offered before I actually explored it. And we had decided against adoption so the truth is that surrogacy with my sister was the only way we could go.

"Having experienced this, I know that infertility is a big problem in this country. It doesn't get the attention it deserves. And why isn't it covered by medical insurance? It's too expensive for many women to consider. I know how many women can't afford it and don't have sisters. My sister made it possible for me. It was my pain that made her realize she could help. She was able to reach out to me and it bound us together. This is what sisters can do for each other."

Lucinda suffered terribly because she was unable to have a baby. Her sister's empathy was such that she decided on her own to help Lucinda, long before Lucinda saw it as an option. Coming from a strong family despite the one sister who has gone her own way, everyone supported the decision.

What is interesting is that Lucinda decided that although her eggs were intact, it would be better for her sister to avoid the necessary hormones. In this instance, there is a balanced give and take in the sisters' relationship. Another point is that Lucinda and her sister understood from the start that the delivery would be a scheduled cesarean. That the sister who was pregnant found it acceptable is a further example of her selflessness.

It seems that Lucinda's sister who made the commitment to surrogate mother her child was the only sister available. The sister who is a drug addict was obviously not a possibility and the other sister sounds as if she might have been ambivalent about her attachment to the baby.

Pamela

"My sister did not want to be listed as a surrogate mother on legal documents."

Living in Anaheim, California, Pamela, at the age of thirty-eight, has a sister who is two years younger and has two foster sisters who are eight and ten years older. Several weeks ago Pamela's sister gave birth to a baby girl which she surrogate-mothered for Pamela. Pamela and her husband provided the egg and the sperm and her sister provided the incubation.

"I come from a very close family unit. We were raised to believe that the family comes first and to be a good sister is sublime. Being good sisters was viewed as the testing ground for being a good citizen of the world. I think that the foundation with my sisters was the groundwork for what was to follow.

"I've been married for twenty years. Around six years ago, I began trying to have a baby. After four miscarriages, including twins at four months, I learned that my husband and I have an immune system disorder which caused my body to attack and reject the fetus. My sister never had a problem with her pregnancies and has healthy children. She watched what I went through and couldn't handle my miscarriages. Our husbands, who are best friends, were completely drawn into the process. We live ten miles apart and our parents are also nearby."

Pamela's sister offered to carry her child.

"Once my sister realized the depth of our disappointment, she made the decision to be a surrogate mother. We went to a fertility center where they were thrilled that we were sisters. It was fortunate that I was able to use my eggs because then my sister really became a carrier. We got pregnant right away—it was a tremendous experience.

"Some surrogates have to make many attempts, but this happened the first time for us. We had discussed how many embryos would be implanted. I couldn't ask my sister to do a multiple birth, although her pregnancies had been trouble-free and she was confident about this one. She's not a complainer and we're so friendly as couples, it seemed the right approach from the start. But I felt asking for a multiple birth was pushing it."

Pamela, her sister, and their husbands drew up a covenant.

"We didn't go to an attorney but something had to be drawn up or I would be required to adopt the baby that my sister was carrying for me. My sister didn't want to be listed as a surrogate mother on legal documents. She saw herself as a carrier and was firm about this. Each person reacts differently to the system, and that's how she felt. I saw her as more of a participant; she provided the muscle and the blood and that goes beyond just carrying the child. But I never had any concern that she'd want to keep the baby. She shared our sentiments about that part of her role.

"While there's no doubt I would do the same for my sister if it was necessary, I know how enormous the task was. On a cellular level alone, what my sister did for me was amazing. She had to give a tremendous amount of time to the pregnancy. There was some physical pain and at the end of the pregnancy her priorities shifted in terms of her work and time away from her kids. I took care of them often during this period. I'm very close to them and it was a rich experience for all of us. There were so many caring people involved with this pregnancy—that made it even more special.

"Another piece of the pie is that our friendship as sisters has become deeper because of what we shared. Our mother and father, my husband, and her husband were there for the birth. Each of us had different attitudes toward the whole process, but it worked out smoothly. For the delivery, we hired a labor assistant and drew up a birth plan ahead of time. Everyone was included in some capacity. I had real sympathy pains and I'd even had morning sickness early on. But I'd had so many miscarriages that I didn't want my own personal fears to be contagious during her pregnancy. My sister and I learned how to work through all these different issues."

Pamela and her sister were not alike in approach.

"We have the same values but my sister and I go about things differently. I'm more organized and down to earth, she's more spontaneous. We had to blend our styles as women and as sisters. In this way, it was a real growth experience for both of us. The most amazing part of the entire thing was that my sister took the pregnancy so in stride. She was just her usual sweet, wonderful self. She gets flustered when people compliment her because she feels it was something I wanted badly, so she did it for me. She was born with this loving attitude—she's always been as supportive as possible. Our parents also embody this kind of positive belief.

"Today I feel closer to my sister than ever. What she did for me fills me with love and gratitude. While our foster sisters were quite helpful and behind us all the way, as were our husbands and parents, what happened was really between my sister and me. I believe that my sister was my only hope of having a baby of my own. It was a window in time and she was there for me. I know now that I can adopt another child or pursue surrogacy with another woman. We still have five frozen embryos. But this happened first, at the right time for the right reasons. We all knew each other so well and that's why it worked so easily. I marvel at how my sister and I run our lives so differently and yet as a team we were perfect."

Pamela and her sister have been sought out by women who have heard about their story.

"Based on our experience, we've encouraged other women to do it. Especially sisters. Working closely with one's sister and being in counseling and in the proper hands medically can be the best experience of one's life. It's the ultimate gift from one sister to another. I look at my baby and I want to give my sister everything. I have this urge to bring her something special every day. There's no way to thank her for what she has done."

There were several ingredients that worked in Pamela's favor. The fact that her sister would provide her body, but not the egg, was probably the deciding factor for both sisters. What also worked in their favor was that Pamela, her sister, and their spouses were so close and lived in the same town. Everything just seemed to fall into place. Lastly, the pregnancy "took" immediately, without the pressure of disappointments and repeated efforts.

From beginning to end, everyone was supportive. When Pamela mentions that she and her sister have very dissimilar styles, the pregnancy and birth plans were not affected. Everything ran smoothly; as Pamela describes it, the "team effort" paid off. There was no doubt about the baby belonging to Pamela and her husband; from the start of the surrogacy plan it was understood by both sisters that it was Pamela's child.

Lea

"My sister's doctor had actually recommended a third-party pregnancy and I was the likely candidate."

Thirty-five years old, Lea is the mother of two young children. Living in a town in Michigan, she is a secretary for a small business. Recently Lea gave birth to her sister's baby.

"My sister and I have been best friends since we were small. I am a few years younger and I was always the baby. Although we were together all the time growing up, I'd say in the last ten years we've become even closer. This is because our husbands get along and we're like one big family. There has never been any competition and we had a normal, happy childhood together.

"It came as a shock to all of us that my sister was having trouble getting pregnant. I'd had no problems with either pregnancy, and it was difficult for me to relate to what she was going through. I thought that if I could help in any way, if I could do anything at all, I would. At first, the question of being a surrogate mother did not occur to me. Then the issue came up, and I knew I'd be the carrier. My sister did not need me to donate an egg. That made it an easy decision."

Lea never had to consider the possibility that she'd be the egg donor because she became pregnant quickly with her sister's egg.

"It was very clear in my mind that I was carrying their child. From the start I never considered this baby mine—I was just helping it grow. I had no maternal feelings as I'd had with my own children. My relationship with my sister is so established that I understood everything: my role, her role, our husbands' roles. We spoke daily during the pregnancy but we usually do that anyway.

"People in our town knew what was going on and we were not shy about it. I felt that everyone was behind me and I was thrilled at how it worked out. It was such a terrific thing to be able to do. My sister is so grateful. And my children understood what was going on, too. My husband and I explained that I was carrying a baby for their aunt. The baby is so special to all of us and my kids are happy to have my lap back. But I don't think I'd do it again, because I don't particularly want to have another baby, even my own. What I did was absolutely for my sister."

During the pregnancy Lea felt quite well.

"I felt fine throughout and I wasn't afraid. I never thought anything would go wrong. There was no reason to believe it would—and no indication that it would. I didn't have an amnio although my sister's eggs were the right age for such a procedure. She didn't want me to have to go through it. I had an ultrasound and one blood test. Not until the very end did I have a feeling about the sex. On the way to the hospital, I believed I knew. But in this story, what counted was a healthy baby, not the sex."

Lea feels that the pregnancy was a joint experience from the beginning.

"My sister would come to all my doctor's appointments. It was an entourage—my husband, my sister, her husband, and me. When the doctor would say that only my husband could be there at certain times, I'd say that they all needed to be there. And when people I didn't know would ask me about my baby, I'd explain it all and watch how they reacted. My sister and I liked to tell our story because it is a story for all sisters in a similar situation. This can work for them.

"What made this such a successful venture was that we all were so involved with each other to begin with. It was something I could do for my sister and something she wanted desperately. I never dreamed until I saw her struggling with pregnancies that I'd be doing what I did. It kept floating around my mind as I saw her disappointment. Then I began to understand what I could do. My sister's doctor had actually recommended a third-party pregnancy and I was the likely candidate."

Both sisters felt that it was an ideal situation because it could be kept in the family.

"I'm so happy I was there for my sister and that she did not have to think of another option. I see her happiness and I know that it was the only thing to do."

Lea's surrogate-mothering experience was very positive. The sisters come from a very supportive family where their parents were behind them. Their husbands were friendly and everyone lived in the vicinity. It seems also that there had never been any serious problems between the two sisters and Lea describes her childhood as a pleasant one. The foundation was solid.

What is interesting to note, coming from the surrogate mother's point of view, was how detached Lea was from the baby. She describes herself as the vehicle, a means to an end. Since she felt this way, there was no confusion over whose baby it was. When she says she doesn't want any more children, it becomes evident that this was an isolated incident, an act of love and generosity for her sister.

Gail

"What was so bizarre about it was that not for a minute did I want this baby to be mine. After a while, my sister saw it was the truth."

The mother of two children, Gail lives in a small town in the midwest where she works full-time as a laboratory technician. Several years ago she was a surrogate mother for her sister's child.

"My sister was unable to conceive and had many 'female problems.' I was taking a genetics class at the time and I knew how close siblings are, genetically speaking. When she told me she was planning to hire a surrogate mother, I made the offer. I knew that a baby that I carried from my egg would be much closer to her than anyone else's. Once I'd made the offer, I had to explain my plan to my husband and children.

"As young girls my sister and I were not as close as we became in our adult years. We were adversaries and didn't come from a nurturing home. Our family was not particularly affectionate and I'd describe them as semi-dysfunctional. Our mother had problems and she was not a touchy/feely sort of woman. I think it was when I had kids of my own that my sister and I became involved with each other.

"I watched how she was with my children—I couldn't believe how much love she had for them. She loved them as if they were her own, but they weren't. No matter what the occasion, my sister was always there for them. Then, I watched how she would try and try again to become pregnant. She would call me to describe a medical procedure and her hope and determination to become pregnant once it was over. Then she'd call, devastated when it didn't happen."

*Gail believed that her sister had so much love to give and a
tremendous desire to have a family.*

"I knew what she wanted. By then we were extremely close
and I began to understand that we hadn't been close as children
because of the kind of family we'd grown up in. Deciding to do
this was a reflection of our new-found closeness; I made the offer
because I saw how tortured she was. Our family had come together after our mother died. We all had some reservations
about my doing this; my father felt that if something went
wrong, there'd be another break. Eventually everyone was behind us.

"We had something written up by an attorney, then my husband and children as well as my sister and her husband saw a
psychologist. The papers stated that no matter what happened,
this baby would be theirs. I assured my sister that I had no desire
for more children. I had made the offer because it would have
been criminal for me not to. It was so easy for me and it was the
one thing my sister desperately wanted."

*Gail realized that her pregnancies and deliveries were easy and
uncomplicated.*

"I knew I could handle this. My sister was so paranoid that I'd
become emotionally attached to her baby, but that was never
even a possibility. Finally she began to realize that I meant it; I
didn't want this baby or I'd have had my own. One reason I was
so enthusiastic is that I have easy pregnancies and didn't anticipate any problems. I saw this as babysitting for nine months; it
was never my baby. I understood that for the entire pregnancy.

"After the baby was delivered, I stayed with my sister for a
few days to nurse. I felt I was a wet nurse and while I was very
emotional, it was hormonal; intellectually I still did not want the
baby. But my sister felt so guilty, as if she was taking something
from me. That wasn't the case, and after a few days of being

home and continuing to weep, I was fine. What was so bizarre about it was that not for a minute did I really want this baby. After a while, my sister saw it was the truth."

Today Gail feels she did the right thing and that everyone is pleased.

"It's wonderful. It's hard to say who is capable of doing this. I think that what I did for my sister is one of the great accomplishments in my life. I'm very proud of myself. When I think back to the day that I first agreed, I recall wondering how I'd get through it. I also wondered how I'd explain it to my clients. But there was never one negative comment. I would always tell people it was my sister's baby because I was so aware of the fact that my husband had no part in it. That helped to make my feelings clear-cut.

"My husband was amazed that I did it. He was so supportive—that's part of the storybook quality of the whole experience. My entire family embraced the pregnancy—it was like a fairy tale. I feel that what I did was a natural reaction. Women should not be denied these longings; I wanted to do this for my sister. We're closer than ever, and she still can't believe it really happened. It's our miracle."

Gail and her sister had established a strong bond before the question of surrogacy arose. And while Gail made the offer, the closeness of their relationship set the stage. Once the family was consulted and the legalities taken care of, the surrogacy was under way.

There was not a moment's hesitation on Gail's part that this was her sister's baby. Yet her sister felt concerned and guilt-ridden, as if it seemed impossible that Gail could resist the baby. Gail understood her own motivation and was able to separate her role as surrogate from her role as a mother and wife. What she did for her sister was an extraordinary gift but Gail also saw it matter-of-factly, a role that had a beginning, a middle, and a happy ending.

Claudia

"On the last day, I pulled through and this time my sister's levels, which were fine until then, had dropped."

Claudia lives in a suburb of Philadelphia. At the age of twenty-nine, she has one sister who is a year younger and lives nearby. Claudia is a paralegal and her sister is a computer programmer. Having known since her teens that she cannot have children, her sister, who is unmarried, has been an egg donor twice for Claudia.

"I needed an egg because twelve years ago I developed a spinal cord tumor. It was treated with radiation and although my ovaries were to be lifted out of the area of radiation, my eggs have been damaged. I was only able to get my period with medication. Meanwhile, my sister, who is only a year younger, was very close to me during this illness. I really think it brought us together."

Claudia's sister and she were very different types when they were growing up.

"We were typical sisters in terms of our fights and bickering. She was always more outgoing and we had different lifestyles. I always stayed home. After I got sick, I married my high school boyfriend. My sister and I were very close at this point. What really drew us together was our disappointment when she and I learned that I couldn't have children. My husband was very supportive but he knew that I wanted a home and children. We agreed that we would adopt a baby. The wait to adopt was so long and there were so many false alarms. Finally we went to a Fertility Center. We had come to the conclusion that *in vitro* might work.

"I did not plan to use my sister as an egg donor originally. But my hesitancy about using an unknown donor was that I was afraid that one day my child would meet up with the donor's child and marry him or her. So, after counseling and soul searching, we decided to go with my sister. I would never have even considered it if my sister had shown an iota of interest in keeping the baby. If I had believed for one second that my sister would want the child back ten years down the road, I'd never have done it. She had offered early on and I'd refused. My husband asked me to reconsider her offer and so I did. The three of us spoke of any possible repercussions and again, I had no fears that she'd change her mind. We did not exchange money as in some surrogate situations, and papers were not drawn up. My sister was not looking for money—she just wanted to give me what I didn't have."

At this stage, Claudia and her sister went to the clinic together.

"The doctor thought that it was so wonderful that my sister was donating her eggs. And so we began the process, which we went through twice and which did not take either time. They had to make sure I'd be able to accept the egg. Both my sister and I were put on injections, which altered our hormone balances. My system was to believe it was getting pregnant and she was to overstimulate her ovaries so she produced a lot of eggs. My sister was monitored very carefully and had blood tests and other procedures all the time. Donating eggs is a big deal. She felt moody and crampy some days. The day they took her eggs the first time, I felt very guilty because it was an invasive procedure and she felt sick. My sister stayed with me that night.

"Once the eggs were fertilized, they were transferred to my womb and I was sent home with medication. When the lab discovered I wasn't pregnant, I called my sister even before I called my husband. I was so devastated. I felt like I'd let everyone down. My sister left work immediately and came to my house. I was hysterical. When I called my husband, I said he didn't have to bother coming home because my sister was already there. She was that kind of comfort to me."

Four months later, Claudia and her sister made a second attempt.

"The second time we knew what to expect. The doctor felt that everything was going nicely, except that my uterus was not responding to the medicine. On the last day, I pulled through and this time my sister's estrogen levels, which were fine until then, had dropped. I was called immediately. I was even more hysterical because I hadn't had the chance to carry the child. My sister was the one who felt guilty this time, as if she'd let everyone down. It was no one's fault but she felt she had failed me. It was a hellish period for both of us.

"We had considered having my sister carry the baby. She had offered plenty of times to be a surrogate. My husband and I hesitated because my sister has not yet married and had her own children. I don't know how we can ask that of her at this stage in her life. Now that she is about to get married, I suppose it's a possibility that in the future she could carry a child for me."

Recently Claudia adopted a baby and is very happy.

"Finally we have a baby through adoption and everything has quieted down. I feel the pressure is off and that my sister and I can resume our lives. Although we plan to try again, it seems less critical if it takes or not, and I think that means it might take. I'm not so preoccupied and I'm beginning to relax. But I will never forget my sister's efforts. Whether it took or not, I know what she did for me and what she was willing to go through. Those two chances were very emotional for both of us and we feel so close. No matter what, we see our future together, as sisters."

The guilt that both Claudia and her sister experienced as a result of unsuccessful pregnancies might have strained their relationship. *But they are such kind, supportive sisters that it has not affected them. The bond is so strong that Claudia sought her sister's solace before her husband's when the fertilization did not take. Intertwined and single-minded during the process, the sisters only wanted it to work.*

In a most positive relationship, the two sisters have weathered the demands and stresses in an attempt to give Claudia a baby. Claudia is sensitive to her sister's lifestyle and found it difficult to ask her to donate her eggs before she'd married and had her own family. Yet Claudia has full confidence that there will be no after-effects if her sister carries Claudia's child successfully. Claudia's sister, who suffered with Claudia during her illness, has been willing to do anything she can to help.

Rachel

". . . I believe that the media plays up surrogacy, especially with sisters, as being fraught with all these conflicting feelings. That isn't what happened with us."

At the age of forty, Rachel, an accountant, has been married for ten years. When it became obvious, after seven years of unsuccessful attempts, that she was infertile, her thirty-four-year-old sister came forward to surrogate-mother Rachel's child. Rachel and her sister are part of a family of eight children. Both sisters live in a city in the midwest.

"It appears that I could not have children although there has never been any explanation for this. For that reason, after five *in vitro* pregnancies that did not work, I was very relieved when my sister called and made the offer. We were so close and she wanted to do something for me. She also wanted to experience a pregnancy but was not in the position to have a baby. She was divorced and not ready to be married again. It was a totally compatible situation.

"Although we were close as we grew up, it wasn't until adulthood that this sister and I became really attached. She is six years younger and as kids I always thought of her as my baby sister. Our family was divided and she belonged to the second, younger half of the family, while I was part of the older group."

Rachel donated the eggs and her sister was the carrier.

"This baby was my husband's and my genetic child, so that was very clear-cut. My sister and I were not living near each other when she was pregnant. We were living on the west coast, but we spoke weekly and visited often. I was there for several weeks before the birth and for the actual birth. Since our baby was born, my husband and I have moved back to be nearer to our family. I feel so close to my sister after what she did. She sees my baby the way she sees her other nieces and nephews. There were fifteen children born into our family from the time I began to try to be pregnant and the time my sister gave birth."

Rachel and her sister were not aware of the thirty percent success rate when they first began the surrogacy.

"We went to the best clinics and were very fortunate that this happened the first time. I had a large number of embryos and could have gotten pregnant at the same time as my sister in theory, but it didn't work that way.

"We drew up some papers with a family attorney but I did not pay my sister a fee. We were able to get an order declaring the child as ours and our names were on the original birth certificate. It was the first time it had been done this way in our state. I know that an order can be accomplished in California also. If one doesn't do something, then the mother's name will be on the birth certificate, not the parents' names. For insurance purposes I needed proof that this was our child."

Both Rachel and her sister are seriously considering the possibility of doing this procedure again.

"My sister wants to do this once more and I certainly want to do it again. What is prohibitive is the cost. *In vitro* is very expensive and I find it so frustrating to have a willing surrogate but the cost such that I have to find a way to do it. My sister has a window of time in her life right now and I have to hurry because of my age. If she gets into a relationship with a man, a meaningful relationship, she can't have 'my' pregnancy going on. I do believe that this sister likes being an aunt, to be with her nieces and nephews, and then return to her own life. She does not have an overwhelming desire to be a mother."

As a result of the surrogacy, Rachel and her sister are closer to each other than to their other siblings.

"This experience brought us together. I have a different perspective on my sister than I did before. I admire what she did—I consider it a courageous act. She took on quite a task and she was absolutely wonderful through the whole thing. She had tremendous power over me, if you think about it, and she never abused her power. If she even had a back ache, she would not consider taking a Tylenol without first calling me. It's as if she handed over her body and was respectful of me, first and last.

"If there's anything to add about what my sister and I went through, I'd emphasize that it was not a drama but a happy situation with a great ending. There was no trauma and I believe that the media plays up surrogacy, especially with sisters, as being fraught with all these conflicting feelings. That isn't what happened with us. My main message is that it doesn't have to be traumatic. In fact, my sister and I understood from the start what was expected of each of us.

"So while it was intense, it wasn't bizarre. She's not confused about being the mother—she understands that she's the aunt. There were really no problems with this."

In a practical manner, Rachel sees the relationship that she and her sister share to be positive and successful. Rachel is acutely aware of her own biological clock and her sister's desire to carry a child without the responsibility of parenting. The power that she speaks of, while her sister was pregnant, is a perspective that no other sister in this situation has mentioned.

What is most meaningful to Rachel, however, is that her experience was a basic agreement between the two of them, a functional means to an end. A happy story all around, and we are interested to see if Rachel and her sister will make the unusual decision that many of the sisters in her position want: to create the sister surrogacy again for a second child.

PART TWO

The Prevailing Bond

INTRODUCTION

by
Dr. Robin Hirtz Meltzer

Many sisters are very close but for as many of those as one comes across, there are others who are remote and uninvolved. In our society, there is a tremendous focus on the parent-child unit and the sibling relationship is often overlooked. As a result, the impact that these sister relationships have on psychological and emotional development is relatively unexplored. Similarly, the power of sibling relationships to influence personality and subsequent adult relationships is too often overlooked. As we all know, there are sisters who are close and sisters who are detached.

We cannot generalize about sister relationships but it is possible to view them in a case-by-case context. While sisters can be positively connected, there are many variables. For instance, if one sister is very beautiful and there are only two sisters, although they may be very close, there is a built-in resentment. The less attractive sister may constantly suffer remarks about her sister's beauty; she may feel jealous and yet may love her sister.

Older sister/younger sister relationships often are quite complicated. The older sister is pleased with her role and yet usually controls the situation. While she feels gratified she might become angry at her mother that she's been assigned the task of looking after her younger sister. The younger sister is less affected by any conflict and usually enjoys the extra attention. As the baby in the family, she has a special position. Thus her mother lavishes attention upon her and she also benefits from the older sister's attention.

With larger families there are many alliances among sisters, and they often remain strong throughout their lives. Occasionally these bonds form by age, although what it is really about is *dependency*. The bonds center around issues of need and dissatisfaction that were never properly handled by the parents. These "leftover" feelings are often channelled from sibling to sibling, but not always equally. Where and how this reservoir of feeling settles among sisters is what motivates the groupings.

In the case of a favorite sister, she is thoroughly aware of her role, as are the others. While the favored sister may feel guilty about it, she certainly does not want to relinquish her position. The other sister or sisters may remain annoyed and disappointed but the relationship between the favorite sister and the parents doesn't change. The reason there is a favored child is often unconscious. She may remind the parent of him- or herself or of the spouse, or this daughter may simply pick up on how winning she is. If this child pleases the parents more than her siblings, then the tension increases as time goes on. How the favorite sister is chosen may be serendipitous, without real rhyme or reason.

It is difficult to overcome the imprint of a parent. Thus, if the parent thinks that one child is better or smarter than the other, that child is marked for life. In the case of sisters, which entails the same sex, it becomes more difficult and the marking never really goes away. While it is conceivable for the other sister to succeed as an adult, and to the outside world all seems well, the imprint remains within.

Another factor besides beauty is achievement. If one sister is tremendously gifted or talented, it is another invitation to rivalry. What begins early on persists with painful consequences. It is never really flushed out.

When sisters are totally estranged or dysfunctional, the awareness of the other's existence remains. However, hostility and anger may build up in the case of feuding sisters. Whether it is positive or negative, the bottom line is that the attachment remains.

When a sister dies, the surviving sister is changed forever and the results are devastating. It is a very powerful experience when she wrestles with the question of why her sister died and not her. It depends to some degree at what stage in one's life a sister loses her sister. If there is only one survivor, it becomes more destructive—she has lost not only her sibling but her identity as a sister.

Sisters are sisters for life and regardless of the happy or unfortunate stories, the bond prevails. If it works out positively, the sisters, however many there are, are blessed with an insulation against the unknown. Women from the outside often envy sisters as they see how, regardless of their ups and downs, they almost always put their sisters ahead of everything else. Even if sisters are separated physically or emotionally for a time, the closeness still exists. The bonding is that strong, often one of the strongest familial ties.

Dr. Meltzer is a graduate of New York University. She holds a Ph.D in Counseling Psychology and has published articles in professional journals. She is in private practice in New York City.

EXCLUSIVE SISTERS:
Shutting Out the World

An important part of growing up is the ability to separate from one's family to become strong and self-supporting. Some sisters hang on tightly to their childhood relationship, shutting out the rest of the world. These sisters have difficulty making friends and developing intimate adult relationships. No one else seems to be able to fulfill their emotional needs.

—RONNIE L. BURAK, PH.D

The Royal Sisters are Queen Elizabeth and her younger sister by four years, Princess Margaret. A fraught set-up from the start, Margaret, by the age of seven, was well aware of the fact that three relatives stood between her and her sister in succession to the throne. Nonetheless, the sisters spent their early childhood as equals.

Raised almost as twins, Elizabeth, called "Lilibet" for many years, was granted certain privileges. Margaret showed signs of being the more intellectual, curious, and imaginative sister early on. Lilibet, however, spent more time with her father. Margaret responded to this either by behaving badly in order to get his attention or by amusing him so that he laughed.

By the time she was sixteen, Lilibet had met Philip. During their first meeting, Margaret was included. Then Elizabeth and Philip became more involved and Margaret was no longer invited. She was precocious and a rebel to begin with, and once her sister was married with babies, she became resentful. On Elizabeth's twenty-first birthday, neither sister was very happy. Elizabeth was consumed by her many royal duties, limiting her availability to Margaret. Philip's attitude toward Margaret had also changed. It is believed that Philip became critical of Margaret once he and Elizabeth were entrenched in their lives. Elizabeth observed, in turn, her sister's whirlwind social life and romances that she never had the opportunity to experience herself.

During the time that Elizabeth was crowned, an event drove a wedge in the relationship between the two sisters. Margaret's engagement and subsequent break with Peter Townsend was quite painful for both sisters. Elizabeth understood how much her sister loved him but as a divorced man, he was unacceptable. Elizabeth caused the end of the affair, putting the demands of protocol ahead of her sister's happiness. Elizabeth acted first as the Queen. After she denied her sister, Elizabeth felt responsible and made a tremendous effort to please Margaret.

From the start, Elizabeth's and Margaret's childhood and adulthood were most unusual. Their universe was small, royal, and exclusive, consisting of Elizabeth, Margaret, the King, and the Queen. Once Elizabeth became Queen and had several children, Margaret was no longer included in the same way and was less comfortable being with her sister. It became a requirement that she be formally announced, and she was not even allowed to knock on her sister's door. To Margaret's eyes, duty came first for her sister and the mutual trust which once governed their relationship was finished. The political decision that her sister made in terms of Townsend was the final blow.

* * *

Kate Cushing deliberately raised her three daughters, Minnie, Betsey, and Babe, to marry well. Her goal was that they ensnare husbands of great importance and wealth, be they European or American. Betsey, the most similar to her mother of the three, was very determined. The first to marry, she chose James Roosevelt, son of the president, and gave birth to two daughters. She then married Jock Whitney, who subsequently adopted her children.

Throughout both marriages, Betsey made sure that her sisters were exposed to the proper men. When she introduced Minnie to Vincent Astor, she saw it as nothing less than her duty.

There was a brief interlude for several months in 1940 when none of the three sisters was married. Betsey was divorced, Minnie unmarried, and Babe, the youngest, was ripe for the role of a young bride but resisted, working full-time at *Vogue* instead. She chose to marry Stanley Mortimer—the union lasted six years and produced two children. When Minnie married Vincent Astor, he was considered the best catch of all. Her sisters were determined to benefit from this liaison and while Minnie might personally have preferred to be Astor's mistress, she could not disrespect her sisters' and mother's wish that she establish herself socially.

Not only was each sister destined to marry well and to marry twice, but to make her mark on society. When Babe's marriage to Stanley Mortimer dissolved, she married William Paley. But Babe and Betsey were united in their disappointment when Minnie dissolved her thirteen-year marriage to Vincent Astor, who represented American royalty at its best, in order to marry James Fosburgh, an artist who was known to be a homosexual. Breaking the Cushing sisters' reputation for marrying rich, then richer, Minnie made the decision that suited her personally. Rumors flew that she chose this second marriage because of her own sexual proclivities.

Minnie was the least attractive of the Cushing sisters, and her marriage to Fosburgh created a rift among the three and broke the chain. None of the sisters was as close in later years. As for Minnie and Babe, who as the oldest and youngest had been quite adoring of each other in childhood, their dramatically different lifestyles forced them apart.

Lisa

"My oldest sister . . . is twelve years older . . . so she really is a second mother to me."

As the fourth youngest in a family of five sisters, Lisa lives in a suburb of a large midwestern city. She has three daughters and has chosen to give up her career as a paralegal to raise her family. All of her sisters are married and two of the five live nearby.

"I loved all my sisters growing up. The second oldest, who was eight years older, was my favorite from the start. To this day I idolize her and we have remained the closest. That has never changed—she feels the same about me as I do about her. The other sisters knew it. I think we paired up before the youngest sister was born, when I was five years old. The four of us divided into two and two. Number one and number three were a team, as were number two and number four. It wasn't rivalry, just a closer connection. If I had a fight with number three, I'd run to number two for sympathy.

"My mother treated us unfairly and unequally. Each of my parents had an obvious favorite and I was never one of them. Number one was my mother's favorite for a while and number three has always been my father's. Later, when number five was born, she became my mother's absolute favorite and it never changed after that. In retrospect, the child who was the favorite was the neediest, which forced the unfavored to be independent and strong. I always accepted their favoritism—my father made no bones about favoring number three and so it was an unacceptable condition that was accepted in our family."

Once Lisa became a parent, she realized how hurtful her parents' attitude had been.

"As a parent, I know now how thoughtless my parents were to do what they did. Even now, I don't know how the favorite sisters felt. I suppose that the two favorites were very attached to the parent who favored them—and still are today. I feel that my mother was divisive, maybe not intentionally, in allowing secrets and by badmouthing us to each other. She was not direct and there was lots of hostility as a result. I hold their behavior against both of my parents. In a large Italian family, I expected it to be different.

"I felt very loved growing up, despite my parents' attitude. No matter what they did, there were lots of sisters around and it was very reassuring. Initially, I did not notice who got the most attention from our parents and who did not.

"Later on, as adults, each of us got married and our family became more complex. The diversities and demands that came with marriage, plus having children of our own, intensified the way our original family functioned. Spouses got involved and voiced their opinions and grandchildren were an added factor. My parents resented the influence of any spouse, yet there were five sons-in-law, each with strong ideas. For the youngest sister, who remained under my mother's wing, there was nonstop attention. She was the baby so everything she did was all right. She was considered the most deserving and was always forgiven by our mother. It was nauseating. The others concentrated on their own families to compensate."

Lisa thinks of her oldest sister as another parent in some ways.

"My oldest sister had much more of a relationship with my mother than the rest of us did. She was motherly and interested in my life, but not nurturing. She is twelve years older and by the time I was seven, she had a baby. So she really is like a second mother to me. I am very close to this sister's child. I see her as a sixth sister—she was raised like that. For many years I resented my youngest sister. I know there's a price to pay for being my mother's favorite, an emotional price. I think of her as handicapped and hindered, a crippled adult. I resent the fact that my mother chose any of us to be her pet. It's a reflection on her marriage that she needed a favorite. Whatever was lacking in the marriage was evidently fulfilled by fixating on a child.

"I never wanted to be the one closest to my mother because I knew how it had to turn out. The one molded by my mother would have to be shallow and selfish. What I'm really saying is that my mother is shallow and selfish. I'll always believe, in any family, that the favorite child becomes handicapped. Today I don't feel much connection to the youngest but at least we stay in touch. She makes dutiful phone calls to all of us. The truth is that no one feels close to her, but my mother is still obsessed with her."

Three of Lisa's sisters live within a half-hour of one another. The two other sisters live in Atlanta.

"We speak on the phone a few times a week. As I said, the youngest is out of the loop but might not even know it. Because we all know about my mother's obsession with her, no one wants to be in her shoes, and none of us reach out to her. Personally, I feel I escaped my mother's tyranny, and I think my other sisters would agree. Now that we're older we've all forgiven her, but none of us has forgotten."

Lisa tends to side with her second sister during family rifts.

"The youngest sister is so superficial she hardly ever notices anything. With my second sister, the one I'll always be closest to, we're there for each other and we know it. I had a long-standing quarrel with my youngest sister. As a result I was excluded from her child's christening—my parents hosted the event. It had to do with a business dealing with our husbands, and my parents took sides. I know now that I should have been angry at my mother, not my sister. My sister and I did not speak for years. Now I understand where the message came from: my mother actually approved of my sister not inviting us to the christening. It's incredible.

"I've decided to put this incident behind me, because recently our mother became deathly ill and everyone was reconciled at her bedside. We each found a way to mend fences. I don't want to be like her and hold a grudge. My mother is much relieved. She doesn't see that she fostered these feelings all along, but it no longer matters what she sees. What counts is that we're reconciled, after a fashion. In other words, for my mother, what matters is that we appear to care; whether we really do or not is another story."

Being part of a large family of sisters has affected Lisa greatly.

"I've been forced to be independent, to make my own way. I've never sought approval because I knew it wasn't there for me anyway. I learned early on who counted. One negative was that at a family gathering none of us ever counted as an individual. It was an event, a roll call. My parents were never able to focus on one of us at these times. They couldn't get away with it. They were exclusive whenever they could be and hierarchical, but not during Christmas or Easter. Of course, my mother wouldn't have anything if her favorite daughter wasn't a part of it.

"I look at my sisters and know that only number two and number three would be my friends today if they were not my sisters. Not number one or number five. The oldest is so different from me that I cannot really relate to her. She has an extremely successful business and is very prominent in her field. The second oldest and I have purposely chosen not to work and that binds us together. We identify most closely with each other. I take the best part of her and try to apply it to my life. I suppose we take what we want from any of these relationships and do with it what succeeds. But with my second sister, there is the most for me to strive for.

"There's no jealousy or rivalry among us today. It was never a big issue. The focus was about how our parents treated us, not how we treated each other. I'd say that sisters number two and three are absolutely my best friends today. I never had to have a lot of friends because I was surrounded by sisters. I was safe and always had someone to talk to, someone to listen. Each sister filled a different need."

Lisa feels she has learned a great deal about her sisters from observing her three daughters.

"Once I entered my thirties I began to understand my children's sibling rivalry. I think I had some insight into what comes from the heart. I know now that it might not have taken me so long to get along with all my sisters if it hadn't been for my parents. Because it was too painful to be angry at or disappointed in my parents as a child, I would be hostile toward the favored daughter. It took a long while to heal the pain and learn whose fault it was. It came full circle for me when I had my own daughters and saw how I could help them become lifelong friends. As sisters, they have to respect each other, to go beyond being sisters, which is not easy. The message has to start with me."

Ambivalent and tortured, Lisa has come to terms with her place in a family of five sisters. She claims she never wanted to be the favorite, and feels she benefitted from having to make her own way. Realizing how her parents failed their children has been a struggle for Lisa. Her self-awareness is admirable and brings her full circle. Through enduring her parents' favoritism and raising her own children, Lisa has gained the compassion and understanding that makes her able to enjoy the camaraderie of five sisters. She is a mother who knows what is required to establish equality and trust in her children.

Amelia

"When my father died my mother came to live with me immediately. My sister was not really there for her . . . I noticed that there was no guilt laid on her, only on me."

In her mid-forties and living in southern Florida, Amelia has one sister four years younger. Both women work together in the printing business, and have done so for over fifteen years. Each has one son and one daughter.

"My relationship with my sister while we were growing up was very difficult. We never hated one another, but we fought constantly. It was a typical situation, in my opinion. I always saw her as younger, cuter, more easy-going. Academically, we were both good students. She dated more than I did and as the older child, I was the one who listened to my parents. If they said to be home from a date at a certain time, I was. My sister was more rebellious—she did as she pleased.

"My father insisted that as the oldest I marry first. I was eight months ahead of my sister, who was forced to wait for me. Our husbands had actually bought our engagement rings together and initially, the two men were friends. I met my husband through my sister. Today we are not socially connected in any way although we see each other daily at work. As adult sisters we continue to be so dissimilar that this works out for the best. My nature is to let things ride with my sister, which I always have. She is not as conscientious as I am. Her husband cares very little for the rest of us."

It bothers Amelia that her sister arrives at work late.

"My sister and I do not argue but it is irritating that she comes to work when she does with the attitude she has. Her lifestyle and mine are not the same, either. She knows we both need to work to make ends meet and she ought to be more motivated because her lifestyle demands more material things—vacations, cars. On the other hand, money doesn't trouble my sister. She loves to go out and spend and not worry about where it comes from. I don't need to go out and I worry constantly about money.

"I'm closer to my sister than I am to anyone, despite our differences, and I assume she feels the same about me. However, we have no friends in common. Our relationship has improved recently since both our parents are gone. We know that we're the only immediate family. Our children get along but are not close. Somehow I don't think their relationship is so important. I'm pleased they get along as cousins, but my kids are more like me and her kids are more like her."

Amelia believes she is so responsible because she was the oldest child.

"My parents depended upon me and not upon my sister, for some reason. They were from the old school and leaned on me, as the oldest. They also knew that my sister didn't attend family functions or make time for them. My husband was the kind of son-in-law who put up with my parents' demands. My brother-in-law would not. He's getting a little bizarre as he ages, a throwback to the sixties. My sister has been influenced by him, undoubtedly.

"When my father died my mother came to live with me immediately. I felt very pressured for the years she lived with us. She had no interest in anything and leaned on me constantly. My sister was not really there for her, only occasionally. I noticed that there was no guilt laid on her, only on me. My sister saw how difficult it was for me but she did not try to help. She tried some of the time but not enough. She didn't have the patience. I tried to smooth things over—I was the peacemaker. My mother and sister had huge fights. Then our mother died and I've felt less burdened in the past few years. Now my sister and I will take our girls shopping or to lunch or a film. I have less guilt about things now that my mother is gone. But my sister's husband and mine do not get along and it's uncomfortable. We live in the same town and our kids attend the same schools."

Amelia's husband resents her sister's attitude.

"My husband sees my sister as slovenly and not concerned enough about the business. I no longer get upset with her, because we've lost two parents and I know what's really worth being upset about. I know what my husband means, though. When we first got our business off the ground, my sister was too laid-back for me. I still don't believe she makes work the priority she should.

"My kids are more focused and goal-oriented than hers and that's another issue. They are not as influenced by peer pressure and tend to do their own thing. Meanwhile, she waits on her kids for every little thing. So there it is again—we're opposites and our kids are, too. The part that makes it different is that we're sisters and complement one another. I'm the one who cleans up her mess in the office. I suppose we see each other's faults but still remain connected. I think of my sister and myself as just another relationship which requires constant attention. The attachment is not the same as you'd have for a husband or a child; it's unique. She'd be there for me and I'm there for her, despite our squabbles."

The attachment that Amelia and her sister share is based on a reaction to their mother.

"Our parents were the ones who made our commitment so special. My sister and I laugh when we remember that although we didn't get along as children, today we're very tight. Our mother always let her friends come first, before her sisters. We put each other first, ahead of our friendships. I would definitely feel alone without her. I'm closer to my sister than I was to my mother. My father and I were the close ones, growing up. My mother had quite an attitude; it was her way or no way. I couldn't take it.

"I can't say that my sister's my best friend because my daughter is, but my sister comes next. With my mother, she never saw her daughters or her sisters as that important. We learned what to do and what not to do from her. I watched my mother, as the oldest of three sisters. The middle sister was always on the outs. Of course, there are only two of us, but my sister and I don't have the same priorities."

Opposites by nature, Amelia and her sister have found a mutual ground as adult women and partners in business. Although her sister's habits and values continue to annoy Amelia, what she has come to accept is that her sister is her sister. She's grateful for the essence of that relationship.

Amelia and her sister exemplify a situation where the lack of rapport with their mother drives the sisters closer together. It is noticeable in Amelia's case, however, that her primary attachment is to her daughter, and her sister comes next. Yet she and her sister have found a comfortable place for each other—that of living in the same town and running a business together.

Sandra

"Today we share our own world, and while we are very different, we are also connected."

Younger by four years, at the age of sixty-five Sandra has been living in the same town as her sister for the last twenty years. Having grown up in a northeastern city, Sandra is divorced with children and grandchildren. Her sister is widowed and also a grandmother and mother. Both women work freelance jobs, Sandra as an illustrator and her sister as a journalist.

"We were not close growing up. We fought constantly but I also knew she was there to take care of me. She always hovered over me like a mother and obviously I needed it because our mother worked and was never around. Our father was a manic depressive, sickly man. We had a terrible childhood and it was my sister who comforted me and made it all right. We became adults prematurely. By the time I was ten I wasn't a kid anymore. We had so little money that the lights were often turned off because my father didn't pay the bills."

Neither Sandra nor her sister was able to go to college.

"Both of us wanted to go to college but our father lost what money he had. That was why he was so depressed, I think. We were Depression kids, the product of a very bad time. I was younger, so I never asked many questions. But our friends' fathers were jumping from windows—that was how bad it was. Meanwhile, my sister and I lived at home, joined at the hip but not exactly close. Although my sister felt a strong obligation to keep taking care of me, we still fought. I don't know if it's a by-product of our generation or just personal, but neither of us was very thoughtful. We weren't introspective because it was too frightening. No one ever discussed anything.

"Then my sister got married and moved out. For some reason, we became closer then. I liked her husband and she lived nearby. I didn't feel jealous or upset—she was very supportive and continued to watch out for me. Again, I don't know if I allowed myself to consider the possibility that she might not be available for me. I was fortunate that she stuck around."

Once Sandra married, her husband, sister, and brother-in-law all got along.

"We traveled as a foursome and spent a lot of time together. Our kids were close and, in fact, continue to see one another today. I was divorced in the seventies, which was not my choice, and I was devastated. My sister was so sympathetic—she really saved me. When she was widowed several years ago, I was there for her. We've taken care of each other as adult women, as sisters.

"Today we share our own world, and while we're very different, we're also very connected. She's the more glamorous one, and always was. Although we look alike, I think that we didn't when we were growing up. I often look at my sister and think of our mother and feel like I'm my mother's sister. I see that age changes and mellows all of us, especially women. The gap seemed so wide at the age of ten and fourteen and now it no longer exists.

"We continue to fight, though, because of our personalities. An underlying competition exists, based on our women friends and how we've lived our own lives. We see each other on a daily basis, yet my sister has expanded her horizons recently. She now travels in the winter and has made it clear to me that this is something she must do. I don't go and I miss her when she's gone. But I also understand, she needs to have a life of her own."

The life that Sandra's sister seeks bothers her.

"Women friends are a big deal with us. I don't infringe on her friends. My sister is the more social one and has all these support-group friends. I try to create boundaries so I won't impose. She can be very possessive with her friends; she does not appreciate my presence at times, so when it comes to the women she spends time with, I try to stay clear. I have my own friends. For me, though, my sister comes first—before anyone else. I feel that together we are impenetrable. Then I think she shies away from our closeness—it seems to smother her.

"I really do understand why she travels alone and her need to be on her own. I've adjusted. I'm not a particularly involved mother or grandmother—it isn't my thing. Neither of us is very maternal. We put each other ahead of our kids and our spouses, too, when they were around. It has worked for us. At this point, my sister has had it with taking care of me. She has been supportive her whole life and now she's ready to have a life without me, but it doesn't change how I feel about her."

Sandra loves her hometown and doesn't like to travel.

"I could make my whole life right here in this small town. My sister has had bitter experiences and needs another kind of life. She wants to be free, to savor whatever time is left; what she missed needs to be found. I don't feel like that. But I know how careful I have to be about all this and her friends, her separate life. She has no intention of sharing it. Then I remind her—we're the only family we have.

"Perhaps my sister and I are both looking to have our own lives late in the game. We can get very competitive about our work and our friends, but we always come back to each other. Sometimes I get very frightened about the future. What if something happens to her first? I don't know what I'd do."

Sandra and her sister realize that they have been together during every aspect of their lives.

"We were looking at a photo album from our younger days. We've always been there for one another. I think it's because our mother never could be there, so we had to be everything. My sister, as the older one, was more experienced, a bit ahead of me. I looked up to her. She seemed to know a lot more than I did about life. Now I see that she was also lost and mixed up. But she seemed so strong. And the bottom line is that we are our own support system.

"In her own way, my sister needs me to be there and I need her. Being a sister goes beyond any other relationship I've ever had. While friends remain a touchy issue between us, I know my sister comes first, beyond my own children. If I need her, she's there for me, too. I know it, even if she doesn't."

The unhappy childhood that Sandra experienced was buffered by her sister's love and affection. As adults, the relationship continued to unfold as Sandra entered the world behind her sister, looking to her for advice. She required no one else; her sister's protection was all-encompassing. Where the sisters differed in experience was in their marriages. Sandra's marriage failed and she was crushed; her sister's ended in widowhood.

Their approach to mothering is similar, having had a poor role model in their mother. The most valuable relationship for these two women seems to be that of sisters. Yet their exclusivity is interrupted with periods of competition, surrounding their work and friendships. Both women struggle for an autonomous existence while they cannot truly untie the knot that binds. For Sandra, it seems it is a more difficult task. Her sister, in most instances, has been able to make the break. Sandra is adjusting, slowly and deliberately. Her frailty is evident, as is her dependency, when she speaks of how fearful she is of a life without her sister.

Cathy

"We were too free-spirited as children. The four of us.
We spent time mostly with each other."

*Cathy, the second oldest of four sisters, lives in Atlanta today.
Her oldest and youngest sisters live on the eastern shore of
Maryland, where the family grew up. The sister closest in age to
Cathy lives in New York City. Now forty-one, Cathy believes
that none of her sisters has been attached to the others from
childhood onward.*

"I'm closer to my youngest sister than to anyone, because she
and I have gone through some medical problems together. We're
both extremely anxious. She gets more depressed than I do but
both of us have emotional problems. The other two are not like
that—I can only discuss this with my youngest sister.

"My oldest sister and my youngest are married. The sister
closest to my age is divorced and living with someone. I have
lived with the same man for twenty years and it's a common-law
marriage. Lately I'm sorry that we never married and I'm aware
that all three of my sisters have been married. My youngest sister
has been married twice. I've been in my common-law relationship longer than anyone has been with a husband, but I sense the
difference."

Cathy sees her sisters once a year.

"There is an annual visit to our parents in Maryland, and I see
all three sisters then. It's a ritual. As we get older, I always look to
see how we've aged. The oldest sister is three years older than I
am, then I have a sister who is one year younger; the youngest is

four years behind the second youngest. Growing up, the oldest sister felt maternal toward the youngest. I never felt that. As kids, when we played together in grade school, the sister closest in age to me is the one I spent the most time with.

"Only recently have I sensed that this sister, the one right behind me, might be competitive. I have the feeling that she's aware of what I have without actually wanting it. In the last few years I think she has become more conscious of my belongings. Until she met the man she's with today, she had very little. She has worked every day of her adult life to support herself and was in a bad marriage without any money for a period of time as well. From what I understand about her ex-husband, he was not good to people. It was a marriage of convenience that destroyed her self-esteem. Now that she's with a man who appreciates her and can provide her with nice things, her self-esteem is improved. I'm very happy for her."

The situation with Cathy's common-law husband has been secure from the start.

"I've been comfortable all along. The man I live with has done quite nicely. When I'd travel back to Maryland to see the family, my sister closest in age to me would notice I had nice things to wear and she had nothing. She never opens up—she's like a clam, but I understand. She might have chosen the man she's with today for comfort. He's older and not very attractive—my sister is quite pretty. I'm relieved that she seems content. We never competed as kids, and I didn't like competing, even in subtle ways, as adults.

"We were too free-spirited as children, the four of us. Most of our time was spent with each other. My mother made mistakes but she never made us competitive. She definitely favored the sister I have described, but it's the youngest sister she feels sorry for. This sister, the baby, married very young to get out of the house. It was a very bad marriage and she had children at a very young age. Now she has a second husband and it's rough raising her kids because they have financial problems. There's no question that my youngest sister has a difficult life today. My impression is that she'll do the best she can even though she's miserable."

Cathy's mother and her younger sister see one another often.

"My mother lives near her and tries to be available. The oldest sister lives nearby also but is no longer close to my baby sister. A lot of this has to do with her husband. The oldest sister's husband is judgmental and successful. He forces their three kids to succeed and they're little replicas of him. I admit he's very smart and so are the kids but his disapproval of our family is unfair. He makes us feel we're not good enough for him, and it's hurtful to the rest of us. My older sister has made a choice to concentrate on her husband and kids. She pushes the family aside, and that's the way her husband wants it."

Cathy blames her father for much of the dysfunction within the family.

"I've come to the conclusion that our father is a sick person. He is antisocial, verbally abusive, and extremely cruel. I remember as a kid dreading how mean he'd be to me. He would criticize me for whatever I did; no matter what the task, he'd say it was wrong. He was unrelenting and had us all in tears most of the time but no matter what the problem was we stuck together. In a middle class upbringing, it's surprising that our father never even offered to send any of us to college—he never made it an option. That was quite a disservice.

"Our mother was from an extremely poor background. She was programmed to marry right out of high school and have babies immediately. She was taught to keep her mouth shut and go about her life. I've always felt so sorry for her. Yet she was not that close to us; we had to look to each other instead. Our oldest sister took care of us and on many occasions she mothered us. She was the typical big sister, but she never taught me anything about boys or dates. She never dated so I had to learn through experience. No one ever told me anything about anything. That's the bottom line."

There was no bonding among the sisters.

"I was always aware that I had sisters but there was nothing really tight and secure about it. The second youngest and I did the most together because we were only a grade apart. Even when we dated two guys who were best friends, in high school, we never shared intimacies. It wasn't the way our family was structured. Our youngest sister was left at home once we were all gone. She couldn't stand it and married immediately. She was the only rebel among us and had always hung around with a bad crowd in high school. She got into a drug scene, which the rest of us had avoided. In retrospect, I think it was out of a sense of abandonment. She felt alone. She dropped out of high school because no one told her not to. At fourteen, this little sister was so much slicker than I'd ever been in my whole life."

Despite a lack of closeness with her sisters, Cathy believes that during her childhood she was more involved with them than with her friends.

"All my play time as a kid was spent with my sisters and family, cousins who lived nearby. My second youngest sister was the only one to have a friend. I was the sidekick, the third wheel. Whenever they'd get into trouble, I'd disappear. Her best friend was a real troublemaker. I suppose that was the draw. Today I realize I'm attracted to strong female friendships. I think I'm making up for what I missed. These women friends and I have a good chemistry which I never really had with my sisters. I'm closer with these women than I ever was with my own sisters at any time.

"I do remember that as teenagers my sister and I would have physical fights, but I think of it as the usual kid stuff. Maybe I was protected by my sister and didn't know it. The sheer good fortune of having them was something I took for granted. I was protected and safe but somehow I didn't realize that. What I do now as an adult sister depends on the sister it affects. For instance, I send my youngest sister all my old clothes because I know she really needs them. I wouldn't do this with the other sisters, and they're less needy anyway. No one has ever asked me for a loan—that is, not the youngest sister or the second youngest, even when she was in dire straits."

Cathy wishes she lived closer to her sisters.

"I have this need for family as I get older. I suppose that's normal. Looking back we have a better understanding of what we had. I also see that for whatever reasons, there's no real closeness with any of my sisters. Even the one I identify with the most, my youngest, seems remote. I only speak with her about twice a year—it's very upsetting because she's so manic and depressed. I speak with my mother once a month and with my two other sisters once a year. I know it sounds strange, but if I reached out beyond this, it wouldn't work anyway. The family isn't ready for me to be there.

"My sisters don't respond to my efforts. I'm not blaming anyone. Each of us might have some bad genes from our father. Or maybe we simply took our cues from our mother, who has eleven siblings and sees none of them unless there's a funeral or some tragedy. It's the example my mother and my father have set for us. For instance, I've invited all my sisters to come visit me, but no one will come. These are the choices they make—not to try, not to stay in contact. We're all so scattered and I wonder, is it simply the way our lives took us? We were young and living in a small town and met these boys who became men and we followed them. Two of us returned to our hometown and two did not."

Cathy has no real relationship with her sister's children.

"I send Christmas and birthday cards and that's as far as it goes with my sisters' children. They do know that I'm Aunt Cathy. I have no children of my own but what bothers me is not the relationship with the children but with my sisters. I'm sorry that I see no hope for the future. I just don't know how it could improve. What we have in common is the feeling that we come from a very scattered family.

"I wonder if my mother would do it differently if she had it to do over again. Perhaps with more positive reinforcement, she would give us the love and attention that sisters should give to one another. Although she did her best, she was unable to show us how to be good sisters. We never learned."

Although Cathy does not blame her mother for the lack of relationship with any of her sisters, she does note that her mother failed to set an example. Cathy seems to see it as a loss that cannot be regained. Growing up in a dysfunctional family such as Cathy describes, each sister was preoccupied with finding an opportunity to escape. Being close as children was defined by play time and school time, but there was no true bonding. Instead each sister waited for her ticket out.

The fact that Cathy's oldest and youngest sisters were perhaps the closest of the four growing up and no longer connect is unfortunate. Cathy's take on this, that it is her brother-in-law's choice, might make sense, but the pity is that the older sister cannot compromise on some level for the sake of her sister. This typifies the manner in which each sister lives her adult life. Cathy firmly believes that had it been a tighter family from the start, the possibility of connection would exist. She sees the situation as hopeless because there was never a firm foundation in the first place.

Antonia

"The oldest was always jealous of everyone and everything. There was no jealousy between the youngest and myself."

At the age of sixty, Antonia is the middle of three sisters. Growing up in a metropolitan area, she purposely chose to marry a man from the midwest and move there. Her two sisters have remained in the northeast, which Antonia views as pivotal in their exclusive relationship. Antonia works part-time in the fashion industry.

"As children, the relationship the three of us shared was definitely on the rough side. My youngest sister had a hot temper and was impossible. No one wanted me to bring her when we went out because she beat up other kids. My oldest sister was very aloof and snobby—she ran with her own friends. The three of us fought often. Our mother was the only common enemy. Once she came after us, we reunited. We fought over everything—there was never any particular reason. The oldest and the youngest stuck together and I was left out. The oldest was the apple of my father's eye and the youngest was the beauty, the darling of his eye. My father always came after me whenever there was a problem; for years I was scared to death of him. My sisters, on the other hand, had a close relationship with him.

"My feeling about my father was that you can't make yourself love someone. I respected him because he was my father but I did not have the rapport the others had. I didn't realize how he saw me until I had my own children. I was the middle child, so stupid I behaved like a contented cow. My oldest sister never wanted me around—it was my younger sister I got along with. We played together often and I was so proud of her."

As adults Antonia and her sisters have become friends.

"My older sister has said things that I have resented. For instance, when my mother wanted to have a large wedding for me, my younger sister helped plan it while the older one accused me of demanding a large wedding. It wasn't like that at all. It was what my mother wanted. I was the second to marry. My youngest sister was first, my oldest last.

"Only as we grew older did we become really close. My older sister was never really interested in my children, but we got along superficially at family get-togethers. Once I provoked her at a dinner table and she threw a plate of food at me. Yet we never stopped speaking; throughout our arguments, we remained on speaking terms. And I never asked her to be involved with my children—I understood how she felt.

"When we were young women, my oldest sister and I shared a room. I resented her attitude that she always came first and that everything should be done for her. Her food preferences came first, my mother did her ironing but not mine. Why my mother catered to the oldest that way is beyond me but it made me very angry. I was never treated as an equal. I watched my oldest sister make demands and get them. I had no problem with my younger sister, who, of course, had married so young that she was long gone. But once she left, things didn't improve with my older sister."

Antonia's younger and older sisters got along from the beginning.

"I was never much like my younger and older sisters, and that was part of the bond for them. Both were more highfalutin than I was. My older sister didn't criticize the younger sister but she constantly criticized me. She always imitated the youngest, which really baffled me. She wanted everything the youngest sister had: lifestyle, wealth, material things. My older sister was very judgmental and jealous. She wanted to be treated like royalty.

"Once I was married and had moved out of town, I didn't see my sisters often. I liked the distance. I was content to live in a smaller city and content to have a life where we managed and were satisfied. My sisters wanted more and I was relieved not to be a part of it. Throughout all this, I was much closer to my younger sister. She was so pretty and attractive that I would brag about her to my friends, but I didn't feel good about my older sister. We never saw eye to eye and only lately, as she is widowed and has no children, has she mellowed and begun to make more of an effort. But we were not close as young women. Occasionally the three of us would do something together, go to a play or to lunch. The oldest was always jealous of everyone and everything. There was no jealousy between the youngest and myself. Once I asked my parents to babysit for my kids, who were still young at the time. My older sister thought this was really inappropriate."

Antonia has often felt excluded from her two sisters' plans.

"They get along so well and do everything together. The youngest does everything for the oldest since she's been widowed—I can't figure it out. The youngest makes me feel inadequate because I am unable to provide for the oldest in the way she does as I don't have the means. I think there's a lot of guilt tied up with my older sister's behavior. I know how she treated my parents. I was the good daughter, so she can't really face me. My mother always liked to have me around because I didn't fight with her or give her a hard time. I listened to my mother. The other sisters fought with her. I was the peacemaker.

"My older sister feels sorry for herself. I remember what a snob and social climber she was—her fate was inevitable. She married late and had no children. She made her own bed. I also think she cared about material things because my mother did. Her values were passed on to two of her daughters but I escaped somehow. I see myself as the simplest sister. I was content and didn't want the social life of the younger sister or the intimidating friendships that my older sister sought.

"I feel close to my younger sister and respect her advice, but I ask nothing of my older sister. I know she mimics my younger sister so why not get it straight from the horse's mouth? I'm more comfortable with a relationship that reestablishes itself. My own children were not as close as children as they have become as adults. My sisters and I have grown together as adults. It doesn't mean I forget who they are—it means I'm able to handle it better. My older sister is still competitive. If I say I work hard, she works harder. My younger sister is not like that—she's a very happy person. My older sister has no sympathy for anyone, she's done it all. But she was like that many years ago when we were children. I understand as an adult that she lacks introspection. To this day I can't relate to her and she will not listen to me. The difference is, I know we're sisters and so it's not worth the fight.

"I continue to be only partially available. Living out of town, in Ohio, was my goal from the start. I can see my sisters today for who they are; the older sister still the taker and the younger still the giver. The two of them are locked in battle while I simply go my own way. The youngest is the one I've always wanted to be close with. And my older sister feels the same. It goes around and around; we're older and wiser and it continues anyway."

Antonia needed to carve a niche for herself and escape the tyranny of her older sister. Given this awareness she moved away

as soon as she married. Yet the triangle of these three sisters has
not ceased to exist. Although Antonia claims she and her sisters
are more mellow with the passing years, one wonders. Has she
really grown closer with her sisters, or simply developed a better
perspective on the relationships?

When Antonia explains that she felt left out from the
beginning because of her father's exclusion, she might never have
recovered from such pain. Her decision to be non-confrontational
is partly her nature and partly a deliberate choice in order to
survive. The wounds do not seem healed—her preference for her
younger sister and disdain for her older sister remain a factor.
Despite these feelings, she also recognizes the unity that sisters
provide for one another. Antonia has a keen sense of who each
sister is and what she can expect from her.

Andrea

"As her sister I understand why she sells drugs; that is,
I understand how money is at the heart of her
problems. But as an onlooker, I think it's a crime. It has
ruined her."

The oldest of four sisters, Andrea never knew her father and was
raised by her stepfather. Having grown up in a northeastern city,
she currently lives in a small town in New Hampshire. Her three
half-sisters live in Cocoa Beach, Florida. Andrea, in her
mid-thirties, is seven years older than her next-oldest sister.
There are three years between this sister and the next, three again
between the second youngest and the youngest. The second oldest
is the most troubled of the four sisters and Andrea believes she is
a drug dealer.

"My sister closest to my age ran away by the time she was fourteen and got into a bad crowd. Although she eventually returned, she has always been in trouble. She had a baby with a man she has split with, and he provides for her to this day. This man is a drug dealer and a bookie. I think her problems began when our mother and father divorced. She was the first child for my father and he saw her as the apple of his eye. Her feet never touched the ground. No one in our family knows how she learned to walk. And then the divorce came and she was thrown for a loop.

"I always felt a part of this family although I knew he wasn't my real dad. I was a smart kid, and I understood the difference. But I knew he had a favorite among his own three girls and that made it easier—I wasn't the only one left out. As a kid, I remember when my mother brought the babies home from the hospital—three times, three sisters. I'd tickle their feet and try to wake them up in their cribs so they'd play with me."

Andrea thought that the sister born first was spoiled and occasionally bratty.

"The oldest sister and I fought constantly growing up. She'd go into my room, go through my clothes, and do all those sister-type things that make you so crazy. Sometimes I was asked to keep my eye on her and she was a terror because she was so spoiled. In the end it is sad—she is definitely the unhappiest of all of us and has many problems."

Andrea traces her sister's unhappiness to her parents' divorce and their subsequent move to another area of the country.

"I tend to believe that as kids we were a tight ship, a bunch of sisters, strong and proud. We lived a very comfortable life in a nice house in a suburban town. Then my mother divorced my stepfather and the move threw everyone. Each of us, as sisters, had to make her own way. I was a teenager by then and my mother, who had always worked, had my grandmother take over. The oldest sister got in with the wrong crowd for sure. I think the loss of attention, our father's absence, upset her badly. To this day she's in search of what she missed. The other two sisters, the younger ones, had each other.

"My mother began to tell me that by the time she was in high school this sister was not coming home at night. One time she actually left the country. That was how she got into drugs. She needed money and became part of a whole different world. We all worried about her but she wasn't approachable. Meanwhile, I felt motherly toward the other two sisters because they were younger. I watched them grow up."

Andrea married by the time she was eighteen and continued to help with her younger sisters.

"I'd go home to the house to help them get ready for the prom and tell them what to wear on dates. I saw that they finished high school, like I had. My other sister, the one who ran away, had not completed high school. She took an equivalency at some point, but she wasn't like the rest of us. By this time she was on drugs and had an illegitimate baby. She is still on drugs. After the relationship with the father of her child didn't work out, she met someone and married him within several weeks. That marriage failed and there was a quick divorce. Again she tried to live with the father of the first child and again it didn't work out. Then she met someone else who was unmotivated and poor. She got pregnant and married him after the baby was born. It hasn't gone well and the financial problems remain. As her sister I understand why she sells drugs; that is, I understand how money is at the heart of her problems. But as an onlooker, I think it's a crime. It has ruined her."

This particular sister has never held a conventional job as Andrea and her other two sisters have.

"She sells serious drugs. She has a secret life and it makes her a liar. She steals from my house. If I hear she's coming to visit, I panic. I know she'll steal what she wants, whatever it is she needs, even from her own sister. I try to be nice to her because she's my sister and I feel sorry for her because of the life she leads. I don't really judge her. Still I know what her responsibility is because I have kids of my own. She has to bring up her kids so they don't do drugs. That's her responsibility just like it's mine. I'm not condoning what she does, but I understand that if she doesn't do it, someone else will. Except in this case, it's my own sister doing it. That's the heartbreak.

"My other sisters feel as I do about her. My mother knows the truth but denies it—she won't listen although she's very worried. We all sort of keep our distance from this sister to protect ourselves. I don't pick up the phone to call her because I don't want to be associated with her."

Andrea's next sister has three children and leads an ordinary life.

"This next sister won't even drink. I find her very dull and I think if her husband left her, she'd fall apart. She's not strong enough and not street smart like the other sister, or like me. It so happens that this sister and the drug-dealing sister are very competitive. Despite their different lifestyles, they compete about their kids and their homes. This sister is so jealous that she says something bad about everyone and everything. All she can talk about is hair, clothes, and her mother-in-law. That's it. Sometimes she describes her hair in such detail I have to get off the phone. She has no global view, this sister.

"Every two years she gets a new diamond ring and she always wears designer clothes—all gifts from her husband. I find it very surprising that my drug-dealing sister and this sister have the same objective—to be as materialistic as possible. But their tactics are certainly not the same. The drug-dealing sister with the poor husband has little in common with this sister who depends on her successful husband for everything. I suppose it's the materialism that keeps them together."

The youngest sister in Andrea's family is the baby and remains unmarried.

"I worry about this sister. She has no motivation and is so immature. She is such a nice person and I feel the closest to her of any of my sisters. I have always had a soft spot for her but she has to get a life. I feel protective of her. I know she might party some but she would never do drugs. I see her more often than the others.

"I have never exchanged one unkind word with this sister. She is the dearest to me. The other sisters are not as involved with her as I am but they can't help but like her. Even though they tear each other apart, she's immune, she's the baby."

Andrea and her sisters are not alike in any way.

"People's eyes light up when I say I'm the oldest of four sisters and then I explain how unalike we are. Still, there's an identification with the clubbiness of four sisters. We're a part of something, united we stand. Recently, on Easter, the four of us and our mother went out together and we drew quite a bit of attention. My sisters are very beautiful. It's such a waste for the sister who deals drugs. My littlest sister and my youngest daughter are very close and that means a lot to me. It's that kind of connection between a sister and a daughter that you hope will happen.

"When I've had tough times, when I got divorced, my sisters loaned me money. I'm attracted to motivated people but my sisters don't operate that way. Nor are they hardworking like I am.

So the fact that they were willing to lend me money meant a lot to me. I'm not disappointed that they don't think like I do because they were there when I needed them. Ultimately I see them as relatives; that is, I didn't choose them but I accept them.

"The bottom line for me is that I'm proud of my sisters, happy to be a part of the foursome. They're very attractive and my mother is proud, too. It sounds superficial but beauty is a family characteristic. The sister who deals drugs is very good looking. In a picture of the four of us, you'd think everything was perfect."

Andrea's sisters are not as they seem. She is most concerned with the sister who is a drug dealer, but ambivalent about any relationship they might share. Coming from a broken home and never knowing her own father, it has been difficult for Andrea. Her attachment to her youngest sister, the one who has needed her and offers unconditional love, is the safest bet. Her identity with the middle sister is limited—she finds her too materialistic and banal. It is the entire canvas that means something for Andrea, rather than the individual interaction, when it comes to her sisters. She is a realist who sees them for who they are and treats them accordingly.

Suzanne

"Having sisters is definitely more demanding than having friends. . . . My middle sister and my oldest are not as close. I'm the glue for both."

Suzanne lives in Larchmont, New York where she works in a family business and is the mother of three small children. The youngest of three sisters, Suzanne sees her family often.

"When I was growing up, our house was always full of action. My oldest sister, who is eight years older, was very social and my middle sister, who is five years older, was very quiet and academic. She tried to teach me everything she knew. I was considered cute by the oldest sister, who was a cheerleader and very involved with her social life. Both sisters were very protective of me and treated me like a baby. To this day, they treat me that way.

"I am equally close with both sisters but I definitely spend more time with the one who's only five years older. As adult sisters, they have each needed me in different periods of their lives. When the oldest got divorced or when the middle one was still single and I was already married, for instance. Also, when my oldest sister was married, her husband and my husband were like brothers. So that split has been difficult for everyone."

Suzanne does not see herself as similar to her sisters, but as her own person.

"My middle sister has kids my kids' ages and our lives are more similar but I don't identify with her more than with the other. Actually, I identify with neither. I feel I'm not like my sisters but I'm connected because we *are* sisters.

"I've never liked anyone my sisters have ever dated and that's because we're so different. But our closeness has its own reality. For instance, I've been accused by a certain friend of putting my sisters ahead of our friendship. This friend probably needs my friendship more than I need hers. That's because I have sisters and she doesn't. Deep down, I know that my sisters are there for me and I don't need friends. My sisters and I have a family history. I don't see friendship in the same way that I see sisterhood. I'm a good friend to my friends and I also have sisters."

Suzanne visits her sisters at least once a month.

"I see my middle sister more often than I see the other, who is divorced and lives out of town. However, she is now moving closer to be with us, and I have very ambivalent feelings about it. I know I can't fill the void created by her divorce. I don't think she'd make those demands on a friend. Having sisters is definitely more demanding. The other pressure on me is that my middle sister and my oldest sister are not as close. I'm the glue for both.

"My own family, my three kids and my husband, come before my sisters but I've set it up so my middle sister's kids and mine get together often. There are lots of cousins and doting aunts in our family. My husband likes the fact that I have a constant support system. He appreciates it and realizes that my sisters are my confidantes and that I can always reach out to them."

Suzanne believes she was her parents' favorite child.

"My oldest sister was the most demanding and so she got the most attention, but I was the favorite because I was the easiest. My middle sister was a typical middle child. To this day, the three of us talk about being sisters and where we fit into our family. My middle sister chose a certain kind of husband in order to break free. She made a conscious choice in lifestyle and culture because she wanted to be able to stand on her own two feet. She has succeeded at it and is hitting her stride in her forties. I believe she might have felt disliked by our parents in her twenties but it wasn't the case. Now she knows that. She no longer feels overlooked, and is close to our mother.

"As sisters we do exclude our brother's wife. We do it all the time and it isn't a matter of not liking her, it's about not being in the loop. She really isn't one of us. The three of us have a long-standing pattern and there is no room for her. We realize this and don't purposely exclude her but we know she feels cut out. My one sister and I do share friends though, but she isn't our friend. She's family 'on the side,' if you will. The friendships that are mutual work because two of us live near our hometown."

The assumption that Suzanne's sisters will be there for her as she grows older is absolute.

"I know that my sisters will be my safety net in my old age. I don't think we could live together, but in the same community. We could do something together every day, that's how I picture it. But forget living together—I know my sisters too well for that to work.

"I'm so happy to have my sisters, but the truth is, I know no other way. I feel I'm giving the most at this stage in our lives, as if I grew up and everyone finally let me be the nurturer. I don't see them as the buffer that outsiders believe they are. I know they're there, but I feel my own strength."

Suzanne makes no bones about the fact that she and her sisters have been known to exclude her sister-in-law and that her friends resent her closeness to her sisters. Although she plays down the bond, it seems to be at the center of her life. She is motivated by family and her identity is wrapped up in being the youngest of three sisters. She doesn't say it, yet it appears she is in search of a way to prove to her sisters that she is an adult. Suzanne's concern that her divorced sister will lean on her makes us question how responsible she really feels. When Suzanne claims that her own children come first, her sisters are still very much in the picture. Subconsciously she still seems to need their approval.

$\mathcal{Allie}$

"Both my sisters hated my husband for what he did to me. The affair lasted several years."

The oldest of three sisters, Allie and her entire family live in Cleveland, Ohio. At the age of forty-four, Allie is six years older than her middle sister and ten years older than her youngest. Allie is a teacher and her sisters are full-time homemakers.

"We grew up in an abusive home. I was abused as a child and so were my sisters. It was physical and mental abuse, lots of neglect in the name of something else. I was the oldest and so I took care of my two sisters and tried to protect them. I have always been closest with my middle sister. With my younger sister there was such a generation gap that I feel an entire world apart from her.

"Today my kids are grown and my sisters' children are not. We all live in the same town. My middle sister and I speak all day long. My day doesn't begin until I've spoken with her. It is a truly unique relationship—she's my best friend and we never argue. I think I was a role model for her. I can see through the years how she has identified with me. My youngest sister isn't the same as we are. She has a different outlook and values. I suppose she suffered the most because she was home when we had

gone and had to fend for herself. Our parents thought they were
wonderful but they weren't. My father was addicted to tranquil-
izers and spent most of our childhood drugged out. I never felt
that my father was there although he was certainly present. Our
mother was a hypochondriac and complained nonstop.

"It was a strange family. The three of us never really rebelled
but have remained very close, ending up as solid adults. We
were petrified of our father, especially me. I was the oldest and
he wanted to make sure I was safe. He instilled a fear of men in
me. Growing up in that house was so difficult, and I had to lead
the way for my sisters, I had to protect them. To this day, I feel
that they need my protection. My middle sister has an illness and
my youngest sister is very naive. She married an ordinary guy to
get out of the house, just anybody, rather than be left alone with
our parents. This husband of hers is extremely dull. My other
sister married a sincere guy who does fairly well. He loves her
very much. It's my youngest sister who feels she's reliving our
mother's hellish life because she and her husband have such a
struggle financially."

*Allie's parents had financial difficulties throughout her
childhood.*

"My parents, who never had money, are still in poor shape
financially. Now, as they've grown older, they've become de-
mented. I've always been a perfectionist, even when they belit-
tled me as a kid. I think because they had such serious problems
I didn't quite know what to do to prove myself to the world. I've
always wanted to display my talents, and they were not supportive.

"My life has not been exactly as I expected it to be. I really feel
it's a reflection on my parents. However, something else happened several years ago. My husband had an affair. This had
nothing to do with my family—it had to do with my marriage.
My marriage was fine until this took place. We had married very

young and had gone to high school together. Ever since, I've viewed the marriage like a coffee cup; once there's a crack in it, it can be repaired, but it's never the same. I sensed something was not right and my instincts were correct. I knew he was having an affair. I went crazy; I hired a detective and wore men's clothing to follow him. It did no good at all. I think I had to prove something to myself, or why else would I have done it? I felt so humiliated by this affair."

Throughout the affair, Allie's sisters were there for her.

"My middle sister gave me all the support she could. She came to the detective's office with me, nauseous from pregnancy, to help me get through the meeting. She understood my uncertainty about whether I was doing the right thing. She told me that I had to do what I had to do. She's very strong and she stood by me. My other sister also supported me and my decision to hire a detective. Both sisters hated my husband for what he did to me. The affair lasted for several years. I threw my husband out of the house. It was like *The War of the Roses*. He was very upset when I threw his clothes out after shredding them.

"Now that I'm reconciled with my husband, I know that my middle sister comes first. I'd do anything for her and she'd do anything for me. Of the two sisters, she had the true empathy. I simply don't feel as attached to my little sister and she's not my friend, but my sister. She comes after my other sister in terms of my loyalties, yet I continue to mother and guide her. For example, she called me to wish me a happy Mother's Day.

"I feel so lucky to have my sisters. My parents couldn't have raised a son. We raised ourselves and I know that a son could not have coped with them. The fact that we had to find our way and the degree to which our parents failed us is an all-consuming subject that we continue to discuss, my sisters and I. Once my youngest sister and I had a fight and ended up not speaking for a few years. She alienated herself from both of us and then when we got back together, she explained that she needed the space away from us. I think that she feels outside the closeness that I share with my middle sister. We're so exclusive. I admit it. We're like twins. We protect each other. We do try to include the youngest but the age difference is tremendous. She was ten when I married. Somewhere along the way we've failed to connect.

"I have friends who have sisters and describe the missing ingredient. They're not close and really suffer. When you have that closeness it's a wonderful thing. I don't believe that three sisters have to have an odd man out. In other words, it isn't because we're three that I'm not as close to my youngest sister. It's because I'm more attached to my middle sister. When I learned of my husband's affair, I had a nervous breakdown. Both sisters helped tremendously. And my mother, who had never been there for me, was surprisingly there then. Maybe because she was so anxious for me to remain married. She looked at it in terms of money. If my marriage had failed, there would be less money and as I've said, she has none to offer."

When Allie's daughter was born, she wanted her to have a sister.

"I don't have two daughters, but two sons and one daughter. I know that my daughter is missing out on a big life experience. My sisters have been my buffer against the world, and my middle sister is my soulmate. It is truly a thrill that I live close to both sisters. I'm a very private person and having my sisters around means I only need a few close friends. They fill my needs. The younger sister continues to be guarded and wants her own life. She sticks to her own agenda, but I see that we're slowly bridging the gap. It's interesting that the middle sister is closer in age to the youngest sister, yet they're not very close.

"There have been circumstances that forced us to be there for one another. Not only our parents, but years ago, our youngest sister was raped. Our mother refused to believe it, but we did.

Our mother has been an example of what not to be as a mother. As mothers, each of us has made great attempts to give our children all the emotional support we never had. So although it's sad to think of the childhood that my sisters and I never had, we can still have great fun together. We still act immature and crazy. With my middle sister, our family and friends get in the way. Sometimes we really only want to be with each other."

Allie's story is filled with sadness and disappointment, the blows softened by the presence of her sisters, especially the middle sister. Between her parents' dysfunctional nature and neglect, as she describes it, and her husband's affair which devastated her, she has suffered from the actions of those close to her. Her middle sister has been stoic and at Allie's side, regardless of the reason.

As for her youngest sister, one wonders how she must feel about the exclusivity of her older sisters. It is obvious from the fact that she broke away for several years that she has needed her independence. Allie and her middle sister do not seem particularly concerned about the feelings of their youngest sister. Allie's rationale is that she has made herself available and protective of her, if necessary. However, the loop consists of Allie and her middle sister, to the extent that we wonder where her children fit in. Due to her husband's affair, we know where he fits into the picture.

TWIN SISTERS:
Double Bind/Double Bond

If sisters are strongly connected by virtue of their birth from the same womb, twins are even more strongly connected, having shared the womb together. Identical twins have not only shared the womb but are the same genetically. Being an identical twin is the closest thing to having another "me" in the world.

Twins have a truly unique bond. Researchers have found that some sets of twins develop their own language as toddlers. Other studies have shown that twins separated at birth develop incredible similarities in behavior and taste. One set of these twins was found to be using the same very obscure brand of toothpaste. Another set discovered that their spouses and children had the same names.

Twin sisters have to deal with all the usual sibling issues but in an intensified form. For example, competition between sisters may be a fierce version of competition between non-sisters. Devoted twin sisters may face the world as an inseparable team.

One twin acts as a mirror for the other, reflecting her image of herself in the most powerful way imaginable.

—RONNIE L. BURAK, PH.D

Born the Friedman twins, Esther Pauline, called "Eppie," and Pauline Esther, called "Popo," were deeply attached to one another until their wedding day. After their double wedding, these twin sisters became very competitive. The rivalry began because Eppie Lederer's husband had less money than Popo's but it has long since ceased to center on the success of their husbands. For the last thirty-five years Eppie and Popo have competed over their syndicated columns. Eppie, also known as Ann Landers, and Popo, also known as Abigail Van Buren, vie for the position of queen of syndication.

Eppie/Ann Landers began her career at the *Chicago Sun Times* when the previous "Ann Landers" unexpectedly died. At that time, her sister, Popo, helped her with the overwhelming amount of mail she received. Popo believed that Eppie was not appreciative of her help and Eppie felt that her twin took charge. Within several months, Popo began her own advice column at the *San Francisco Chronicle*, modeled after Ann Landers. Popo's deal confirmed that she owned her name, "Abigail Van Buren," while her sister did not initially insist upon ownership of "Ann Landers."

When "Dear Abby" became the most popular column in the country, Eppie was beaten by her sister again. By 1958 the twins' battle became public, written up in *Life*. Several years later, when Eppie's daughter was married, Popo attended the wedding although the sisters did not speak. Afterward, the sisters found themselves together for a stint at the *Chicago Tribune*, in a situation where the competition escalated rapidly.

Today the twins continue to compete, despite the fact that each has established a daily readership of ninety million. The sibling rivalry persists beyond fortune and fame.

Dedicated to one another, Gloria and Thelma Morgan, notorious twin sisters, were considered the epitome of café society beauties at the height of their glory in the twenties. Growing up with little besides their looks, the twins were encouraged by their mother to better their stations in life through the husbands they sought. When Thelma eloped with Lord Furness, Gloria found herself alone for the first time. However, she was not alone for long. At the age of eighteen, she married Reggie Vanderbilt, the most eligible bachelor in New York. When he died several years later, he left behind a beautiful widow and a beautiful daughter, "little Gloria." Thelma, as Lady Furness, had begun a long-standing affair with the Prince of Wales.

While Thelma was considered the stronger of the two sisters, both had a noticeable stammer and were almost impossible to tell apart. As explained by the twins themselves in their autobiography, *Double Exposure*, the sisters felt so closely connected that at the age of thirteen each chose the same gift for the other. When Thelma went into labor, Gloria, separated by an ocean, experienced birth pains. And when Gloria contracted diphtheria, Thelma suffered an intense sore throat. Describing these experiences as a "psychic bond," the Morgan twins were much less involved with their older sister, Consuelo, who had no such hold on them.

Once they emerged as young women without husbands, the Morgan twins were known celebrities. It was Thelma's sheer devotion to her twin that cost her the love affair with the Prince of Wales. With Gloria begging Thelma to return from abroad, she asked her good friend Wallis Simpson to look after the Prince during her absence.

The great tragedy for Gloria Morgan Vanderbilt was her custody battle for "little Gloria" and a lack of a rapport with her only child. Because her mother was absent often and the twin sisters inseparable, "little Gloria" often mistook Thelma for her mother.

What is sad about these twin sisters is how they brought on their own unhappiness. During the celebrated custody case, they were defined by the press as narcissistic, adventure-seeking women with little sense of responsibility. Facing great adversity, the twins grew more attached to one another. As their notoriety began to wither in their later years, the sisters lived together in poverty, the romance and excitement of the twenties long gone.

Shelley

"I'm aware that people saw us as having created a wall, as if we had our own little world."

Sixty-eight years old, Shelley lives in Seattle as does her twin sister. Shelley is married and has two grown children and four grandchildren. Her twin sister has never married. Shelley continues to work in a retail store and her sister is a recently retired receptionist.

"We are identical twins and were very close growing up and are very close today. We have always lived in Seattle and so we are known around town. I see my sister often, almost daily, and have done so my entire life. We have never really discussed why she never married and had children. At one time I thought it was going to happen, but it never did. She has been totally involved with my children from the start.

"My husband likes my sister and I'd say that forty percent of the time, he's with me when I'm with her. She thinks of my children as her own, and my grandchildren as her grandchildren. Being twins makes us doubly close and that feeling extends to my family. I provide the family that she never had."

As children, Shelley and her twin sister shared a bedroom and were dressed alike until they were fourteen years old.

"We have always been put together. We are identical and in our day, there weren't many of us. One might expect us to be very different in personality, but it isn't the case. Of course, we've always been mistaken for one another. People will say hello to me, thinking I'm my sister and vice versa. It's easier to smile than explain. One gets used to it.

"My sister and I have stuck together always. Because we had each other, we never really needed anyone else. We have friends, but basically my twin sister comes before anyone. We are no longer identical but those who knew us well years ago could tell us apart. I have salt and pepper hair and my twin dyes her hair."

Shelley believes that her twin might have missed something by choosing not to marry.

"My sister has the benefit of my family and knows it's her family, too. But I think that's because we're twins. As just plain sisters, the tie would not be as strong. I've never felt guilty that my sister has chosen the life she has. I have always included her in any family event and I respect her decisions in terms of her personal life. We have always helped each other and in her case, that meant that when my kids were small, she would babysit. Our lifestyles, because I'm married and she isn't, have not been the same.

"I have never known anything but being a twin. I know how people see twins of the same sex. I'm aware that people saw us as having created a wall, as if we had our own little world. In some ways it's true. There hasn't been a week in my life, even if I've been traveling or if my sister has, that we haven't been in touch. We're so close that I can't imagine not having a twin sister. I would tell my sister things I'd tell no one else and we would do things for each other, that we'd do for no one else. While I might confide in my husband, it's a different relationship. I put my sister ahead of any other woman."

When they were younger, Shelley was anxious for her sister to settle down.

"Although my sister's lifestyle has not come between us, I always hoped she would find someone. She never did, so our way of living was always very different. So while we stayed close, her decision to remain single in a day when few women did was always there. It makes quite a difference when you reach our age and one has been married her entire life and the other hasn't."

As identical twins, Shelley and her sister are deeply bonded and engrossed in each other. Although she denies it was out of guilt, Shelley included her sister in many aspects of her married life—mainly childrearing and the joy of grandchildren. What is unusual is that identical twins of their generation would end up living such divergent lives. Shelley's sister has had the benefit of Shelley's family without any of the responsibility. It is almost as if she never needed to pursue what her sister had, because her sister had established it so nicely and generously offered it to her.

Amanda

"From fifth to eighth grade, we were identified by our peers as twin one and twin two."

Amanda, at the age of twenty-one, grew up in a Chicago suburb and later lived in Boston. A fraternal twin, she and her sister purposely chose to attend different colleges.

"I have always thought that my sister looks just like my mother and that I look just like my father. We definitely look like sisters but not like twins. My sister looks older, and people think she is. She is shorter and has a big chest and gives the impression that she's very mature.

"We're extremely different and we're best friends. I cannot live without my sister. We're connected as twins. It isn't like anything else. You have to be a twin to understand. She is my other half. When she left for college, a week ahead of me, several years ago, I sat at home and cried and cried. I couldn't function."

The only competition that Amanda and her twin have experienced is school-oriented.

"I have always had superb grades and was very academic. She was the party girl and we ended up with different friends and different guys. I would never have taken her boyfriend and she would never have taken mine. That isn't how we treat each other. This has been a rule of ours since we began to date. We're also attracted to very different types.

"There was no competition for my parents' attention when we lived at home. I happen to get along better with our father and I was the sister who did the right thing, while she did the wrong thing. I was the better daughter. This was more difficult for both of us because we were not just sisters but twins. It made it a really impossible situation. Our mother was always a friend to us. But my sister would behave badly so she got into more trouble. In the end, she also got more rope because she was so much trouble. It's almost as if she got away with so much that they were lenient with her. Maybe they were afraid. As for me, I was on a short rope."

When Amanda and her sister were small, they were not close to each other.

"From fifth to eighth grade, we were identified by our peers as 'twin one' and 'twin two.' This drove us so crazy that we went completely separate ways. And then in high school we became closer because we moved to Boston. Once we established ourselves, we were able to find our own sets of friends. It seemed like we have had our own groups but we had to discover each other first and that closeness has stayed. By the time we moved to Massachusetts we learned that being a twin sister is really special.

"My sister and I know now that we're always there for each other and that neither of us is going away. We're there forever. That's the bond. The only fights we've had in the past few years have to do with my sister's habits. She drinks and smokes and I'm an athlete. It really bothers me. I've gotten very angry at her because she took up these bad habits to please her friends. The smoking still goes on and I finally decided to accept it because I don't want the separation nor do I want her judging me. Eventually we came to realize we're not one person. Our entire lives we have been thought of as twins and people expect us to do exactly the same things in every instance. We know we may be twins but we have two different bodies and two different brains and two sets of emotions. One of us is good at what the other isn't."

Amanda sees her twin sister and herself as two halves of the same whole.

"We come first for each other. When we applied to colleges and I wanted to leave Boston, we originally agreed my sister would come to the same college. But I knew it wouldn't happen in the end because of our grades. She was angry at first that I chose a school halfway around the country. It turned out to be good for both of us. We needed that space.

"My sister and I shared a room growing up. I had no idea what it would be like to be so far away from her physically. We had even gone to summer camp together and slept in the same bunk. We adjusted to being at colleges that were not close but we spoke on the phone nightly. My day doesn't end until I've talked to my sister. I know how strong our connection is. I have wondered sometimes about how the rest of our family feels. I don't see us as excluding our parents or our brother, but I don't know how they feel from the outside. Our bond will grow stronger and stronger as we get older. I cannot imagine anything else. I'm aware constantly that I'm a twin sister."

As fraternal twins, Amanda and her sister have established unique identities for themselves. Having chosen separate sets of friends and interests, they remain devoted to one another. As young women, they already have a sense of how special and invaluable their connection is. There seems to be very little that Amanda would allow to get in the way of her relationship with her sister. This is evidenced by her justification of her sister's smoking and drinking habits. Amanda is so determined to have their relationship be solid that she's willing to look the other way.

Sally

"The first time that I got pregnant I do believe that my sister intentionally got pregnant."

Living in Los Angeles and raising two small children, Sally, at the age of thirty-seven, has a fraternal twin who lives in Pennsylvania. Although they have not lived near one another for several years, their children get along well, as do the two sisters. Sally's sister's children are close in age to her own.

"Growing up as a twin, whether I knew it or not, was the most pivotal relationship in my life. We are fraternal, not identical, and I think that's a stronger bond because we don't look alike. There's none of that inherent competition that comes with having a mirror image of yourself. At one point, my twin sister was nine inches taller.

"We were very different from the start, with separate but equal goals. She was academic and I was not. It was not a terrific childhood because our father was an alcoholic. Yet we were blessed with two sets of wonderful grandparents and a fabulous mother. And I think, in a way, that having a father with a problem might have bound my sister and me closer together. We shared an experience and a tragedy. Today my sister and I, as twins and sisters, understand how his drinking affected us. The result is a kind of legacy."

Sally has missed her sister since she moved to the East Coast.

"Although my sister and I attended different colleges, they were only an hour apart. And I knew, always, that she was the more academic sister, the more intellectual. But once we'd finished school, we lived as singles in Los Angeles together and had parallel, equal lives. I worked in public relations and she worked in advertising. We had some of the same friends and then we had other friends from our jobs. That made for the right balance. She was always my best friend—she's my best friend today.

"I'm one of those women who loves women. I'm still close to my friends from college days. I always had such great women friends, which is a reflection of the closeness my sister and I experienced. I've met women who don't like other women. I have a difficult time with those women because that hasn't been my orientation. I appreciate strong, positive women, like my sister. I know I can trust certain women because my sister is so trusting."

Sally believes that it is serendipitous that her twin is her twin.
They would have been best friends in any case.

"I think if I met my sister socially we'd become best friends. I love her mind, her sense of humor, and the friendship she offers. We are so connected—even our children sense the bond. We are godmothers to each other's children and our kids are very close, despite the distance.

"The first time I got pregnant I do believe that my sister intentionally got pregnant. Then it's progressive, and we both just planned our families and ended up with kids very near in age. So we're a pair, as twins and sisters, and it extends to our children. As for our poor brother, he has definitely been left out. When my sister and I were little, we shared a room and were dressed alike. Our mother, ironically, had identical twin sisters so she was in the same position as our brother. For this reason, she was adamant that we were not to be treated alike, but each as our own person. Even dressing us alike was a charade; she realized how different we were from the start."

Sally was married three years before her twin sister.

"I met an older man and knew right away that I loved him. I realized I had to seize the opportunity. My sister was not competitive and she was happy for me. Our spouses get along quite well, so it's a good arrangement. There is not much competition or I simply don't see it. My sister has a great personality and she's very beautiful. We look a lot more alike as adults than we did as children. Our mother was an actress and we both look like her. People often comment on my sister's beauty which does not make me jealous. I'm pleased for her.

"As an adult woman I'm very aware that I'm not only a sister but a twin. Now that she and her family are moving back to Los Angeles, she's hesitating about living in the same suburb, and I agree. As much as I love her, I don't like being pigeon-holed. Neither of us appreciates being lumped together. She's very conscious of it, as am I; it's a valid concern. There's some ambivalence, despite the fact that we love being twins. My husband, because he isn't a sister or a twin, does not understand my feelings. He thinks she should move next door, but she and I know it won't work. My sister has chosen a town an hour away and that's perfect for both of us.

"I never look at the big picture with my twin sister. I hope we'll continue to live near one another as we grow older. I feel that we will and that it's the best thing for both of us. She and I have shared a special identity our entire lives. I'm blessed to have a twin sister. It has worked out so well in our case—we've really worked to keep it together. We're close not only because we're twins, but also because we're sisters. It's a double commitment. I only hope my daughters can have half of what I have with my twin."

Sally's story is a positive one, which speaks to female strength and loyalty. She and her twin sister, self-sufficient and independent, are also dedicated and trusting. Sally establishes this early on in the interview, and only later does she bring in her ambivalence about her sister's return to their hometown. While she's pleased that her sister will be close by, she makes it obvious that she did not want her living next door. Territorial and determined to remain autonomous, the threat of proximity loomed very real for her. Fortunately, her twin sister felt the same way, and her decision to be an hour away suits them both perfectly.

Despite the positive forces, the sisters continue to desire their own lives and identities. Yet Sally never denies the bond and believes that she and her sister are united for life.

Anne

"After the rape, things changed for my twin sister. . . . She was in and out of psychiatric hospitals from that time on."

Living in San Francisco at the age of thirty-four, Anne is one of four sisters. The mother of one child, Anne is currently pregnant with twins. She works in a doctor's office part-time. Her own twin sister died several years ago, a suspected suicide.

"My twin sister and I got along very well as kids but we also fought a lot. Overall it was a good relationship. We looked exactly alike but my sister always did things to make sure we didn't look alike. There was definitely a time, while growing up, when both of us disliked being twins. We were compared to each other constantly while the older and younger sisters didn't have to put up with that. Today I'm close to the younger sister but not so much with my older one. My twin didn't get along with our older sister either. This sister never liked being a small child with smaller twin sisters. She resented us from day one."

Anne's sisters live nearby and have children.

"No one was favored by our parents when we were growing up. I've made attempts to get along with my older sister but it hasn't worked. I used to be sorry but now I don't care. My youngest sister doesn't even get along with the oldest and one would think that this relationship would work. The oldest has really distanced herself from us.

"My twin was never married. I got married when I was twenty-eight and I think she might have been jealous. But our relationship had been competitive at certain stages anyway. We had gone to camp together and were in the same classes in school so we spent a lot of time together. As we got older we had friends who became more important but as kids, we definitely put each other first. What happened was that my twin sister became too demanding. She wanted my full attention and I wasn't able to give it to her."

Anne and her twin sister attended separate colleges in different parts of the country.

"She was miserable and called to say she wanted to transfer to where I was. I said no because it was the first time in my life that I'd been on my own, without my twin or my other sisters. It was very important to me. I knew that if she came, I'd feel burdened and I'd worry about her, making sure she was busy and happy. I wanted time to grow up on my own and be alone.

"I had tremendous guilt because my sister stayed at her school. If I had said, okay, come, she would not have been raped on campus. That was what happened. After the rape, things changed for my twin sister. She was in therapy and did not date much. First she disassociated and had problems, then she went to a hospital for a year, and then she had a breakdown. She was in and out of psychiatric hospitals from that time on.

"My sister became a bit of a patient activist and when she was lucid, she made a fuss if patients were not treated properly. One of the diagnoses was that she was schizophrenic. Her problem was that she had different personalities—she'd suddenly lose touch with the present and become someone else. This tendency might have existed before the rape, but it was triggered by that experience and drove her to her end. I believe that if there had been no trauma, no rape, she could have functioned."

As children there was no evidence of Anne's sister's problem.

"We were together so often and I saw none of what came afterward. I always felt closest to this sister because she was my twin. It is a closer relationship than with regular sisters. We could tell each other anything. I was more connected to her than to anyone else in the family and even after she became ill, I felt that way. It was a heartache that she was so sick—it broke my heart. I sensed this especially when I got married and she was there, but she wasn't healthy. By the time I had a child, she was dead. Until the end, I kept hoping she'd snap out of it.

"In the past few years, until her death, I didn't see my twin as much as I had before that. We spoke often on the phone but I was living in New York then and she was still in San Francisco. My younger sister remained involved with her, and lived nearby. She saw her often in the hospital and my parents visited, too. My oldest sister, as I explained, did not; she was not involved with any of us on that level."

Anne's twin was not interested in men.

"It had crossed my mind that my twin might have been gay but I'm not sure. She had a few male friends but they were from the psychiatric community and had their own problems. She stopped coming into contact with normal people—that was the tragedy of it. Meanwhile, my life was flourishing. I was with the man who later became my husband and I kept thinking how unfortunate it was that my sister could not have the same kind of life. When we were young it always seemed that we'd be together, happily.

"What finally happened to my sister was that she'd caused such issues at the hospital as an activist, they refused to let her return. She was in a severe depression and suffering from insomnia. She needed medication and still the hospital refused to admit her. She overdosed on whatever kind of medicine she was taking at the time. Her doctor said that she knew exactly what the consequences were of taking too much and that it was intentional. He believes it was a suicide."

To some degree, Anne's twin's death was a relief.

"The illness spanned a ten-year period in which my sister was not herself. She had not been the twin I had known in childhood and it was so very painful. She had constant problems: alcoholism, anorexia, attempted suicide. When I got married, she was very thin and had to be rehydrated in order to be able to come. My youngest sister married a few years later and my twin also made it to that wedding but it was hard on her. For some reason, the fact that our baby sister was married made her depressed about her life. Perhaps the combination of both weddings did that. In any case, my twin sister died several months after our youngest sister's marriage.

"I've always thought that because she was my twin it has been a deeper loss for me. As kids, we were the twins, known as that, and everything was absolutely fine until we were fourteen. We rarely had conflicts then and never over boys or the family. At this stage things began to change and by college, they were irreversible. I'm glad I have other sisters because her death has been such a blow."

Anne believes she has faced her twin's death to a certain extent.

"Sometimes I try to forget what happened with my twin sister. I can face a good deal of it, but the enormity is there. I've buried some of it but it surfaces sometimes. What happened with my twin wasn't about the two of us but about her, that much I know.

"Recently I was told that I'm pregnant with twins. I'm very nervous about this and noticed that my parents have not said much. They're haunted by what happened and I'm sure they're freaked out by my news. I understand, and I know how they suffer. I know how it is, because I miss my sister too. I miss her now and I miss the memory of how we were as kids. I dream about her, I dream about her all the time."

Full of pathos, Anne's tale is a modern-day tragedy. Her twin sister might have been able to lead a functioning life had she not been raped on a college campus. From there it was all downhill, and since Anne's primary attachment was to this sister, she has suffered tremendous guilt and loss.

Although Anne is grateful that she has other sisters because her twin is gone, there is no real solace anywhere. The eldest sister became estranged from the family long ago, for reasons we do not really know, but partly in reaction to the attention the twins received. The youngest sister and Anne have a rapport, but Anne remains tormented by what happened to her twin. She has repressed and denied part of what transpired in order to cope.

Pregnant with her own twins, Anne will have to resolve certain issues in order to ease the pain and move forward in her own life as positively as she can.

Jennifer

"We have done coincidental things, such as send the same card to each other or buy the same gift for someone."

One of identical twins in their early forties, Jennifer is a research scientist living in Virginia Beach. Her twin sister lives in New England and is not working at present. Both sisters are married; Jennifer has two children and her sister has three.

"As far as our children go, it is an interesting situation. My sister adopted a child and then ended up having two kids of her own. Those children are the same sex and ages as my children. If anything, as mothers and adult twin sisters, we're closer today than we've ever been before. We're not inseparable but we always had each other. By not living in close proximity, but by having parallel lives at present, there's a sense of contentment.

"My twin sister is one person I don't have to explain myself to. No matter what I do, she understands. So while we were not in the same classes until high school, when we both took advanced placement, and while our parents emphasized our individual strengths, we are still closely linked. We've never been competitive about anything, not sports and not academics. But that's because my sister has always backed off. I was the more dominating twin and have a more competitive spirit. She never felt the drive to compete."

After college, Jennifer and her twin went very different ways.

"I immediately sought an advanced degree while my sister married a lieutenant in the army. I did not marry until six years later. She lived in a military environment all that time and so while I bounced around the academic world, my sister did the same thing from a military perspective. Only recently have we come to lead similar lives. Our spouses are very different but compatible. My husband is more competitive and more academic than my sister's.

"I never gave much thought to how our lives would work out. When she married I really did have a sense of loss but I was so preoccupied with my own life. I didn't lose the intimacy because our relationship is about comfort and that remained. The comfort level provided by having a twin sister is unlike any other sibling relationship. Being a twin is something I'm constantly aware of. When people talk about siblings I realize I've never had an experience with a sibling who isn't a twin. It's not the same."

As children, Jennifer and her sister did not rely on their being twins to get attention.

"In my hometown there were several sets of twin sisters, so we didn't feel unique. But our relatives always called all the other children by their names and called us 'the twins.' If anyone confused us, it was because they didn't know us well. Once we were close to someone, they could tell us apart.

"My twin has always been the one person I could tell anything to, and we're definitely connected when we aren't together. We've done a lot of coincidental things, such as send the same card to each other or buy the same gift for someone. We still look pretty much the same. When one sees adult twin sisters and they wear their hair the same or dress alike, it's probably caused by the fact that what flatters one undoubtedly flatters the other."

Jennifer's children and her sister's children do not get together too often.

"I only see my sister three times a year and I wish we lived closer. We speak on the phone once a week, but it doesn't have to be a long conversation. We can pick up wherever we left off. We speak to touch base. But our children don't see one another as a result of the distance and that bothers me. When they're together, it goes well and I wish we did it more often. As they grow up, I wonder if they will stay in contact. If I have any concerns, they center around their relationship as cousins. I worry that one set will be more successful than the other and it'll drive a wedge between us. It's a sensitive issue, who does well academically.

"I've worried over the years that my sister might be jealous of my lifestyle. I've never felt envious of her but she has a right to feel that way because we have more money. Yet our bond is so far-reaching—beyond anything, including material goods or any other family tie. I suppose that really sums up the relationship."

Jennifer does not admit that there is much competition between herself and her twin sister. However, when she mentions her fear that there will be tremendous upset over whose children succeed academically, it seems that this would be the result of a residual competition passed down to their children.

Having initially chosen very different types of husbands and lifestyles, there is a contentment in realizing that they now lead similar lives. What Jennifer feels that most twin sisters share is that specialness by virtue of their relationship: a sense that their twinness comes before other friendships, despite distance or disparate lives.

Nadine

"When my twin sister got married and was no longer at my side after having been roommates, even in college, I was lost."

In her late sixties and the mother of four, Nadine is an identical twin whose sister also has four children of similar ages. Having lived in New York City their entire lives, Nadine and her sister have one older sister who lives nearby but is not as involved with them.

"It's gotten to the point, even now, where I need to wear a name tag to tell which twin I am. Our sister, who is six years older, had her own life from the beginning. She was almost a mother figure to us and apart from our day-to-day experiences.

"We've always shared a nice group of friends. We never competed for anything, not for dates and not scholastically. I'm more outgoing and my twin is less gregarious. She married three years before I did. I didn't want to be married because I was having too much fun. She definitely wanted to be married. We both had kids at the same time, though, and rather quickly. They're close in age and very friendly. As cousins growing up and to this day, they're very involved with each other."

Nadine has had a career most of her married life and her twin has not.

"My husband didn't want me to work but I wanted to. Today I have my own company while my twin sister is involved in volunteer organizations and charities. So each of us is busy in our own way. We speak every day no matter where we are and if we're both in town, we see one another four or five times a week, if possible. We're always in touch. My twin sister's husband died a few years ago. Our husbands were not so compatible and over the years we stopped seeing each other socially. Originally we had done so, and today my sister and I travel together whenever we can.

"So many times strangers smile at me because they think I'm my twin. We're so close that often we'll be in a different city at the same time and buy the same dress in different colors. It's psychic and compelling because I know I'm not alone. My sister is out there, even if we aren't together physically."

Nadine's worst fear is that she'll be alone someday.

"When my twin got married and was no longer at my side, I was lost. The first walk I took by myself made me feel so alone. Then, when I was first married, my husband and I were in a plane during a terrible storm and the experience of coming in for a crash landing was sobering. There I was, holding my husband's hand; but when I closed my eyes, I saw myself alone. I wasn't with my sister. The fear of being alone is worse for me than the fear of being dead. People say you're born alone and die alone. But I wasn't born alone and I can't go out of this world alone. This sensation is the most significant thing about being a twin.

"I have a great marriage and I've been involved with my husband on many levels for many years, and I'm extremely attached to my children, but being a twin is a separate element in my life. It's a wonderful feeling of belonging and being in tune. I don't feel that my twin is exactly my 'other half,' but I feel I could tell her anything. We're part of one another."

Nadine and her twin sister have suffered the same health problems.

"Several years ago, my twin sister had her gallbladder out and two years later, I had the same surgery. Sooner or later, we catch up with each other, even in terms of health. Our lifestyles and values are similar and our lives are quite parallel. We practically live together now, in the sense that I always include her. Someday we might live together down the road, but I don't like to think of it. It's kind of like thinking of living in a nursing home, something you don't want to consider. Another thing is that my sister and I have such independent lives. I'm not sure that living under the same roof wouldn't spoil it.

"Our older sister fits into the picture as a good sister, but not as a twin. The experience is entirely different. She is very nurturing, but she does not see life as we do and we don't share as many interests as my twin and I do. The real attachment is my twin. It's very complete."

When Nadine speaks of her fear of being alone, we gain perspective into how twins operate. While she is close to her own family and has a relationship with her other sister, her twinness fills a large portion of Nadine's life. Despite each having four children, Nadine and her sister don't seem to have had any obstacles to their commitment to each other. Their common energy is such that regardless of their marriages and children, they are totally engrossed in each other. Any individual interests either twin has is complemented by the other's particular orientation. In this way, they are a balanced pair, familially and occupationally.

The psychic experiences which Nadine describes, those of buying the same article of clothing at the same time while apart or enduring the same surgery, is a phenomenon common among twins. Both as sisters and twins, Nadine and her sister enjoy an uncompetitive, undying affection for one another.

Lori

"She drinks, out of unhappiness . . . I get very upset with her. I do not drink at all."

At the age of forty, Lori lives in Memphis and her twin sister lives in Maine. Both sisters work full-time, Lori as a receptionist in a large corporation and her sister in a clothing store. Each sister has three children; each child was born within three months of the sister's child.

"My sister and I see each other three or four times a year and speak on the phone once a week. I feel very close to her and I'd say she comes before any other female relationship I have ever had. Being sisters and being twins makes it that way. The bond is very strong. We were born identical but we no longer look alike. As we grew up we began to look like sisters and less like twins. Our personalities are not at all alike."

As children, Lori and her twin sister fought constantly.

"We fought all the time but we were also each other's best friend. We never fought over boys, though. She was more sophisticated and dated at an earlier age. She dated my husband before I did but in the end, she preferred his friend. That was how I got to know him. I was married two months before my sister. We married very different kinds of guys, but both of us got married so young we never knew many men. Our husbands went into the service soon after we married.

"Even though so many similar things were happening to us, I began to feel separated from her. Our husbands were not one bit alike. Hers was so confident while mine was unsure of himself. It was as if my twin and I had chosen the opposite side of the same coin. I saw from the start that my sister had goals in life and I didn't. She's also better off financially and was from the start. I'm not jealous nor do I resent her. Only for one hour that I can remember have I ever felt jealous. Mostly I see my twin for who she really is and I never envy her."

Lori's twin sister has a drinking problem.

"My sister is very insecure. No amount of money can make her happy. She wants to fit in with a certain crowd and torments herself about it. Her husband doesn't even care. It matters so much to her and I keep thinking that if she would only realize what a good person she is, she'd be less frustrated. I don't share her values and it causes a breach between us. When she drinks, out of unhappiness, I get very upset. I don't drink at all, and I cannot discuss my sister's problem with her. Her children have asked me to but I'm afraid it will push her away from me. She doesn't see it as a problem and I don't want to risk losing her friendship. I'd rather be sure of what I have now.

"I don't believe that I can reach my sister. Because I'm her twin, I understand her well enough to know that she would run away if I approached her. The drinking problem has been going on for her entire adult life. She sees herself as inferior to her husband. He doesn't make her feel that way, it comes from her."

Lori believes that being a twin did not draw much attention in her hometown.

"We grew up in a middle class family—our mother was equally kind to all of us, to me, my twin sister, and my brother. Being twins had little more impact than being sisters. There was another set of twin sisters in our neighborhood who were identical physically, and they elicited attention. They were known as the first set of twins and we were the second, because we were not difficult to tell apart.

"When I think back to our childhood, I remember that until we were seven or so, our mother dressed us alike. But we hated that. Our mother must have picked up on it because she stopped. After high school, before we got married, we both worked. A lot of our friends were getting married, and we did the same. Being pregnant at the same time was fun and made us feel special. To this day our children have remained close—especially the oldest kids because we lived in the same town when they were born. By the year we had our third babies, my sister and I no longer lived close by."

Lori is devoted to her sister.

"I do things for my sister that I would do for no one else. As twins and sisters, we never competed in sports or in school. We've been so close growing up and she has always come before friends—we always had each other so we didn't need so many friends. Today, as adults, I know that my sister is there for me. And we're much closer now when we get together because we don't have our six little kids running around. Those kids have grown up and we go out as couples—our husbands get along well.

"When our mother was so sick, my sister took care of her because she lives closer. She knew I was too far away. I felt as if we both did what we could. This is a sore point for sisters, definitely, the question of who takes care of the elderly parent. But I don't think the distance was a problem for my sister—we handled it successfully.

"Because we're twins, our identity remains the same no matter where we go. I've often thought how odd it is that we're identical twins, yet we don't look exactly alike. Being identical twins is a tremendous link, stronger than any I've come across in sisters.

"Our kids have gotten a kick out of it. They'll point out that our gestures are the same or our smile. My sister was more outgoing than I was when we were teenagers. Then we got married and did a complete about-face. Now she's the insecure one. She behaves in a forced way in a crowd while I'm completely comfortable. I really understand my sister, but I can't make her problems go away. Even though she's my twin, she has to stop drinking and give up her need to be accepted in society. It's often on my mind that my twin sister is not really leading a healthy life. It bothers me."

The link that Lori and her twin share, as sisters and as identical twins, is impenetrable. Despite distance and their contrasting lifestyles, the fact that one has financial success and the other does not, there is little jealousy or judgment. Instead there is a deep connection that many of us, from the outside looking in, would have difficulty understanding.

What is interesting to note is that as Lori became more confident, her sister became less so. They switched roles as a result of circumstances. When Lori confesses that she cannot help her sister with her problems, it's because she is too afraid to jeopardize the relationship. She understands her twin so well that she can anticipate her reaction. The separate peace she has made over the drinking problem is not a totally comfortable one, but it is the choice she has made for now.

JEALOUS SISTERS:
In Search of Power

Jealous sisters have not resolved their feelings of childhood rivalry. Struggling with low self-esteem, a jealous sister continually compares her life to her sister's. Each sees the other as having had all the parental love. As an adult she may continue to envy her sister's life. Rather than competing actively with her sister, the jealous sister obsesses about how unfair it is that her sister should have more than she. The jealous sister has no sense of self and continually focuses on her sister as a way of avoiding the responsibility of growing up and living her own life.

—RONNIE L. BURAK, PH.D

The three Gabor sisters have fascinated the public for many years. Due to Jolie, their amazing mother who was compelled to make her daughters into special women, the three sisters were newsworthy for years. Jolie set her sights high for Magda, the eldest and most complacent sister. Zsa Zsa was the most ambitious and singleminded, while Eva was the most intellectual of the three. The sisters searched desperately to find proper—and prosperous—husbands. By the time Magda was eighteen, she was married to an aristocrat. It was Zsa Zsa, however, who logged seven marriages and was the only one of the three to have a child. Francesca, as the single offspring of these three devoted sisters, understandably became the focus of her aunts as well as her grandmother.

Jolie's ambitions never ceased; she was hellbent on having three famous, wealthy daughters. In 1967 it was Eva who would excel with the success of the top-rated television series, *Green Acres*. Jealousy raged among the three sisters. Eva detested having either sister mentioned, but at the same time she disliked her sisters to be criticized. It was a territorial relationship—the sisters were basically connected but envious at the same time.

As they grew older they became more committed to each other, their awareness of their status as the Gabors never waning. They carved a world around themselves formulated by mutual goals and desires. Jolie never ceased to be the cheerleader in the Gabor sisters' quest for fame and fortune.

Growing up in Main Line Philadelphia, Princess Grace of Monaco believed that her oldest sister, Margaret, was favored by her father. As the middle of three daughters, Grace was jealous of her baby sister, Lizanne. Realizing that her father was unsympathetic toward her, Grace turned to her mother for love and support. Despite the fact that her parents were rarely available, a bond did not form among the three sisters and Grace resented Lizanne for years.

Grace felt misunderstood and taken advantage of by her sisters. While they were boisterous, she was fragile and gentle. Self-described as the "brat sister" who made life unpleasant for Grace, when Lizanne locked her in the closet, Grace did not tattle.

Opposite in every way from both her sisters, Grace Kelly sought refuge in her acting career. Unable to compete, she realized her own achievements would set her free.

Lily

"I felt protective toward my sister because I was the successful one, the popular one."

Lily is the older of two sisters by five years. Growing up in Sarasota, Florida, both knew from an early age that they were adopted. Their upbringing was upper middle class and both sisters are college educated. Today Lily is a writer and her sister is a secretary. Lily is divorced and her sister is married with three children.

"As young children, my sister and I were close. I was five years older and had wanted a sibling. Then my sister came along and I was crazy about her. I don't know when or how the problems arose. Perhaps she never adjusted to the rejection of being adopted. She had been adopted at a much younger age than I—she was only a few months old when my mother brought her home. I had been in foster care, and by the time I arrived at my adoptive parents' home, I wondered where to put my suitcase. That was the difference.

"My mother didn't know anything about sisters. She had been an only child and was unaccustomed to sharing. And for the first few years, she just had me to take care of. Even then, I was always holding her hand because not only did she know nothing about sisters, but little about how to be a mother. When I study the old photos and home movies, I see fear in her face. She was wild about both of us, although unsure of herself as a parent."

Lily's mother had tried to become pregnant for ten years.

"I appeared on the scene and was treated like a princess. I went from foster care to practically being royalty. My sister became the second princess. I took her around with me as if she were my doll. I dressed her up and she was my toy. But we were never compatible. I was always the intelligent one and she was not. She realized early on that she would not be able to keep up with me. I was the straight-A student, the cheerleader, the achiever.

"I thought my younger sister was pretty. We look alike because in those days when people adopted children, they had the opportunity to mix and match. We had the same coloring and eyes. It made us seem a real family because back then, adoption was less common, I think."

Lily's mother attempted to bring Lily's sister to her level.

"I felt protective toward my sister because I was the successful one, the popular one. My sister was taken to a psychiatrist and tested to see if she simply didn't try or didn't have my brain power. I loved her then and yet I can't say if she loved me. In high school things began to fall apart. She became jealous of me. I was probably jealous of her, too, as I look back on it. She was younger and very good-looking.

"My sister invaded my space. She came into my room and opened my letters. I was furious. At the same time, I wanted a friend in her, I wanted more than a sister. I did not, though, want to give up any of the family attention. My mother really suffered—it was hard on her. She was overwhelmed. For starters, she was from a poor family and my father was successful. She didn't know quite what to do with it. Meanwhile, my father pretended that everything was absolutely fine."

At this juncture, Lily's sister became "aberrant" and the family began to break down.

"She destroyed the family with the choices she made. She would have boyfriends who stole from our house and used drugs. She took LSD at the age of thirteen. I think ultimately she was just being who she was, I mean, it was in her genes. She would lash out at my parents, screaming that they weren't her parents at all. When I went away to college she said she wanted to be with me. Maybe I didn't hear her because I told her I needed to be alone for a while. Why didn't she come to me anyway? I think I let her down. I told her not to come because I didn't realize how badly she needed to. In retrospect, I wonder if she'd been abused. She was so desperate. I look back on it and I feel terrible. She had nowhere to go but I just didn't get it. I was only nineteen at the time."

Lily and her sister have not discussed what transpired.

"There is always this weight upon me. I think I disappointed my sister. I saw her for the first time after nine years recently. We're both grown now, and in our thirties. I feel she was cruel to our adoptive mother and yet at her funeral she accused me of being the one to break her down, as if I was responsible for her death. It's very complicated because my sister has had to put her children in foster homes because she has a recurrent drug problem. I had thought that if she didn't get the kids back, if she put them up for adoption, I would take them. There's the link as a sister, the link to her children.

"I feel that my sister owes a lot of people an apology. I have yet to hear a note of gratitude or repentance. Nor has she acknowledged my efforts on behalf of her children. She will take to the grave all the things she never said or did. Then I remember she has no one to talk to. I'm able to express myself through my work, as a writer. It really saddens me that I have a sister who is not really present."

There is confusion for Lily surrounding the concept of sisters.

"Often I'll hear myself describing a woman friend as a sister to me. I must say it because I don't yet have a sister. So it festers,

this story of mine that feels so southern in spirit. I still write letters to her but there's no response. I keep recalling how as kids
when she made reference to our parents, she called them 'my'
mother or 'my' father. To me they were ours, to her they were
hers alone. But we are still sisters. We come from the same family
and ought to be close. That's how it should be but hasn't been
since we were young.''

*As Lily looks back on her relationship with her sister, she believes
that being adopted is a part of the problem. Her sister reacted
very differently toward that adoptive family than Lily did.
Because Lily was so attractive and intelligent she realized she had
a special place in the eyes of her parents. Although she very much
wanted a cohesive, meaningful relationship with her sister, she
was also unwilling to relinquish her position.*

*Lily's sister attempted to get attention by taking drugs and
running away. It was a cry for help that seems to have been
misunderstood by Lily who was wrestling with her own issues
concerning adoption and her way in the world. The relationship
between the two sisters fell apart and the promising start was
lost. Lily seems to feel regret and guilt while she longs for some
kind of reconciliation. The fact that she has no children and her
sister has three, who she may or may not be able to care for, is
another issue. Lily intends, if need be, to come to the rescue for
the sake of her sister. This intention is what speaks to the bond
that still exists.*

Jeanie

"I love her because she's my sister but I would never have chosen her as a friend."

Living in a suburb of Detroit, Jeanie and her sister are located several towns away from one another. Jeanie works full-time, is the mother of two, and her sister is also a full-time mother of two. Thirty-nine and forty-three respectively, the two sisters have gone through periods of non-communication.

"There is one story in particular that stands out when it comes to my sister. The Christmas my child was born, I invited my niece over. Then I took both kids to Macy's. My niece was so excited about my baby that I thought she'd simply stay with us while we went shopping. We'd been gone an hour longer than I'd said we'd be when my sister actually paged me at the store. There I was at the checkout with loads of Christmas gifts, having waited in line forever. So I had to give up my spot and drag the children to the phone. I found this very bizarre. She knew I was new to the neighborhood and still she carried on. She made my neighbor break into my house to see if someone had harmed us. That was when she decided to call the mall. She had no idea where I was so she tracked me down by calling every major store until she got me.

"My sister is a college graduate but when it comes to her kids, she's irrational. She doesn't even trust her own sister. Needless to say, we didn't speak for years after this incident. She said I had attempted to kidnap her child. I never heard anything so ridiculous."

Jeanie and her sister experienced diverse lifestyles in the same household.

"My sister would describe it as lower middle class while I saw our family as middle class. Nothing was ever good enough for my sister. Despite her attitude, which hasn't changed, we tolerate one another today because of our kids. We do celebrate the holidays together and I do as much for her kids as I possibly can. But I work full-time and have my own children to look after. There I am, working forty hours a week while my sister's husband is the only breadwinner necessary in her family.

"When I look back on our childhood I think of it as great, yet my sister loathed it. We are such different people—we surrounded ourselves with very dissimilar people. My friendships with my peers were very important to me. My sister is and was too eccentric for her friends to matter as mine did. I've always been the realist. I love her because she's my sister but I would never have chosen her as a friend."

Jeanie feels that despite the fact that her sister is older by four years, she was treated as the older child.

"As the pragmatic child, I was the adult. My sister is so emotional. If traveling abroad would placate her, she got to go and I didn't. I never really felt denied but she expected certain things and the result was that she got them. Because we were treated differently, there were different outcomes. I thought of my sister's world as fantasy. She was a constant reader. She did much better than I did in school. I wasn't a student and I didn't finish college. My sister would not go out and get a job—she wanted to go to college forever."

Today, Jeanie feels, her sister is overly involved in her kids' activities.

"I love my kids dearly but I don't monopolize their lives. My sister stays home just to be available for her kids, but I'm raising my children another way. I can't be involved to the extent that she is. I don't see how it helps anyone. Her children are not allowed any of the nineties paraphernalia. No ninjas, no Nintendo. One of her children is extremely bright. My kids cannot compete. And this child is so lovely, why would I want to?"

Jeanie wishes that her sister would allow her to be closer.

"My kids play soccer and tee ball, baseball, and collect baseball cards. Her kids are artistic and I cannot get near them. There's no common bond, unfortunately. Then I remember that my sister was the smart, bookish one and that I never wanted to be. My kids aren't like that, either.

"I think it's all tied up with how we were treated as children. Recently my sister told me that my mother liked me better, and that she secretly suffered and craved my mother's attention and affection. My mother always leaned on me because I was so practical. As the older daughter, my sister wanted to be consulted.

"My father died many years ago but when you talk about it with my sister it's as if it happened three weeks ago. To her, he was the center of the universe. And he was kinder and more patient with her and with me. My mother was not so patient. Once our father died, I think my sister expected her husband to become the patriarch, but it wasn't going to happen. She fought and fought this issue, and never was able to accept our stepfather as a father figure."

As children, Jeanie recalls being dressed alike and treated as a pair.

"Each of us is a physical combination of both our parents. Her coloring is more like my dad's but she's built like my mother. But it's internally that we differ. I wish my sister were more normal. I wish we could go shopping together. But she would never put me first, never has in the past. When we were children, she resented my friends and wanted me to be closer to her. She was sarcastic and nasty to my friends. She had very few friends and I happen to have gotten along with them all. Now I'm ready to be close, ready for that closeness. I do feel we're missing something by not having it. I would have liked a real older sister, one who could have taught me how to put on makeup, one I could have watched go out on dates.

"Instead I married first and became the grown-up sister. I was slotted for that role and the years made no difference. I say, if you have a big sister, why be treated like you're the older one? I suppose that everything aside, my sister would be there in a crisis. It's the day-to-day living that keeps us apart."

Jeanie has probably resented her sister's place in the family for many years. However, as the "practical" one, she has never felt entitled to express herself. Today, as adult sisters with children of their own, their pattern persists through the lives of their children. What disappoints Jeanie the most is that she was never treated as the younger child. Not only is sisterly camaraderie missing from her story, but Jeanie has also lost the ability to claim her rightful place in the family.

Susan

"What I do admire is how our mother recognized our individuality."

At the age of fifty, Susan is the middle of three sisters in a family of six children. Living in upstate New York, she works in the real estate business. Her younger sister is a teacher and her older sister is a travel agent. Both sisters live near one another while Susan lives several hours away.

"Today my relationship with my sisters is fine but growing up, it was impossible. My older sister was the eldest child and very sophisticated. My younger sister was difficult from the start and she is difficult to this day. I see her as a stereotypic middle child. Each of us had our own place in our family life. That was how our mother established it. But even with this great setup, my younger sister was cranky and unhappy.

"When my little sister was very small, she was so helpful and lovely that she earned the nickname 'Red Hen.' She learned everything very early and then she rebelled. I paid for being the middle sister who makes everyone do for her. My little sister wanted to please me and then she realized it didn't pay. She became uncooperative and has remained so.

"Due to our age difference, three years between each, we had very separate worlds. I have always admired, respected, and loved my older sister. I feel that had we not been sisters, she could have been my best friend. However, our mother made such a point of encouraging us to have our own best friends. She always had her own best friends, as an example. I also knew, no matter what, that my sisters and I could depend on each other."

The youngest and the oldest in Susan's family stayed away from one another.

"I think that all that took place with the three of us, as sisters, began with our mother. My older sister and I have our mother's ways. She is really quite beautiful to this day. Our baby sister rebelled—she did not want to be a good student and she became reclusive as a teenager. She was very pretty but her style was different. She was jealous and competitive. It's interesting that the youngest and oldest look so much alike and yet there was such friction there. Even now, my little sister will make inappropriate demands on me and my oldest sister.

"The oldest and youngest, due to proximity and mellowing through the years, have actually come to terms with each other.

But this youngest sister still confronts me; why didn't I call, why didn't I remember? I sort of laugh but I know she's not kidding, she means it. And the competition never goes away. Competition was our family religion, the name of the game. My youngest sister never wanted to be compared and my older sister was always comparing. The choice my little sister made was to do it on her own terms."

Susan's father was madly in love with her mother and not interested in the children.

"My father distanced himself from all six of us, sisters and brothers alike. His attitude was that it was my mother's idea to have all these kids. He married her and that was what she wanted, part of the package. He had his own agenda, though, and the aim was to find time alone with my mother. Meanwhile, my oldest sister had no motherly instincts nor do I. Each of us was very independent and never babysat for anyone in the family. We felt no responsibility toward one another. It was a hectic household with loads of stuff going on and no one was particularly concerned about the next child.

"Ironically, I love kids, but they don't have to be my own for me to feel this way. I was never motivated to be maternal. Nor are my sisters maternal. We are very independent, strong women. I identify with my older sister but mostly I identify with my mother. I look and act like her. My older sister acts like her, too, but she and the younger one have become close. That doesn't bother me, but what the younger sister expects from me continues to irritate me. I doubt the oldest plays her game, but perhaps their relationship can get beyond it. Mine cannot, that I know. And with my older sister, I'm completely at ease but feel I miss nothing if we're not together."

The oldest sister and her husband are very much in love.

"I love to watch my older sister and her husband. She married a prince and they are still such lovers. My baby sister married a foreigner who is very attractive—they have an extremely competitive relationship. Even in her marriage this sister has to be competitive. She knows no other way to behave. What I do admire is how our mother respected our individuality and always encouraged us to treat each other according to our needs. With my younger sister my mother would let me be the stronger one, coaxing me to let her have her way. She'd tell me to set my limits and stick with them but play the game as best I could.

"I do believe that having these sisters has taught me to deal with the world. I feel I have a greater understanding of human nature. I know how to interact with other women because I've had so much practice. An only child or a woman who has never had a sister has to learn the hard way. I know I can be manipulative if the situation requires it since I had to make my way with my sisters and had to know how to make it work."

Susan makes no bones about the fact that she's not enthralled with her younger sister. She also doesn't resent the closeness that has developed between the youngest and the eldest. She seems genuinely relieved to be separate from both women. In fact, Susan has a high regard for her older sister but the real bonding for her does not apply to either sister but to her mother. One wonders if this is a way to avoid the competition and demands that the two sisters would place upon her if she were to connect totally.

Having struggled with both sisters during childhood, especially the younger one, Susan is relieved that all three of them get along today. Yet she seems quite content to have gleaned what she has from each relationship and apply it to her own life.

Audrey

"I have married the prototype of what was expected of me and she has gone the other way."

Audrey is four years older than her sister. She lives in a suburb of Chicago and has two daughters. Her sister lives in a suburb of Detroit and has two very young sons. Although their lives are very similar at this stage, Audrey feels that the relationship has never improved since childhood.

"My sister and I never got along, not for a second. She was always depressed and pulled back when we were kids. I was the one the family admired, the one who excelled. I think she was jealous. My parents obviously didn't prefer her and she knew it, so the envy was there constantly. My parents had a busy lifestyle of their own and were preoccupied with their friends and their club. While my sister felt abandoned on some level, I never felt left on my own. I had friends and I was happy.

"As adults we somehow blame each other for what happened, for the way my parents were focused on their own lives. They must be trying to make up for it because today they are more involved with my sister and her babies than they ever were with mine. It's a matter of timing. When my kids were small, my parents were not ready to be grandparents. Now they are."

For Audrey and her sister, the competition persists.

"I watch how my parents treat my sister's children and how they are so willing to spend time with them and it bothers me. It's simply a further manifestation of our poor relationship. To this day, she and I argue about it. She's jealous of the money my husband makes and she's acutely aware of what I have that she hasn't.

"When I see my sister as an adult, I realize how much we look alike. Yet we're not really alike at all. My early memories are of how remote she was and resentful of my friendships. I've always surrounded myself with good, close women friends. I find my life very full, so I've never missed having a sister as a friend. I cannot say if I've missed being close as sisters because it simply did not exist."

Audrey has developed a close rapport with her sister-in-law.

"I've gotten very close to my sister-in-law and find it gratifying. In some ways she embodies what I never had with my sister—a closeness, a give and take. I think my sister is better off today, more verbal and introspective. I'm sure she resents me, however; that has not disappeared.

"There have been painful incidents in our adult life, as sisters. One Christmas she actually wanted to have a fist fight with me because she was so angry. To this day we fight over the stupidest things. She and I argue over everything. If I say black, she says white. One always thinks she knows more than the other—that's the problem."

Audrey sees her sister as seldom as possible.

"I don't spend time with her. In fact, I'd say I see her two or three times a year at the most. I see it as a relationship I never had and therefore can never miss. My sister gave me custody of her kids and then changed her mind. She decided I wasn't still capable since my kids are older now. I very much wanted to mother one of her children, and I'm disappointed. So when it comes to her kids, I really did hope for some kind of special relationship, but it hasn't happened.

"My sister is married to a man from another culture and another religion. Religion was never a main concern for her. I have married the prototype of what was expected of me and she has gone the other way. She was definitely the more difficult child growing up and this was one way of continuing that. She did it on purpose, I'm sure of it. It isn't that this guy isn't nice, he is. He's also a hunk and she was determined to have that sort of husband. I have a more cerebral, less physical husband and that definitely wasn't for her. I don't believe my sister chose this husband as an escape but I do believe it was deliberate."

There is hope for Audrey and her sister.

"I honestly think that since she's married and has kids there's a better chance for us to bond. Distance is a factor—the trip to her house is a long one. We do it and stay in each other's home. Actually, staying in each other's home and not in a hotel is not any more stressful than any other aspect of the visit. It's all rather demanding, but we make the effort because we're sisters.

"What I'm aware of is how hurt my parents are that we're not closer. My parents dream that one day my sister and I will get along. I have tried to make peace to some extent only to please my parents. My mother is getting older and wants so much for me to try. I also understand more about how things are with my sister. She's a remote person to begin with and now she's no longer part of the religion we were raised in. She has chosen another life and it obviously eliminates certain opportunities for closeness. Then I remind myself she's my sister and the only one I've got. That's where we are today."

Audrey's relationship with her only sister has not improved with the years and was not close initially. Yet as adult women, there is a glimmer of hope. Whether it is to please their parents or because they are finally in some ways sharing a similar existence—that of child-rearing and marriage—a common thread exists. Audrey seeks close friendships with women, not to replace what she'd never had as much as to enrich her life. Subconsciously, however, she might be looking for what she never had with her sister; the bond with her sister-in-law might be a method of avoiding her sister and any potential that could be there.

Maryjane

"I feel that I have lost her as a sister. . . . When her babies were born, she put pictures of the cult leader in their crib."

In a suburb of Cleveland, Maryjane is married with two children. She is the oldest of three married sisters. The middle one lives across the country and the youngest lives abroad. Today, at the age of thirty-five, Maryjane recalls her childhood as being influenced by life in the deep South.

"All of us were pretty close growing up, our age differences being only two years. We were close partly because of our environment, one of prejudice and bigotry, so that we needed one another. It was my youngest sister who was jealous of me, of my freedom. She felt she was treated like a baby. She was not allowed any independence and she resented it. I was not only independent but I received lots of attention. I was the good girl and the reward was that I got what I wanted. Also, I had the new clothes and by the time this youngest sister got them, they were used for sure."

Maryjane's youngest sister is married to a man from another culture and religion.

"She always had to prove herself, and choosing a man from another country was a way of becoming free. She had a chip on her shoulder about this freedom business. Eventually my parents had to let go. My mother understood and was always closest to me, which made it easier. As adult sisters, my mother related best to me because I had chosen the most conventional path.

"My middle sister is part of a cult. She lives in a community and adheres to the rules. She's completely brainwashed. She and her husband were introduced specifically to marry—they have five children."

Maryjane's parents have accepted her middle sister's decision to be a part of this cult.

"The way my parents chose to deal with this was to accept it rather than lose a daughter. I spoke up because I disagreed with the way it was handled—they should have tried to deprogram her immediately. By then she was firmly entrenched and had married someone from the cult. Something must have been missing from her life in order for her to choose to live like this. She had a very serious illness which kept her out of commission for over a year. During this time she felt neglected and let down by friends. She had to give up her dream of becoming a gymnast. It left a void and she chose this cult to fill that void. I do believe that she's happy because she is brainwashed. She and I were once very close. I was closer to this sister than to the youngest.

"I feel I have lost her as a sister. We speak but I cannot relate to her. When her babies were born, she put pictures of the cult leader in their crib. My parents accept it out of choice. I don't feel guilt, just a tremendous sense of loss. We are polite to one another but not connected. I still send presents at Christmas and for birthdays, but she doesn't seem like my sister anymore. She's in another world."

Maryjane's middle sister was close to both Maryjane and the youngest sister growing up.

"As kids I was close to this sister and the youngest felt even closer to her. The two of them shared a room, out of choice. I didn't ever share a room with anyone. We rarely see each other today and when we do our husbands and families are cordial but distant. The cult husband is totally out of the loop. He may be a brilliant man but he's socially inept.

"I see my sister who lives abroad every few months when she's in the country on business. I cannot recall the last time I was with this other sister. Perhaps a few years ago when the youngest sister got married. I've been married the longest, but only by a few months. When I do see my sisters I reflect on the way we were raised. In retrospect, I cannot judge my parents. There are no rules for parenting. They were very loving and caring and did their best. Our lives were very difficult and the repercussions still exist. The prejudice and violence affected us and we each had to find our own way out. I couldn't wait to live in a city, a place large enough to disappear."

As young girls, Maryjane's sisters were extremely important to her.

"I was closer to my sisters than to anyone while we all lived in the same house. I still love them and I'm aware that they're my sisters, but now we're on different wave lengths. I'm very disappointed because I had hoped for more. I probably look to my women friends to give me what I'm missing from my sisters. As an adult I have become closer to my mother than anyone else in our family—I've come to appreciate her more and more. My own immaturity kept me from doing so before this. She's close to each sister because she's so accepting. She's not as judgmental as I am.

"I also think that because I don't live close to my sisters, I can't be involved in their daily lives. Weeks go by and I don't speak to either sister. I do wish we lived near each other and could be together despite our differences. If we were closer physically, perhaps we would be closer emotionally.

Closeness as a child and distance as an adult have affected Maryjane's present relationship to her sisters. This is compounded by the fact that one sister joined a cult and is no longer available. When Maryjane says that if they were closer physically they might then be able to get beyond their differences, one wonders, under the circumstances, if it might not simply aggravate the situation.

With her sisters almost absent from her adult life, Maryjane has continued to be close to her family through her mother. There are two interesting aspects of sister relationships which Maryjane's story brings to attention. One is the recurring theme of sisters who are close as children, often growing less so as adults. The other is the father/daughter connection, which seems to shift when the daughter grows up. In Maryjane's case, she might have let go of her attachment to her father, replacing it with a closeness to her mother as compensation for losing her middle sister to a cult.

Barbara

"It seems to be a recurrent theme, my sister watching me closely, watching what I have."

Barbara is older than her sister by five years and lives in Santa Barbara. Her sister lives in Los Angeles and is unmarried. At the age of thirty-eight, Barbara is married with three daughters and full-time care of her mother. Her sister works in hospital administration.

"It was fine having a sister when we were growing up—I actually didn't think about it too much. I always had a kid sister, yet she wasn't involved with my life. I was into my own thing and she was younger. We were not particularly close then nor are we to this day. Maybe we're too different. I'm more urban and she's more earthy, although, ironically, we don't live those roles at present. I'm further from the city than she is at the moment. I suppose what happened is that our mother tried to push us together and it didn't work.

"Only recently, as our mother has become increasingly ill, have we gotten together. I see her in another light now. I see that she's more mature than I am and handles things very well. As a single woman she has had to take care of herself for a long while. I'm more frivolous. She's serious and has a 'take care of business' attitude. She might even be brighter than I am in some respects."

Barbara sees herself as floating in and out of her original family.

"My sister is more committed to our parents. She feels I should be more available but I have three kids and a husband. She doesn't really get that. She wants to set a specific schedule so we can take care of our mother and I cannot do it. I'm committed to my own family. We're coming from such different places.

"I don't think my sister and I ever really bonded and that's part of the problem today, now that we're thrown together. We chose alternative lifestyles from the start. She always chose the losers as friends and boyfriends and I always wanted the most popular ones for myself. She might like to marry now and settle down, but she's become more particular and finicky as time has passed. She's been single for a number of years.

"My sister has always blamed me for everything. I was the

firstborn and in my parents' generation, that was always the favored child. She has always resented that. With three daughters of my own, I've learned not to favor anyone. Now, of course, my mother feels guilty that my sister is on her own and not married. But as kids, she definitely made more of a fuss over me and was pleased when I did marry and have children."

Barbara believes that her sister is more sensitive than she.

"I've been observing my sister in this ordeal with our mother's sickness. I think she's a nice, smart woman who gives too much to everyone. She probably resents me because I'm married and have children. She would like to be close to my kids but because she works and the kids are so busy, it hardly happens. The truth is, every time she visits, we have a huge argument. While my girls like her, they cannot get close to her because my sister and I aren't close. I know it isn't great for my girls to see how my sister and I carry on. I don't want to set this example and yet that's how it is.

"My daughters fight among themselves but they're also there for each other. I believe my sister's there for me on some level. Our personalities are so different; we never paid much attention to each other growing up, but the bottom line is, we're there for each other. It would be great if we could be really close, but our priorities are not the same. She's not into material things and I am. She would never begrudge me anything I own but she *is* jealous that I'm married and have a family. She envies my lifestyle, probably."

Barbara is convinced that her sister wants what Barbara has—a husband and kids.

"It seems to be a recurrent theme, my sister watching me closely, watching what I have. She doesn't want to be alone the rest of her life. I would like to think that if she married we could be closer and that we'd have more in common. So while we aren't very involved today, I look to the future. I feel it's special for me to have a sister and while she doesn't come before my family or friends, there is a place for her. If she gets her life in order, I hope we can be closer."

Barbara and her sister have never been close. As if they were assigned specific roles in life, Barbara sees hers as that of the older, favored child. Living out her parents' expectations, she is married with children and her life is comfortable. Barbara intimates that her sister has chosen her own fate. She surrounded herself with losers from the beginning. Barbara has little regard for her sister's life, although she recognizes some of her fine qualities. She is also acutely aware that her sister envies her lifestyle and family. The mother, who sounds unintentionally instrumental in setting up the painful dynamic between her daughters, is regretful today. What Barbara hopes is that all will be rectified once her sister finds some happiness, maybe in the form of a partner, and the two women can then be on a more equal footing.

Penelope

"Again she is divorced and heavily medicated on a daily basis. . . . When I watch sisters who are connected, I know I've lost out."

At the age of forty-five, Penelope works full-time as an attorney. She has one sister and a brother in the middle. Penelope's sister is six years younger than she and works as a manicurist. Her sister has been diagnosed as a paranoid schizophrenic.

"Growing up, there was a big age difference between my sister and myself. When we were really little, I was kind to her. We never spent that much time together and had our own interests. My mother was not very involved with us as kids and one would think, under this circumstance, that my sister and I would have bonded. Instead, we have no relationship today. I'm aware of my mother's lack of maternal feelings because I don't have many myself. However, I'm more conscientious as a parent and that works for my kids. I have to make the effort because it doesn't come naturally. I believe I'm a lot better at mothering than my own mother was. And her generation did little except become mothers. I'm definitely not a friend to my kids—I'm their mother. My mother was neither—she was very aloof. In terms of my sister, I often reflect on that."

Penelope was popular in school and attended an Ivy League college.

"I was away at college, after a wonderful time in high school, when my sister was coming of age. I never had any maternal feelings toward her but I felt friendly. When I went home for holidays, it was the happiest time in our relationship. Before this, when we were both living at home, I saw her as a real pest. She was under foot when I had friends over. My friends came before anyone in my family. That was what my parents did, so I followed their example.

"My brother was my mother's favorite and my father favored me. My sister had no siblings her age to identify with and she must have known subconsciously that her birth was not planned. I learned that my mother had even considered having an abortion when she discovered she was pregnant. Somehow we all absorbed her sensibilities and my sister had to struggle with that."

As children, Penelope recalls being left alone often.

"My brother and I hung out together while our parents went out at night. Our sister had no one to buffer her, so she was sort of floating around the house aimlessly. She ended up choosing the wrong kids at school—this happened at a very young age. She got into drugs and that has been linked to her paranoia and schizophrenia. Also, when she was born, she was premature and my mother came home from the hospital without her. They were not even sure she would survive.

"My sister ended up having so many problems, probably because she lived at home longer than we did. She was the youngest and we were already gone. As a result, she was the only one to develop a relationship with my mother. My parents loved us but they did not know how to be parents. For my sister, it was the worst because she was without any kind of cushion. Then our father died and my sister felt terribly abandoned. She really got lost in the shuffle."

Penelope's sister wanted to marry her high school boyfriend.

"My sister had an illegal abortion when she was sixteen. I was at college but heard about it through my parents. They insisted that she stop seeing her boyfriend. By then she had chosen a boyfriend who was much worse. My parents wanted to send my sister away—essentially, they bribed her to go. In a week's time, she had moved in with a townie who had a drug habit. Her aberrant streak surfaced no matter what they did. However, she was mesmerized by this guy and he was probably the love of her life. She dropped out of the college they'd worked so hard to get her into.

"My sister was with this man for years. They were real hippies and only occasionally held down jobs. She got pregnant just before they split up and the baby was born. By this time, he was gone and my sister and her baby lived at home. I believe she had a baby to begin with because my mother had told her I was pregnant. It wasn't so much competitive as defensive. After her baby was born she fell into a deep postpartum depression. She tossed flowers out of the hospital window and they would not release her unless it was guaranteed she was going directly to my parents' house."

Penelope's mother was terrified that she would end up raising the sister's baby.

"During this time I lived across the country with my husband and my own first child. I was quite removed from the day-to-day drama of my sister's life, but I knew that my mother was having a difficult time. What had begun as a rebellion years before, ended up in serious illness and drug addiction. I saw my sister once a year during this period and we rarely spoke in between. When I was single, she had visited me in Chicago, where I have been for years. Part of me wanted to be close to her but she was absolutely crazy. I knew in my heart it was never going to happen. I didn't sense a loss but a sadness. I have been sad about my sister for a long time.

"I was an overachiever and an excellent student. There was such an age difference between my sister and myself that I didn't see it as competition. I thought of myself as history by the time she got to the places I'd been. I was president of my class, however, and attended an excellent college. I had friends and boyfriends that my parents liked. I really delivered for them and they were proud of me, especially my father."

Penelope's sister has been a source of problems for many years.

"Things with my sister have not improved. Recently she has had a number of episodes. She was married again and has another child, but she's divorced again and heavily medicated on a daily basis to the point where she's sluggish. As a child she was gorgeous—even in her twenties, before she had children. The medicine keeps her bloated. To her credit, she works full-time and has a boyfriend.

"We speak on Christmas and birthdays and get together on a yearly basis. It has not been a great experience and the worst part of it is what it did to my parents. It is as if she had a drinking problem, so severe are her personality changes if she's not medicated. Two years ago we both visited our mother, who treats me with kid gloves and is easily intimidated by me. But she's super-critical of my sister, which amazes me. It's complicated because my mother blames my sister for my father's death—they'd gone through so much before he died. She was an enormous drain on them and soon after she left school he died of a heart attack. Of course, my mother might just be critical, since she's not much nicer to my brother's wife than she is to my sister.

"There were very specific incidents with my sister. For instance, one of her friends almost jumped from my mother's window during my sister's high school years. My mother oversimplified the event; her response was that she was anxious for my sister to be married so someone else would be taking care of her. Today, in the nineties, someone like my sister would have been slammed into rehab and cured before it became an overwhelming problem. But that wasn't available back then. It's a pity."

Realizing that she and her sister cannot relate to each other has been painful for Penelope.

"When I watch sisters who are close, I know I've lost out. Nothing in this world is like the rapport with a sister when it works—no women friends, no brother can fill the bill. I read an article recently about how circus troupes are comprised of family members. The people really have to trust one another to be interdependent. I would have wished for a real connection with my sister, because I think of all familial bonds, this one would have been the most meaningful for me, had it worked."

Penelope's sister had a difficult time from the beginning. While Penelope experienced the usual sisterly reactions to her sister when she was small and both sisters lived in the same house, once Penelope was gone, the situation became more and more complex. Penelope describes her sister's decision to have a baby because Penelope was pregnant as a defensive measure, yet there seems to be a competitive component as well, initiated by her sister.

This is an unfortunate story from beginning to end. Penelope never had the opportunity to relate to her sister. As an overachiever, Penelope was not only older, but set a course her sister could not follow. Once her sister got into trouble, the result of neglect on her parents' part and a possible chemical imbalance, Penelope was already preoccupied with her own life. Had her sister not had serious problems, one wonders whether she and Penelope would ever have found common ground and established the bond which Penelope describes as unattainable.

Diana

"My sister has no morals because she has lived in my father's house with his present wife."

At the age of nineteen, Diana lives in a small town in Pennsylvania with her mother. Her sister, who is three years older, lives in the same town, but with her father and attends a community college nearby. Nine years ago, Diana's parents divorced, dividing the sisters irreversibly.

"As little kids, we both loved each other, my sister and I. We didn't always get along because sisters fight. She never liked the fact that I excelled in sports and she was competitive about that. She was a much better student, though. Our mother was close to both of us but her extra-special relationship was with my sister.

They had similar interests. They liked to shop and do typical girl things. I liked the outdoors and hung out with my father."

Everything changed for Diana once her parents divorced.

"Until my parents' marriage broke up, my sister and I thought they got along really well. They always seemed all right on the surface. Neither my sister nor I was ever exposed to their problems, especially by my mom. I was very surprised they were splitting. I was young, and it was a real shock for me.

"My sister and I were getting along at that stage and doing things together. Then the marriage broke up and she left with my father. He tried to take both of us. We had a big house with a pool and I was only a kid. I loved the life. My sister sided with my father and she stopped talking to me. I know that she thought it was wrong for me to stay with my mother. I stayed because I didn't want to leave. I wanted an anchor and it seemed like being with her would do that for me. I didn't really understand what was going on. I think my sister, who was already a teenager when this happened, went with my father because she understood something I did not."

Diana's mother created a scandal in their hometown.

"My sister sided with our father because of the gossip in town. I was very disappointed that she decided to do it. As her sister I was upset and my mother was really upset that she wasn't on our side. But my sister and I agreed about one thing—we were both angry at the boyfriend who broke up the marriage. Our mother had had an affair, which was why she decided to leave. She was very young when she married and had babies and ended up falling in love with someone else later. Now that I'm older I understand what happened. To this day, when I run into my sister on the street, which is the only way we see one another, she still says she thinks our mother was wrong and I still defend her.

"Because I stayed with my mother, she and I got closer. Part of that came out of the hurt my mother felt over my sister. I was there to get her through, my sister was not. To this day, she and my sister are no longer close. My sister is cruel to me and punishes me for siding with my mother. Although the affair is long over, all this still goes on."

Diana is not close to her father at all.

"I gave up on my father, but not because of my sister. My father was not good to me and finally I had to stop waiting for him to change. I regret what happened, but I'm even sorrier about my sister. She and I missed all those years together, those times when we would have bonded. I'm sad because I should have been with my sister. I know I missed something—I had a sister and I lost her.

"We live in a small town where everyone knows everything. That has made it worse. Rumors abound and we've had to live with that, too. Bad things have been said about our mother and each of us, in our own way, has had to endure it. By the time I got to high school, I had gotten over the stories about my mother. I realized that I couldn't change what had happened and began to realize that my parents' marriage might never have really worked. My sister has not gotten over it, although she's older and is supposed to be wiser. She gets angry about it even now, as if we could change what has happened. I know it can never change."

Diana is unable to read her sister's emotions and cannot judge her sincerity.

"I don't know if it's a front or if my sister wants us to get together. We spend some time with each other now but our loyalties are so different that we can't mention our parents. If we skirt this issue, then we can get along.

"I know that even if our mother had married her boyfriend, it would not have made anything better. The anger that both my sister and I have for him, although I know deep down that it wasn't his fault, would have made it impossible. I needed someone to blame and so did my sister. She blamed both my mother and her boyfriend, while I decided to blame only the boyfriend.

"My sister has no morals because she has lived in my father's house with his present wife. She's jealous of everything I do. We're both the same person in a way, both fun and easy to get along with, but then we're also different because we grew up in separate houses. Also, my sister can be moody and I'm not. We do look alike although I'm thinner. She's bothered by that and worries about her weight. Then I'll see her on roller blades wearing a bikini which I would not do."

Diana feels that her sister is jealous of her.

"When I got my car, my sister complained that she had had a piece of junk for her first car. She tells me that her grades in high school were better than mine. Because I lived with my mom, my sister likes to make me think I was a bad kid. The worst part of all is that my situation with my sister has kept me from being friends with other girls my age. I'm closer to guys because I'm so afraid a female friend will be taken away from me like my sister was.

"My father literally pulled me by the arm and insisted I stay with him. That was when my sister left with him, when she made the choice. It really haunts me. She left without listening to me or to our mother, to our side of it. After a few years, my sister moved back in with us. It was competitive because we both wanted our mother's attention. I'd gotten used to being alone with my mom and then she started paying all this attention to my sister. I was cold to my sister then—I didn't like having her around. Our mother was so warm and generous to both of us."

When Diana's sister lived with her father, she would charge
Diana for a lift in her car.

"My sister gave me rides and made me pay for gas. She
wouldn't do it as my sister but as if it was some sort of job she
hated. I wanted to share secrets and be close but because of being
split up, there was no opportunity for that. I wanted to trust her
but we didn't know each other anymore."

Today, Diana is hopeful that she can impress her sister.

"I want her to know I can do well in college. I plan to get ahead
in life and I'll show her that. Even though she holds it against me
that I grew up with my mom, I'm not the little twerp who
couldn't do anything. I want her and our father to see that I can
do things well. I want to be closer to her, to be real sisters.

"But she has to get along with our mother, too. It has to work
for both my mom and me. If she and I get together, then she has
to at least be civil to our mother. She has no right to treat her like
she does. My sister has to realize that she and I didn't divorce,
just our parents. If she really understood, we could finally make
some progress."

Diana's is a story of divided loyalties. Having been caught in the
crossfire of her parents' divorce, she and her sister became
physically and emotionally separated. The sisters suffered from
the force of the split and took sides in their parents' battle, which
further divided them. On the occasions when the sisters found
themselves together, despite Diana's yearning for a
reconciliation, competition and jealousy surfaced.

Despite the loss and disappointment, Diana seems determined
to make amends. As she comes into her own, she will seek her
sister out, hoping to heal the wounds and make up for the past.

Stacy

"I know that she has an entire life that I've yet to have and I'm available to help her in it."

The younger sister by four years, Stacy is twenty-three and lives in Denver, Colorado. She is an assistant to a photographer and her sister is a bookkeeper. Growing up in a middle class family, Stacy's sister was married at the age of twenty. Stacy is living with a man.

"Growing up my sister tried to be my mother, not my sister. I hated every second of it. She would tell me what to do, what to wear. My mother had to work full-time and my sister thought she could take over. I wanted to be close, but I didn't want another mother. We used to fight like cats and dogs. I resented her manipulations and that was the source of the fights. She would make me do her chores and threatened me if I didn't. She said I couldn't use her blow dryer or curling iron if I didn't obey her.

"These problems didn't improve as we grew older. In fact, it got worse. Once she moved out and married, we never spoke or saw each other. We got closer once my father died, but it didn't last. We would fight and not speak for months. We disagreed about everything, especially the family house that we now live in together. She and her family live upstairs and I have an apartment in the lower half."

Stacy's sister was a powerful force in the family.

"She got my mother on her side and even our brother. Everyone was against me, thanks to her. She used every tactic imaginable because as the oldest, she had so much control. Oddly enough, I didn't understand it until recently. Finally, I see that she's strong and pigheaded. She only cares about herself and her children."

Despite her poor relationship with her sister, Stacy has sought close contact with her niece.

"When her daughter was born we finally got along. I was very relieved. For one year we had a truce, and I loved it. I was so attached to her child and she was attached to me. My sister resented this closeness that my niece and I shared. I'm not sure what happened but we began to argue again. I was not even at my niece's christening but I did go to the party afterward. Then my sister had another kid and the same thing happened. I don't think it mattered as much to me by then—I just wanted the closeness with my niece. The bottom line is that my sister didn't want me to play a strong role in her child's life. We had another huge fight.

"I see that what I've always been after is a sister. I would argue with her because she never calls me to go out or simply to talk. I see that she calls her friends and does things with them and it's very hurtful. After our major fight she did call once or twice but then it was the same old story. To this day, if I don't make the first move, nothing happens. She still doesn't call to say hello or ask what I'm doing. I can't help but wish we had a closer relationship. What compensates for all this is that I do see my niece and nephew some of the time. She's mellowed somewhat because she knows that they love me."

The disappointment has not abated for Stacy.

"I don't know why I feel gypped. After it's all said and done, I have an older sister who has never been able to act like one. Her friends were like sisters to me. They would come to the house and treat me the way I expected my own sister to treat me, but never had. Her friends would get on her case about it. Not that it had any effect. Nothing has. That's who my sister is and I have to live with it. It seems funny that as we get older and establish our own lives the pain doesn't go away. Each incident is a repeat performance. I keep looking for her to welcome me, to approve of me. But it isn't happening.

"I've often wondered if my sister was jealous of me or just didn't want me around. I know that she has a full life that I've yet to have and I'm willing to help her. I'd stay with the kids if she went away or I'd come over after work. I guess I'm still waiting, as pathetic as it seems."

There is an overwhelming sense of loss and disappointment in Stacy's story. She feels that she has tried so hard to reach her sister. There have been junctures in their adult lives where Stacy expected a change would take place, such as when her father died or when her sister's children were born. With the latter, Stacy endured her sister's jealousy over her attachment to her child. However, meaningful and lasting contact has never taken place. Stacy struggles because she is unable to accept her sister as she is and move ahead, nor will she make a clean break or a compromise. Instead she remains hopeful that the healing process lies somewhere in the future.

DEVOTED SISTERS:
Endless Journeys

We have all heard stories about two old maids who have never married, or sisters whose husbands have died, who live together as if they were a couple. They are viewed by the world around them as a unit, their identities meshed. They do everything together and are so devoted, if one dies it is as if the other had been widowed.

—RONNIE L. BURAK, PH.D

When it comes to murder, sisters evoke a different reaction from society than do spouses and lovers.

A very recent sister story occurred in April of 1993 in Toms River, New Jersey, when Blanche Black decided to kill her seventy-eight-year-old sister who no longer wished to live. Pleading guilty to second degree manslaughter, Blanche Black was sent to jail. However, the surviving sister had little regret. Her act, that of killing the one person in the world she loved more than anyone, was one of kindness and empathy. Her sister, bedridden and housebound, begged Blanche not to allow her to suffer. Devoted since childhood, neither sister remained married for many years nor had any children. Ruth, the stronger, older sister, became ill in 1990 and begged Blanche not to place her in a nursing home. Their entire life, a kind of sisterly marriage, was irreparably altered.

Having witnessed the prolonged illness of their mother, the two sisters had vowed never to die in the same way, lingering in pain. Once Blanche succeeded in drugging her sister, then covering Ruth's face with a pillow, she wrote a suicide note for herself. However, she recovered from a drug overdose only to be imprisoned. To this day, her feeling is that she would prefer to be in prison than to watch her sister suffer endlessly.

In another matter of sisterly devotion versus life and death, Al-jiva Posey, who is twenty-three, killed a woman while defending her sister, Sharonda Posey. Convicted of manslaughter in July of 1989, she is in prison today.

On July 7, 1992, teenagers Shannon Garrison, her sister Melissa, and Allen Goul, Melissa's boyfriend, were charged with the slaying of Betty Garrison, the girls' mother. In a plot that took a week to devise, the sisters convinced Goul to stab and strangle their mother as she slept. A forty-five-year-old divorced social worker, Betty Garrison had constant problems with her daughters. Because both sisters frequently left the house in the middle of the night, their mother had nailed their bedroom windows shut. Shannon's boyfriend, Mike Brewer, believed that the plan came about as a result of Shannon's manipulation of her younger sister, and Allen's devotion to Melissa.

One cannot exclude the divine devotion of the Delaney sisters, Sadie and Bessie, ages 103 and 101, when we speak of devoted sisters. Having grown up in North Carolina, the daughters of the first elected black Episcopal bishop, they have both achieved their goals. By choice neither sister has ever married, and both have pursued successful careers. Bessie became the second black woman dentist in New York City and Sadie was the first black person to teach domestic science in the New York public schools. Although their lives have been devoted to one another, the sisters' styles have always differed. Bessie is more outspoken and Sadie is the softer of the two. The hardship and happiness of being pioneer middle class black American women is the story that these sisters share.

Duncan

"My sister and I do things . . . that no one else would do . . . I dressed up as a gorilla to meet her at the airport one time."

Duncan, who lives in New England today, is the youngest of four children and has two sisters and a brother. One sister is impaired and institutionalized and the other has remained in Georgia where the children were raised. Duncan is extremely close to this sister, who is eight years older.

"I often wonder what it was my mother did that made me so in love with my sister from the start. She's my best friend on earth. When my twin daughters were born, I remember telling them they already had a sister. I called my sister up and told her that. I was so glad they were girls. The way I see it, my relationship with my sister was always good but once my own children were born, it was perfect. It bridged the years and now we have it all in common—husbands, children, and the same interests. For years I'd been driven by my career while she was already mothering."

Duncan and her sister live almost a thousand miles apart and speak on the phone twice a day.

"There's nothing we can't discuss. There's no rivalry and the most remarkable thing is that we're both so devoted to our mother. Yet I know that this sister is my mother's favorite child and it doesn't bother me in the least. I admire my sister but I don't envy her. I don't want her life and she doesn't want mine. I think she's the brightest, funniest, and most unselfish person I've ever met. I'm extraordinarily close to her kids and she is with mine.

"We don't even look alike. She's tall, dark, and very thin. I'm blond and more average in weight and height. I know I'm more spoiled than she. She was the one to grow up with our retarded sister in the house. By the time I was born, she was institutionalized. My sister had to cope with our impaired sister for the first eight years of her life and I never did. It's a bond that she and my mother share, the pain and heartbreak. I was never exposed to it and so it doesn't affect me."

Duncan feels that her brother is left out of the circle altogether.

"My sister and I adore our brother but we're not that close with him. The threesome in our family is my sister, my mother, and myself. If you really think about it, the longest relationship in life is with one's siblings—not with a parent and not with a child. I know I'll be devastated by the death of my mother but knowing I have my sister will ease the pain. I'll be more blown apart by the death of my sister. She's my anchor, the one who keeps me grounded.

"Sometimes I wonder what I have to offer my sister. She reminds me to take care when I become too caught up in material things. If my head swells, she's the one to bring me down a notch. She also baits me a lot. I'm smart enough to see right through it, so it all works out. She does feel, though, that my father spoiled me, as the youngest child. I know her feelings were hurt growing up because of this. It was tough for her when she first married because I was the baby at home, and could do no wrong. I stood up to my father and no one else did. She certainly didn't, and it's this difference in our personalities that she's aware of."

Duncan and her sister have special rituals together.

"My sister and I do things when we visit that no one else would do. I have no other friends or family who would get as crazy. One time I dressed up as a gorilla to meet her at the airport. And most recently we surprised my mother by stripping and then gluing playing cards to our bodies. We put cigarettes in all of our orifices. This was for my mother only, since she's a big smoker and card player.

"Living in different cultures, that of the north and south, affects our lives. My sister is married to a doctor in the university system who's extraordinarily intellectual. My husband has a white-collar job and that is reflected in our social life. But what we have in common is the card games we invent—silly card games that we play all night, changing the rules as we go. Family members are imaginarily killed if we make a mistake. It's all part of the fun of these games. If the phone rings or the doorbell, we don't answer. We're so rude and we do know it's juvenile. Whoever loses the game has to run outside naked. How could I share anything like this with anyone but my sister?"

Despite the fun, Duncan and her sister have had their problems.

"In my whole adult life I've fought with my sister a total of five times. Most of the time she's my support system and I'm hers. We're totally there for each other. I often wonder if I could live without her. She's my very best friend and I'm hers. I don't feel as close to any other woman on earth. She's committed to taking care of our retarded sister and I'm not and this is on my mind. While I understand my detachment because I didn't grow up with this sister, I'm still aware of the situation.

"I often wish she lived close by. I only see her four times a year. When we go to my mother's I fly to her house and drive the five hours to our mother's with her in order to be together. We're oblivious to the rest of our family when we spend time with one another. Once my son was having an asthma attack and we were so busy playing cards we hardly noticed. It's an obsession, this attachment we share."

Duncan's sister is extremely indulgent with Duncan.

"My sister is so generous in spirit. She gives so much to her church and her community. She has just switched to a less pretentious church. Her generosity extends to me and I believe she is far more giving to me than she is to herself. She likes her upscale lifestyle but at the same time she denies herself things. She calls me 'Lola' and says 'whatever Lola wants, Lola gets.' She's never critical as long as she thinks I'm aware of this self indulgence. I'm never embarrassed to buy whatever I want in front of my sister while I might hesitate in front of a friend. She's nonjudgmental and at the same moment puts it in perspective. So my sister is the only one who can keep me in line.

"If ever I was in trouble financially or medically, I'd turn to her knowing she'd be there for me without question. However, the silliness is there, too. Once we had a fight over blueberry turnovers. Neither of us likes to share food. The rule we have is that whatever you order in a restaurant you have to eat and cannot share. We wouldn't share the blueberry turnovers on the same principle. In most cases, if we have one of our rare disagreements, I know deep down that my sister is right. I'm so proud of her. When she comes to town, I want to show her off to all my friends. People are shocked by the difference in us. I'm simply thrilled that she's my sister."

For Duncan and her sister, a zany, imaginary world of secret games and fun exists. As diverse as they are in lifestyle and age, the closeness and devotion are there on every level. They are obviously comfortable with one another and committed to the relationship. It seems that Duncan's sister is the one who reminds her of family values and what really counts in life. It's the relationship itself, the respect and commitment they have for one another, that allows each sister to hear the other.

The retarded sister whom Duncan mentions has been absent from her life but not her older sister's. While Duncan is aware of their unique experience due to their birth order, there is no hostility or envy. Duncan and her sister are truly happy, loving sisters.

Joan

"My sister was dead when I got married and when my kids were born. I have been robbed of the opportunity to share my happiness with my sister."

Living in a small town in the midwest, Joan has three children and works full-time as an architect. Fourteen years ago her sister died. Although Joan is close to her brother and involved with her own family, there is a tremendous void left in her life by her sister's death.

"I remember when we were young, my sister was very maternal and loved having a younger sister to take care of. My mother's sister had two girls also, and it seemed like a perfect symmetry. My sister and I shared a room and were dressed alike. Although we never really looked like each other, we sounded identical. It was interesting—even as children we had the same voice and the same inflection.

"I loved the fact that my sister had a secret boyfriend when I was in junior high. I kept her secret for many years. I also got along very well with her friends, although I had my own. By the time I was in college, I confided everything to my sister. She was my closest friend. She always included me in her social life and drove me everywhere when she got her license. There was one time when I was in ninth grade and she was a senior. I was invited to the senior prom and she discouraged me from going. I think that was the only time my sister didn't want me around. And I understand—at that stage I was her little tagalong sister."

Joan and her sister had very different personalities and abilities.

"My sister was much smarter—she graduated cum laude from college. I was the artist, the more adventurous one and she was pretty and sophisticated. I was cute and more funky. We complemented one another—it was never competitive. I had my own style and so did she. I was very content with my abilities and she was with hers. Although I was the middle child, our family had no favorites but I was aware I was closer to my father and she was to my mother. There was no resentment over this, it was just understood."

Joan and her sister spoke every day on the telephone.

"My sister married right out of college. I was only a freshman at the time. We became even closer after I graduated. I loved my high school and college years with my sister. I think of them so fondly. She was the smart, sensible, older sister who grounded me. She always brought me back to reality and I appreciated it. Once she became ill and I was out of school, I lived with her. She was so sick and yet she had a baby. She never really discussed her illness but she knew how bad it was.

"The fact that she had a baby was a miracle. She became pregnant and they performed a therapeutic abortion and still she had a baby. The child was a great gift and represented hope against hope. We all loved this child so deeply. My sister was sick for nine years, and I lived with her for the last three. I wasn't yet married and helped her with her daughter. My mother took care of my sister, who was very sick toward the end. She had been so beautiful and was so dehumanized by the cancer. That's the hardest part of all, to think of what my sister went through. It got so that she wasn't even recognized in her hometown. She never broke down and never said much. She wanted me to be with her and so I was. She was definitely afraid to be alone, so I put my life on hold and worked part-time while my sister was dying.

"After she died I found that my sister had kept photographs of herself at all different stages in her life. She kept them in the nighttable. It made me so sad. I knew she longed to be well."

Joan's brother-in-law encouraged the closeness between the two sisters.

"My brother-in-law let us be close. The three of us were together often. He was very supportive. Their child was such an unbelievable joy to all of us. She was the reason we got through it. Everyone is so attached to my niece. Somehow because of this baby, I believed that my sister would get better. I could not imagine how, but I believed she would.

"One of my regrets is that I didn't have more to do with my niece's life. My brother-in-law remarried and it was no longer possible to be with her in the same way. I really did resent his new wife because of the way she took over. To this day she takes all the credit for how my niece turned out. But I see my niece as part of our family and definitely my sister's child. She's the spitting image of my sister, which consoles me.

"I miss my sister. I think of her all the time. My first child is named after her. I do anything I can to have some connection to my sister. One of my good friends was also close to her growing up. I feel good that we're close today and I cherish the link. I've remained close with my sister's husband's family, and I'm civil to the second wife. I realize how she has had to struggle. It isn't so much that my brother-in-law stopped loving my sister but that she died. I cannot imagine that he really loves this woman because she's so unlike my sister. Then again, maybe that's what he needed."

Losing her sister has affected Joan's entire life.

"If one's life is a pie and a slice is taken out and can never be replaced, in fact is irreplaceable, then how can your life be the same? My sister was dead when I got married and when my kids were born. I've been robbed of the opportunity to share my happiness with her. It's left such emptiness in my life. My children will never know her. To think that I had such a fabulous relationship with my sister and she's gone.

"It's especially sad for my mother. I feel responsible for making her happy. I know, at the same time, that it isn't enough. She understands this, too. I look at my daughters and I see how close they are. As my youngest grows older, the whole specialness of being sisters will kick in. And while I'm close with my brother, it cannot be the same. My sister isn't here today to give advice, to put my husband in his place if she knew him. I wonder if she'd appreciate his humor and if she'd approve of him. I believe she would still be my anchor, no matter what was happening in her own life. I'll never get over the death of my sister, never."

Coming from an intact, loving family makes Joan's situation even sadder. Her tragic story shows us how far-reaching and special the relationship between sisters can be. For Joan, her sister's death has changed everything and she will never recover. While she realizes she has other joys, the loss is always with her. The fact that she and her sister were so close, not only growing up but as adults, is significant. There is no regret, no guilt, only tremendous sadness.

What transpired with Joan's niece and brother-in-law is common with a second wife and second family. Although Joan cannot help but resent the woman who replaces her sister as her brother-in-law's wife, she also respects his need to move forward.

However, not being as close to her niece once the second marriage took place is unfortunate. For Joan, it is her one regret. She says little about her mother's loss, but makes it clear that she has tried to compensate, understanding it cannot heal the wound.

Theresa

"My sister had gone along for her entire life pleasing everyone. Then she took an assertiveness training class and left her husband."

At thirty-five, Theresa lives in Miami, Florida, where she works as a stockbroker. Her sister lives in Jacksonville and is seven years older. She works part-time in a real estate office and has two college-age sons. Theresa also has two sons, both in grade school.

"My sister and I are very close and were always close as kids. She has been very maternal toward me because my mother worked and was never around. She took on the responsibilities which my mother could not. She would read me stories at night and bake cookies with me. She was not asked to do it—it was not an assignment but something she liked and I loved. It was all very simple and lovely at first.

"When I turned thirteen and my sister was twenty, I was three inches taller and wore a much larger shoe. Symbolically this was the end of her maternal attitude toward me. She'd been away at college and married right after graduation. I was less needy and more independent than she. I was also creating my own life and interests."

The competition began when Theresa's skills began to surface.

"Not only had I grown older but I was a better student than she'd ever been and was clearly going to have an easier and better time of it. At some point, jealousy began to enter into the picture and the balance was never the same. My sister had attended Florida State while I gained easy entrance into several private institutions. The differences began to emerge. My parents made more money as I got older and not only were they more generous with me but more flexible and easy-going. It was a different period in their lives in every respect. What my sister had been denied, I was offered. She was long gone from the house."

Despite Theresa's promising start in life, she felt abandoned when her sister was first married.

"I felt I was losing her once she was married. It was a primitive feeling because she was more than my sister. I continued to call her before I'd ask my mother when I needed a ride somewhere. Thankfully she still lived nearby. And my mother never minded the attention my sister and I gave each other. She encouraged us. It was in her best interest to do that and she did. She loved our being so close.

"My sister and I rarely squabbled, and there was never any furious fighting. She was settled into her marriage and yet her devotion to me and our family remained. I pity her poor husband, in retrospect. Everything went along nicely and then she had a baby. I was very jealous. It was the first time in my life I'd ever been jealous of anyone or anything. I'd always been the baby in our family and my parents favored me heavily. They didn't even try to hide it. In fact, I often thought my sister was treated like a hired hand. She was so helpful that they gave her the job. That was it."

At the age of forty, Theresa's sister rebelled.

"My sister had gone along pleasing everyone for her entire life. Then she took an assertiveness training class and left her husband. She's been impossible since then. She used to be the one to meet me at the airport, the first to volunteer for any committee or cause. She was the one I could count on. Suddenly she had an identity crisis and a complete metamorphosis. Her pent-up rage at being the good sister and the good daughter and the good mother overwhelmed her. She had watched me and my advantages for years and she'd had it. She had been denied so much that had been lavished on me. She had every right to be angry. No one realized how tame and malleable she'd been or how it couldn't last forever.

"I know how unfair life must have seemed to my sister. She was my surrogate mother, though, and had to eventually resent me as well as our parents for what we'd done. Once she came to grips with it, she really turned on me. My husband and I have money and she has none. She sees that I have anything I want and she can't. At Christmas, when we were together, I bought her a purse that she needed. When we shop together, I always buy her something. She feels it's her due, and doesn't mind one bit that I'm paying. I'm very generous, partly out of guilt, partly because I think it's nice to be able to buy her a gift. She always gets first crack at my old clothes. I lavish gifts upon her sons and I try to compensate."

Theresa admits her ambivalence.

"I do and do not feel guilty about my sister's life. I feel sad for her but it's not my fault that her husband isn't successful or that our parents treated us the way they did. I cannot be angry at them because I was the recipient of their favors. But I don't see them as wise—they didn't make wise choices. Their attitude is that I've given them what they wanted. I work hard and deliver the goods. I'm living the kind of life they imagined for me and so they approve. My sister has fallen short, so we're not treated equally. When I walk into a room, my parents' eyes light up. My mother is always thrilled to see me. My sister walks in carrying the bundles, having done the errands, and they say little to her.

"My parents have helped my sister financially and not me. They see it a duty and it assuages their guilt. My sister's not as bright and was never scholastically inclined. I don't want to be cruel, but it's the truth. She is the kindest person I know and the assertiveness she has developed is just a veneer. Living in the nineties with a fifties mentality was harming her. She would have been the perfect fifties wife, at home with the kids. Instead she needs to work and make money, which is not what she wants to do and I understand that. She would be content to be a full-time mother, which is the opposite of me. My present career as a stock broker is very important to me."

Theresa sees the fact that her sister only recently acquired the skills that Theresa had attained in her twenties as significant.

"My sister's career as a real estate agent is her biggest achievement. She began to do this so much later in life than I did. She sees it as the be-all and end-all, whereas I've lost interest in my career. She now aspires to be what I once was before I discarded it. I was bored with it by the time I had kids and she didn't even pursue it until after her sons were grown. That's the main difference between my sister and myself.

"What is interesting is how our marriages are the same in some ways, despite the fact that I describe us as very different people. My sister married a very domineering person and lets him boss her around. I also married a domineering man, a man capable of doing that, but I won't let him. She's really in a trap. That was why she suddenly became so furious at her husband. Once she woke up to her situation, she began to try to fix it. I never allowed myself to be treated that way. I fought it from day one."

Today Theresa and her sister are more in tune.

"I think my sister and I have found a separate peace. Basically I adore and love her. I know I can count on her. When we're very old, I hope we'll live together. I can see us together, eternally bound and always there for one another. I never feel threatened by her, and I'm so glad she exists for me.

"When we were small, she was the counsellor wherever I was the camper, so I never had a problem adjusting. She'll always be my guardian angel. I always know I can call her. Knowing this, I still understand it's not a peer relationship—her ever-present jealousy clouds it. Perhaps as she gets older and accomplishes more on her own, it will dissipate. My success bothers her—she's actually annoyed when I do well. Had we been treated equally, she would be proud of me today, and there would be no edge to it. She can't help it, really; I suppose it's because of the way she's had to live her life. She even has a problem with my son and his achievements. I know all this but still she's my sister and we're forever tied to each other."

For Theresa, there is an acute awareness of how unevenly she and her sister were treated by their parents. While Theresa does not wish to relinquish her special place in her parents' hearts and actions, she wishes they had not been quite so obvious in their favoritism. At the same time, Theresa understands that despite her sister's jealousy and unhappiness, she is there for Theresa.

As long as the option of leaning on each other exists, the effects of how they were raised seem almost beside the point. The fact that the unfair treatment extends to the grandchildren is not so much a concern of Theresa's, which further illustrates her attitude toward her parents. She sympathizes with her sister's plight without really giving an inch, perhaps thinking it's not hers to give. Theresa's own sense of security comes with the knowledge that both her sister and her parents value their connection to her.

Tamara

"Maybe as a kid I might have been embarrassed, but I never felt cheated, as if I missed having a regular kind of sister."

As a practicing attorney who lives in Sante Fe, Tamara is no longer in close proximity to her older sister, who lives in Omaha. However, the sisters are in constant contact, not because of a strong bond, but because Tamara is the trustee for her brain-damaged sister's trust. On a certain level Tamara feels a need to devote herself to her sister.

"My sister is five years older and has never been okay, yet I really don't know what's wrong with her. It has never been explained exactly, which is part of the problem. For my mother, it has been a lifetime of torture, hoping against hope without any real diagnosis. Although my sister is older, I was always her caretaker. I grew up feeling attached to her, and I remain attached to her. My two brothers, who are older, don't have the same commitment.

"My sister's behavior was too destructive for my brothers to handle. Neither of them seemed able to face it and today, as adults, it's more difficult for them as a result. They simply have to accept the facts. I always felt so responsible for my sister that I never got to be the baby of the family even though I was the youngest of four."

Tamara's mother has not handled her sister's problem well.

"My father was always realistic but my mother does a poor job. The fact that there has never been any tangible evidence, no real medical interpretation of my sister's problem has made it worse for her. The other factor is that my brothers and I are very smart, and all of us are overachievers while my sister was an underachiever. It was very competitive although there was no way for her to compete. It was unquestionably hardest on her, because she was ill-equipped to deal with it.

"I definitely felt that I had a dependent sister and there was no give and take. She was not like a real sister to me, with the rapport and sharing that's part of that relationship. Every once in a while, in isolated moments, I had a glimpse of that normalcy and empathy."

Tamara's sister has always been very proud of her.

"In the fifties when we were in grade school, we all had IQ tests. My brothers were immediately put into a special group for gifted students. I also qualified, but the school wouldn't put me in because it was so obvious that my sister couldn't be included. She knew what was going on and went to the principal's office and demanded that I be a part of it. She said it was only right that my capabilities be recognized.

"My sister's intelligent enough to know that she's not normal but that she's too smart to be with retarded kids. She has a normal IQ and was not diagnosed as mentally retarded, but she's brain-damaged. There are moments when my sister seems almost fine, emotionally and mentally, but not most of the time."

There is a pervasive sadness for Tamara as a result of her sister's situation.

"I feel sad for her all the time. Maybe as a kid I might have been embarrassed, but I never felt cheated, as if I missed having a regular kind of sister. There were times when people would make jokes and I came to realize how evil and cruel the world can be. Adults are mean, too. My parents' friends were not really very kind to her.

"Once I joined a club and then quit because she wasn't allowed in. I know she can be crazy but she also has a sweet heart and is not a bad person. She was never given a chance because she didn't measure up. No one would accept my sister's problems, her imperfections, and it has made her ashamed. My sister feels a lot of shame."

Tamara and her sister have arguments.

"My sister and I can still fight but I love her. I'd do almost anything for her. I'm the trustee of her trust and because she can't make proper judgments it becomes an issue. We fight about money because I am in a position of responsibility for her. She lives alone in an apartment in Omaha and has finished a two-year vocational program. She has a pitiful boyfriend who uses and abuses her—he's emotionally if not mentally impaired. But my sister is provided for by our father and this is important."

For years Tamara was concerned that her sister might become pregnant.

"It's interesting that my sister never wanted to have any children. I think she realized she wouldn't be a good mother. She never became pregnant although we feared that she would and that it would pose real problems. Although I'm involved with her life by long distance—we speak on the phone almost daily—I don't see her more than several times a year. My mother no longer lives in Omaha and isn't close by, either. She speaks to my sister on a weekly basis and my brothers both speak with her infrequently. My brothers continue to try to distance themselves from her.

"I don't really feel close to my sister today. We don't have much of a relationship because we live in different cities and our lives are so dissimilar. The link is that she constantly asks me for things because of my role as trustee and protector. And she continues to resent me, much as she did when we were living at home. It has always been hierarchical."

Growing up, Tamara found it difficult to accept her sister.

"I kept questioning what really happened to my sister to make her the way she is. I couldn't accept her fate until I was an adult. None of us ever really knew what happened to her. Was it in the delivery, or was it something else? Our mother still has a lot of guilt and could never really enjoy her life because of my sister.

"If anything, this has broadened my horizons and made me more tolerant of other people. As a result of my sister's illness, I have taught my children how to treat other children. I'm possessed and preoccupied with teaching them never to tease or hurt someone else's feelings. It's a powerful sentiment and I hold it right up there with telling the truth. It's the most important thing I can teach my children. If they ever intentionally hurt anyone's feelings, they know what I'll do. This is a reaction to my sister, as is my fear of not having healthy babies."

In the past, Tamara's sister would pretend to be Tamara.

"If I tried out for a play in high school, my sister would steal the script. I was five years younger and she'd sneak into my room and try on my clothes. I was the youngest but she was the nonfunctioning baby of the family. I know my sister has had a very strong effect on my life. I really wanted to give birth to a daughter because of my sister.

"To this day, my sister is possessed by my success and her lack of it. Only yesterday she said she'd never want to be a lawyer like me. She continues to do things that are not thought out, such as running up an eight thousand dollar phone bill by calling nine hundred numbers. I just have to accept who she is. My hope is that she can find a non-threatening lifestyle for herself. I want my sister to find some happiness somewhere finally."

Tamara is disturbed by the discrepancy between her life and her sister's. Her sense of responsibility is evident in her role of trustee. While Tamara might dislike the actual task, she feels she owes it to her sister to do it. She also sees herself as the only person in the family capable of helping at present.

A lawyer with children and a husband, Tamara knows that her sister's comparisons will never cease. Her sister is thoroughly aware of how Tamara lives—the pain and sadness is relentless. The physical distance between the two sisters is probably necessary in order for Tamara to balance her own family, her career, and her sister's demands—demands she feels must be met, if possible.

Patricia

"What is interesting is that my mother does not speak with her own sister. . . . My sister and I have a relationship that does not relate to our mother's situation with her sister."

Originally from California, Patricia lives in Baltimore and is forty. Three years older than her sister, each woman has two daughters, close in age.

"I think my sister and I get along very well. We see one another every three months at her home or mine. We talk often and about everything. As kids we had many fights. I don't think it was abnormal, but standard stuff. I remember drawing a line down the middle of the room and neither of us could cross into each other's territory. This was during the period when we shared a room.

"My sister and I don't look or act alike. She's heavy-set with dark hair while I'm blond and very thin. The explanation for this is that my sister was born with a health problem and my mother compensated by overfeeding her. She was convinced that a fat baby is a healthy baby. My mother had this need to have her sickly child appear healthy, a self-fulfilling prophecy. I never felt threatened or competitive about the attention my sister received. I'm not sure why, but it never bothered me."

Both Patricia and her sister have sustained their careers throughout their marriages and childrearing.

"Only recently have I stopped working in a highpowered job and so has my sister. She immediately began her own cottage industry. There have been setbacks with both our husbands in this economy so when I'm depressed I call her. For some reason, she's very unsympathetic, maybe because she's working so hard. She thinks we're not in the same boat because she's making this effort with her own business. Her attitude is, if you're unhappy, then fix it.

"The motivating factor for our closeness comes from the relationship between our daughters. They adore one another and our husbands get along very well, too. We're fortunate that all this works so well. When we get together, everyone has a good time."

Patricia and her sister are not competitive.

"Our mother was so difficult when we were growing up and remains so. We were united against her, and as a result didn't compete with one another. When our father left our mother for his girlfriend, my mother's 'job' ceased to exist. I was already out of the house and my sister wasn't. Our mother lost her identity, that of being a wife. She almost had a breakdown but she pulled herself together. We've always put up with her because she's so needy. To the outside world, our mother appears fine, but she won't consider our problems, only her own. With such behavior, of course, my sister and I had to join forces. What other choice was there?

"I know my sister is more loveable than I am. Or so it has always seemed to me. She and my mother get along very well. She's much sweeter to her than I can ever be. My sister's also very sociable and has lots of friends. She's more in the world, having spent many years in the advertising business. I have a few close women friends but my business is very solitary. I remember double-dating in the sixties. Everything was copesetic so that my sister and I were kind of a team. We both went to excellent colleges and there was still no competition."

Patricia's sister married first.

"My sister has been married several years longer than I have and her attitude is very different from mine. She'll put on a false front, as if she were never upset about anything. I show my feelings. Both our husbands have had job setbacks and her way of dealing with it is so foreign to me. Still, our values are similar when it comes to raising the kids and neither of us is very materialistic. Of course, one can only be as materialistic as one can afford.

"I'm very pleased that I have a sister. If ever there's a problem, I know she would be there for me. My mother has encouraged our closeness without knowing it, by doing nothing. I feel extremely close to my sister. Whatever our mother intended, this is the end result and it's a positive one.

"What is interesting is that my mother doesn't speak with her own sister. I once heard from her sister, my aunt. She had read an article about my work and was trying to track me down. She wrote a note and asked if indeed I was her sister's daughter. I tried to get my mother and her sister back in touch. It worked to some extent. I have no clue, however, as to how her situation with her sister has really affected her approach to mothering us. My sister and I have a relationship that's so different from our mother's situation with her sister. Ours has its own life and rhythm."

Patricia's husband has pointed out that her sister has a specific agenda.

"My sister lives her life at record speed. She doesn't allow adversity to get in her way. If we have a problem, she'll be very opinionated and then stop talking about it—sort of full steam ahead and then a breather. Another common approach for her is to simply gloss over it and then start another conversation. I understand how she operates and I assume she understands how I operate.

"I do think my sister is supportive of me. There's no dirt in our story because we rarely disagree. Although recently there was one incident—this is an example of the kind of argument we would have. When we last visited at my sister's I brought along my juicer because we were staying for a week. She resented it and asked me why I had done that. The next time she visited me, she asked me what kind of juicer was best because she wanted to buy one. I made reference to how she had complained about my juicer. She explained that it wasn't the juicer but that I had imposed on her. On the other hand I know we're there for one another, so I overlook certain things. In terms of family the relationship is important to us both. That's the most important factor."

Patricia maintains that she has an easy rapport with her sister but it appears there are undercurrents. The juicer story would indicate that her sister is territorial. Also, each sister differs in her view of their mother and method of handling her. The problems concerning each husband's career and each sister's career also evoke a unique response. Yet Patricia and her sister personify a modern-day sisterhood, where family values mesh and their experiences as working mothers are parallel. The common denominator is their children and the concept of putting family before friends.

Louise

"The only issue that ever arose was when, as adults, we three sisters got together."

Living in Miami at the age of sixty-eight, Louise is the youngest of three sisters. Her more intimate relationship was with her middle sister, who died fifteen years ago. Louise believes that her life was changed irreversibly by this sister's death.

"My sister and I were very close. We were married the same year and raised our children together. She was very connected to my kids as I am to hers. To this day, I keep in touch with her three children as if they were my own. I see them as my only link to her. I know how important each one was to her and I feel this is the least I can do.

"What haunts me is the fact that my sister might have been saved. She had cancer and died very quickly, probably because her illness was misdiagnosed at the start. The cancer spread through her entire body so fast, and then it was over. I have three children of my own but I have reached out to her children ever since her illness. Tragically, their father, my sister's husband, died several years later. What I feel the worst about is those children. They have always been my focus. I'm doing for her what she would expect of me."

Growing up, Louise and her middle sister were not always close.

"I was favored often by my oldest sister, kind of 'the baby and the eldest' syndrome. As we got older, I became more attached to the middle sister. At one time we shared a house in Miami—that was a disaster. Our firstborn girls arrived within a few months of each other and we lived there with our babies and spouses. That almost finished the relationship. She was very organized and I was very relaxed. She was so compulsive. My husband traveled a lot on business then, so I was left with my sister, her husband, our babies, and her rules. We had so many fights, the kind only sisters can have, because we were also adjusting to having two babies. It wasn't easy. This was the only time we were near to having a rift. After that we became extremely close.

"This sister and I had such similar, parallel lives. Both of us had three children, each born within a few months of the other. Then she moved away. I was upset—she had been the only person I could confide in. I would even say things to her about my husband. She also felt she could confide in me. She was very understanding and would not use any information as a weapon against me. I think my other sister would have, and I have a sister-in-law who I'm very close to, but she also takes the information and turns it around. So, when my sister died, I lost a true confidante."

Louise felt that her sister was a very positive person.

"She was devoted to her kids and her husband, but her priorities were such that sometimes she really didn't see her kids' problems because she was so involved with the marriage. I balanced my priorities differently. When you're sisters and living similar lives, you have these insights. My sister was totally immersed in her marriage—he wasn't like my husband at all, and so the dynamic was not the same. But then, as close as this sister and I were, we had very different personalities."

Louise's children and her sister's children remain in touch.

"The attachment continues and I encourage it. For example, my sister's kids know that when their parents were alive, we celebrated all our wedding anniversaries together. The only problems that ever arose was when, as adults, we three sisters got together—then we would always squabble. Besides that, the middle sister and I had no arguments. We were absolutely loyal to each other. And it's her children who keep me going in some ways, when I miss her."

As adult sisters, Louise saw the sister who died and herself as a pair.

"I don't know how our older sister felt about it. She was very independent and chose not to have children. We had less to talk about and less in common. I was never as close to this sister as I became with the one who died. She and I were a pair. When she became so ill, I stayed with her in the hospital and visited as often as possible. Her death was a tremendous heartache and I will never get over it. My sister just cannot be replaced. I hated watching her suffer. I'll never forget that. Since she died, I've never been as close to any other woman."

Although there were several incidents with her sister who died, for the most part, she and Louise shared an idyllic sisterhood. While she easily expresses her feelings for this sister, Louise says little about her relationship with her surviving sister. It seems that the only deep sister relationship possible for her was the one with her deceased sister. What compensates for the pain is the link to that sister's children. By keeping these connections alive, she finds a kind of solace. For Louise, as a devoted sister, there is no relationship to replace the one she has lost.

Samantha

"I would go out on a limb for her. In an emergency if I was needed, I'd be there."

At forty, Samantha lives in Bangor, Maine, with her husband and three children. Her sister, who is thirteen years younger, lives in Tucson, Arizona. Samantha is a banker and her sister is a college professor.

"I remember being upset at my sister's birth, as if it was an imposition upon me. I was afraid I'd have to babysit because we were so far apart in age. But once she actually arrived, we became very good friends, and it's been that way between my sister and myself to this day.

"My mother was ill and often away while my sister was growing up. I left home for college at seventeen, but those first few years, I was the primary connection for my sister. She and I were the closest of anyone in the family. We have brothers, but they were not there for her, and they're also much older."

Although Samantha and her younger sister did not share a room initially, an incident changed this.

"My sister was badly burned when she was two years old. After she recovered, she moved into my room and we became close. I never felt motherly, it was just close and friendly. To this day I offer her my opinion whether she asks for it or not. But I don't see myself as her mother, more of a mentor. I know she wants my advice and I give it to her.

"I don't see my sister as often as I'd like. She lives some distance away and we only get together about once a year. We speak on the phone twice a month. I'm always aware that she's my sister and pleased about it. Our ages and schedules have always been so dissimilar that we were never competitive. She was the beautiful darling of the entire family, and everyone enjoyed her. I can't recall ever having any real battles with her. We were never on the same ground. For example, her relationships with men can't be compared to mine. She has grown up in a completely different time and the standards and expectations are not the same. She left the woman's college where I went, knowing she wanted to attend a large coed university. I didn't have quite the same reaction to the school, although I wasn't happy there. I chose to remain and she chose to leave."

Samantha is keenly aware that she's available if her sister needs her.

"I'd go out on a limb for her. In an emergency, if I was needed, I'd be there. I'm also conscious of how much less connected she is to my family, to my children, than I'd like her to be. I live in two separate worlds, the world I share with my sister and the world I share with my own children and my life here in Maine. My children rarely see my sister, again because of the distance. The result is that they're less attached than I'd like but when she comes to visit, they treat her as a playmate. She's not married, and is able to bridge the parent-child gap. She doesn't simply sit around and drink coffee with the adults. She sends my kids rocks or stickers because she knows what they really like.

"There's a definite bond with a sister that goes beyond friendship. Blood ties are usually strong, for better or for worse, with all siblings. I consider so much of my family a burden but my sister is a pleasure and a joy. We confide in one another and while she wouldn't call me with a problem, it comes up in a phone conversation eventually. We share a fairly mature give and take. Early on, however, when her only source of information was my mother, it wasn't easy. At that time, when she was still at home and had to listen to our mother, she resented me. Since then we've been able to bond on our own and have overcome my mother's poisoning. My mother is the one who created the problem. I think she suffered from bitterness and felt that no one was entitled to be happy. Then she tried to poison my sister against me. There were many years when I was considered the family 'brat.' "

Their mother spoke negatively of Samantha to her younger sister.

"I was married and away from home when I was described as being spoiled. To make matters worse, my sister lived at home during my parents' divorce, while the rest of us had already left. She often heard me described as an ungrateful wretch. It was intimated that I had usurped my mother's position—not in terms of my sister but in terms of my father.

"My sister's only source of information was my mother, and today we know that my mother also said terrible things to me. She spoke out of both sides of her mouth. Finally we got beyond her warped view of the world, and after all we've been through we found each other again. I just wish we lived closer. Maybe we will someday.

"It's interesting to me that both my sister and I have accomplished a lot, but I suspect she's probably smarter. There was never any competition in this respect, although she felt she had to measure up. That came from my mother, not from me. Now that we're both adults I hope we become closer and closer. I want to get rid of the physical distance so she isn't just my sister but an aunt to my children. That's very important to me."

The most complex issue for Samantha and her sister seems to be the relationship each had with their mother. While Samantha begins by telling us about her "mentoring vs. mothering" approach to her sister, only later do we learn that this also reflects the way Samantha views her mother. She sees her in such a negative light that her relationship with her sister has had to supersede this familial bond, and all others, to succeed on its own terms.

Samantha and her sister love one another and are devoted. However, the shadow of the mother hangs over both women, and the "truth" has taken a long time to surface. Although Samantha does discuss the possibility of living nearer to her sister for their sake and the sake of Samantha's children, she does not mention it as a probability. We notice that her story is filled with various ingredients: a dysfunctional mother, an age gap, a sister who was impaired when very young with its inevitable repercussions, physical distance, and diverse lifestyles. Yet the attachment the two women share is deep and undeniable.

Maria

"Today we are not at all competitive because we are each successful in our own fields."

Maria is the older of two sisters by three years. Living in a suburb of Chicago, where they grew up, both women work full-time, Maria in public relations and her sister in the medical field. Although close today, they were estranged as children.

"When my mother was pregnant with my sister, she asked me if I wanted a real doll or a play doll. I told her I wanted a real one and I got her. But she wasn't a doll to me at all, and for some reason, I believe my mother was the one who drove the wedge between us. She divided us into good sister and bad sister. I suppose, in retrospect, that both my sister and I understand that my mother did it because she needed an ally."

Today Maria and her sister feel close and have discussed their mother's behavior.

"We were over thirty before we formed a real bond. I've often asked my sister why she and I hated each other when we were small. My mother kept us apart and made us competitive. Only as adults did we come to appreciate each other as sisters. We're not sure if our mother did what she did on purpose or not.

"Both my sister and I are married. I have a daughter and she has no children. She can't have children and I've offered to surrogate-mother her child. When I told her this, she cried. I don't want any more children of my own, but I would do this for my sister. I do hope she'll make up her mind soon, though, because I'm already thirty-five. Having made this offer, I know how close my sister and I have become. My sister's attachment to my daughter is amazing. She treats her as if she were her own. That's another reason my sister and I have grown closer as adults, because of my child."

Maria and her sister speak often on the phone and see each other several times a month.

"Our families have grown closer and we spend what time we can together. She lives a half-hour away but she works at night and I work during the day. Also, she works on weekends.

"My family is entangled and entwined. My ex-husband works for my father and has our daughter a lot of the time, so it's complicated and sometimes my sister and I get caught in the web. She's so involved with my child and our family, too, so someone's always upset. But we're getting beyond that, too."

Maria and her sister are not alike in lifestyle or interests.

"We're so different. She's academic and serious, while I'm very social. We're not at all competitive because we're each successful in our own fields. Each of us has finally made our own way. As children it was difficult, because she was the brainy one who got all A's while I didn't care. We were never compared in terms of our looks. In fact, we don't look alike—I look like one side of the family and she looks like the other. We were constantly compared in terms of achievement.

"There was no competition for boys. We were three years apart and it wasn't a problem. We came from such a strict family that boys weren't a part of the picture until much later. By then I was off at school and my sister felt abandoned. I believe she was actually jealous when I left. She resented my leaving her with our parents. With two sisters at home, there's a buffer, even if the sisters aren't that close. Then I was gone."

Today Maria realizes that she and her sister provided a support system for one another without even knowing it.

"We protected each other but didn't really understand what we were doing. We were so caught up in how my mother orchestrated things, we didn't realize we were there for each other. Today we're close, but I have to say, I'm still closer to my best friend than I am to my sister. And my best friend is closer to me than she is to her own sister. I don't know anyone who has a sister who isn't closer to her best friend. I can't judge how close sisters are supposed to be, but this has been my experience."

Maria and her sister fought for their father's attention.

"My father is a warmer, more jovial person than my mother. Both my sister and I wanted to please him, and to this day she vies for his attention. And I sometimes think the other issue is my daughter—because I have a kid and she doesn't, which she regrets.

"I think what happened is that my sister and I have come to appreciate how deep our relationship has always been. Without realizing it at the time, we benefitted from sharing a room, from being sisters. I'm sorry I didn't know what sisters were supposed to be. No one had written a book to tell me. When I was young what I saw as a nuisance now appears to be an important relationship. I wish I had loved her more."

Several years ago, Maria was able to tell her sister that she loves her.

"Today it means something and so I say it. It took so long for me to learn what sisters are all about. They're supportive and close, and there's give and take and real understanding. I look at my own child, however, knowing she won't have a sister, and I don't think she's losing out. It's a choice in life that a parent makes, but for a sister, there's no choice. It just happens. Then you try to make the most of it."

Maria's history with her sister is interesting because it is only as adults that they have come to really appreciate one another. Yet certain themes recur, even in adulthood—jealousy, competition, career pursuits. Their relationship is healing; with Maria's offer to be a surrogate mother for her sister's child, their relationship comes full circle. What Maria laments are their early years, but with maturity, both sisters have come to appreciate what they share. They are fortunate to have discovered each other in their adulthood.

Eliza

"As each of us established our jobs and families, we became more motivated to work on our relationship."

Eliza lives in northern California and works part-time as a consultant. Forty years old, her sister is three years older and a sociologist. They each have two daughters. Eliza and her sister are quite close, but growing up it was a difficult situation.

"When we were kids, my sister tortured me. She was older and jealous. It was the pecking order. She was the firstborn and my father's favorite, and then I came along and took away all that attention. With two girls in a family, it's easy to fall into such a trap. Now that my sister and I have kids of our own, we see what can happen. My sister was manipulative and domineering. I identify with my younger child because of the way my sister treated me.

"I think that two daughters is the worst possible combination. My sister and I didn't get along at all and there was such intense hostility toward each other. Today, we're soulmates. It all changed for the better once I got married and had my own life. Both of us are in stable marriages with very nice guys. We have a lot in common and our way of seeing the world is similar by virtue of how we were raised. When I say that my sister and I are extremely close today, I'm saying to other troubled sisters that there's definitely hope."

Eliza's father favored her sister when they were growing up.

"We were divided. I was with my mother and my sister was my worst enemy. In those days I was much closer to my friends than to my sister. She was so cruel to me. Then I began to act and got small bits on television. That really did it; she didn't like having a cute little sister and it got worse as my television career progressed. My parents did nothing to intervene. They never helped because they weren't aware enough. They had their own life together and acted as if their children were just a small part of it. We certainly weren't a big influence on them.

"When we were in college our parents divorced. By then I was out of the house and my sister had been gone for a few years, too. At this point we turned to each other but not enough, not totally. As a parent I understand now that what our parents did was difficult for us. I realize I'm a crucial role model for my kids and I know my sister and I didn't have that."

Despite their differences, Eliza and her sister were both very studious.

"I might have worked harder but my sister is more successful. She has created an excellent career for herself. As each of us established our jobs and families, we also became more motivated to work on our relationship. After many years in therapy we realized that we wanted to improve the quality of our personal lives. We had to turn ourselves inside out to get there. The bond we have was partly there because we grew up in the same household. The key was to undo the damage and make a commitment to each other. The combination—that of therapy, good marriages, and good lives—really helped us find one another.

"We're very close now. We speak on the phone three or four times a week and our girls are close. My older daughter looks on my sister's older daughter as a role model. I often watch my daughters as they interact and I'm glad that they're closer than my sister and I were growing up. It comes from better parenting. My husband and I have made a stronger commitment to our kids than my parents made. Plus we're in a healthier marriage.

"Basically I feel good about my sister and I rarely look back.

I'm more involved with our mother than she is. Sometimes my sister is relieved that she isn't around because my mother can be so needy, and I don't resent her for that. Our love is completely unconditional and we're too supportive to feel anything but happy for each other. My sister has become a great positive force in my life. We really understand one another."

Eliza believes that although she and her sister did not get along as children that the foundation was laid to become close in adulthood.

"Our mother isn't all bad. She's a nurturing woman and she taught us to be intimate with people. As a result of my mother and my sister, I can be very close to other women. I attended an all-girls high school and I have always had close female friends. An all-girls school felt safe and wonderful—it was that environment that gave me strength. When my sister and I were younger and not close, I had the support of my girlfriends from this school. I've always loved to connect to women. It's an emotional connection that I value, and finally I ended up having that connection to my sister.

"Sisters have to fight for love and attention—I haven't forgotten how my sister treated me. But it doesn't matter anymore. What matters is today and tomorrow."

As Eliza tells us, she has had enough therapy to grasp what did not work out between the two sisters when they lived at home. The jealousy that her sister harbored toward Eliza's acting career made life difficult. The divided family, where each parent favored one child, was another problem. Not until the sisters were married with children did they become close and feel they were on equal ground.

After having so little rapport as children, Eliza and her sister appreciate the bond they have formed as adults. For Eliza, this relationship has given her insight into how she wants to raise her own daughters and what her family values are.

AFTERWORD

Since the day I began this odyssey, researching and writing a book on sisters, I have been privileged to enter a rarified realm which exists only for women who share this bond. While I suspected it existed, having watched my own daughters and observed those close to me who have sisters, I had no idea how intense and important the relationship could be. Nor did I quite comprehend how destructive a negative rapport between sisters can become.

Today I have a better understanding of what is missing if one has never had a sister. When a friend explains that she will not be available because her sister is coming to town, I know exactly what she means. In a positive situation, the sister takes priority over other women. For the outsider who wishes to become close to a twin sister, she is up against a genetic, emotional tie so strong that one wonders how she can possibly fit into the picture.

A common factor in a sister relationship is the almost-invisible mother. She is often pushing her daughters, in a united or divided manner, toward a goal she has chosen. But the range of sisters is so vast, and so intricate, that one cannot generalize. For a competitive sister, there is the counterbalance of a sister willing to surrogate-mother her sister's child. For every jealous sister, there is one who will never recover from the death of a sister and struggles to cope with her loss. There are threesomes with an odd sister out, or those who perceive themselves or others as favorites and the lifelong anguish it creates.

Although the fundamental sister relationship works from a basis of female strength, there is a flipside for every scenario. For sisters who steal their sister's husband or lover, there is an underlying jealousy and competition so strong that it manifests in this ultimate and destructive act. But there is a counteraction to such drama, be it the sister who uncomplainingly cares for an elderly parent while her sister or sisters cannot be available or the affluent sister who ungrudgingly assists her less fortunate sibling. Manifested in a negative manner, the wounds of a sister relationship cut most deeply; as a support system, the results are almost foolproof.

Sisters who shut others out, who share an intimate attachment to one another, finally make sense to me. They have entered the world with this emotional cushion and there is no need to put the same energy into any other female relationship. It is a built-in security, a barrier against the outside that will insulate them all their lives. For certain fortunate sisters, an additional benefit of this same type of sisterly connection is that they are able to interact with most women in a positive and assured manner, encouraged by their early experience.

I now know how women can be born into the same family and find themselves in unique situations as adults. When one sister is gay, the other may be convention-bound. And in these instances, what matters is the encouragement that one sister provides for the other.

The tales we have heard about sisters throughout history and literature reoccur in a modern mode, but with new twists and concerns. Power plays, envy, and dissatisfaction will never cease to exist. Parallel to this are the pluses of sisterhood: devotion, selflessness, commitment, enjoyment, and loyalty. Sisters, whatever their stories, instinctively know how fortunate they are. In the day-to-day struggle of life, the commonality of family braces each sister for what lies ahead. In the nineties, in a world of complexity and evolution for women, sisters can play an even greater role in each other's lives. They share divine secrets, divine pleasures. There is no outsider anywhere who wouldn't appreciate and even envy the tremendous advantage that sisters have, if properly utilized, against all odds.

About the Author

Susan Ripps received her B.A. from Sarah Lawrence College and an M.A. in English and Writing from New York University. She recently published the best-selling book, *A Passion for More*. She is a writer of non-fiction women's issues as well as fiction and screenplays. She resides in Connecticut with her husband and three children.